Born Again Catholic

By
Elma Chopra

Copyright © 2010 by Elma Chopra

Born Again Catholic
by Elma Chopra

Printed in the United States of America

ISBN 9781609573676

All rights reserved solely by the author. The author guarantees all contents are original and do not infringe upon the legal rights of any other person or work. No part of this book may be reproduced in any form without the permission of the author. The views expressed in this book are not necessarily those of the publisher.

Unless otherwise indicated, Bible quotations are taken from:

    The New King James Version. Copyright © 1984
        by Thomas Nelson.
    The New International Version. Copyright © 1986
        by Tyndale House Publishers Inc.

www.xulonpress.com

9/10/10

Dear Ophie,

I am honored to be your co-pilgrim w/ Father Jan & Lucy.

God Bless you!

Elma

P.S. Share this book with Rhoda your sister and your friends.

This book is also available in Barnes & Nobles & Amazon.com.

Table of Contents

INTRODUCTION -- v
CHAPTER 1   MY LIFE BEFORE KNOWING JESUS   -- 1
CHAPTER 2   LIVING WITH JESUS AS
            MY PERSONAL SAVIOR -------------------- 15
CHAPTER 3   LIFE'S JOURNEY WITH JESUS:
            THE CHANGED LIFE ----------------------- 27
CHAPTER 4   MY PRAYER LIFE --------------------------- 35
CHAPTER 5   ANSWERED PRAYERS --------------------- 53
CHAPTER 6   WORSHIP ------------------------------------ 73
CHAPTER 7   THANKSGIVING ----------------------------- 87
CHAPTER 8   WORK ETHICS ------------------------------ 95
CHAPTER 9   GIVING -------------------------------------- 105
CHAPTER 10 FACING ADVERSITY ---------------------- 113
CHAPTER 11 FORGIVENESS ---------------------------- 139
CHAPTER 12 REPENTANT HEART --------------------- 163
CHAPTER 13 EVIDENCES OF DISCIPLESHIP --------- 185
CHAPTER 14 MY SERVICE ------------------------------ 197
CHAPTER 15 RAISING FAUSTIN ------------------------ 213
CHAPTER 16 BASICS OF CATHOLIC FAITH ----------- 243
CHAPTER 17 MY TESTIMONY --------------------------- 325
CHAPTER 18 CATHOLIC SAINTS ------------------------ 337
CHAPTER 19 HEAVEN ----------------------------------- 351
CHAPTER 20 MY PILGRIMAGE TO NAJU, KOREA ---- 377
CHAPTER 21 MY HOPE ---------------------------------- 415
CONCLUSION --- 427
NOTES --- 442

BORN AGAIN CATHOLIC

INTRODUCTION

Every believer of Jesus Christ has a story. I strongly feel that in telling my story I will be able to share my living experiences with Jesus as a born again Christian Catholic.

One day as I listened to a Christian radio broadcast, there was a woman from the Catholic denomination who asked if she was considered "Born Again." She said she loves the Lord, reads her Bible everyday, goes to church every Sunday and holidays of obligations and she truly believes that she is now trying to serve and love Jesus as her Lord.

The Pastor asked her if there was a change in her life and she said yes. She used to say bad words and love to party among other things and she is not doing it anymore, instead she is now a volunteer in their church. The pastor told her that she is now a "Born Again" person. I wonder how many more Catholics out there are asking the same question. A few months later, in the same Christian radio station, another "Born Again" lady asked if her parents are considered "Born Again". Her parents love the Lord, regularly read their Bible and truly live for God. The pastor's response was: "Yes, they are "Born Again" and added that the devout Catholics who practice or live out their faith as Christians are "Born Again." I hope that in writing my story all Christian denominations will understand that Catholics can be considered "Born Again" as well.

I was led to accept the Lord Jesus as my personal savior through another denomination. However, I know that there are many Catholics who did not became "Born Again" the traditional way like our evangelical Christian brothers and sisters. In some ways, Catholics were touched by God and become committed and truly repented for their sins and loved the Lord with all of their hearts, and in essence became "Born Again".

Our Lord Jesus said in John 3: 3 "Most assuredly, I say unto you unless one is born again, he cannot see the kingdom of God." The kingdom of God is the reign of God. It is a divine realm to be entered into, a realm that requires a divine life. Only the divine life can realize the divine things. Hence, for one to see, or to enter into, the kingdom of God, it requires that he/she be regenerated with the divine life.

For the benefit of my Catholic brothers and sisters, who have not yet accepted the Lord Jesus as their personal savior or "Born Again" is realizing God's purpose for all mankind: to be at peace with Him. In Romans 5:1 it says, "This peace can be attained only through our Lord and savior Jesus Christ. We are all separated from God because of sin." The bible also states in Romans 3:23;" For all have sinned and fall short of the glory of God." God has provided us the only way to bridge the gap between the sinful people and God, and that is through Jesus Christ who died on the cross for our sins.

In 1 Peter 3:18 it tells us, "For Christ also has suffered once for sins, the just for the unjust, that He might bring us to God." Therefore, we must trust Jesus and receive Him as our personal savior. As I share my life's story as a "Born Again" Catholic, I will be able to tell you how to receive Jesus and start a new beginning of an exiting, peaceful and joyful life; walking in obedience, enjoying His blessings and following God's ways.

The purpose of this book is to draw more Catholics into a saving knowledge of Jesus as our savior. Hopefully for all denominations, that they will open their mind to learn from each other's doctrine, not to criticize but to welcome what is best for God's kingdom. Christians of different denominations should pay attention of what they have in common rather than their differences. We believe in the same Lord Jesus Christ.

I hope that in sharing my life's journey as a "Born Again" Catholic, others will also grow deeper in their walk with God and genuinely follow Jesus' teachings.

It is also my hope that this book will help lessen the conflict among Catholic families when one family member becomes "Born Again" with the help of our evangelical Christian brothers and sisters.

This book is also my ethical will or legacy to my family since I am the first generation of "Born Again" Catholic in the Montesclaros-Suico clan.

Chapter 1

MY LIFE BEFORE KNOWING JESUS

I came to the U.S. from the Philippines as a Registered Nurse under the Exchange Visitors Program in 1964. When my contract was over, I did not want to go back to the Philippines so I immigrated to Canada. This was during "Expo 67" in Montreal, they were in need of nurses, and Veterans Hospital was recruiting nurses in New York with a promise to give us a Canadian Immigrant Visa within a month. Therefore, my friend Nilda and I grabbed this once-in-a-lifetime opportunity. I know God's hand was in this because my Exchange Visitors visa was to expire the following month.

I met Tony, my husband who was from India, when I was working in St. Anne de Bellevue, Quebec, Canada. This particular hospital had a dormitory for nurses, so when we went out we all went out in groups. One Saturday night, five of us nurses decided to go to Montreal for disco dancing. Because we were afraid to go with just us ladies, we asked the nice young man that worked in our hospital laboratory to come with us. Being a Saturday night, most Disco places were full. We tried three disco places and they were all full so we decided to go to this ball-room type dancing place. While in this place, a Chinese-Filipino man spotted us Filipino ladies, and he came over to our table to introduce himself and his friend Tony, (this is how I met Tony.) When people asked, "How did you two meet?" Tony used to say jokingly, "Oh I picked her up in a night club." It used to be funny in the beginning but later it began to sound irritating to me, but it was the truth. I met Tony again in a Filipino picnic and again in a Filipino party.

To make the story short we started going out, but then after one or two months I found out that Tony was four years younger than me. This bothered me so I called him and told him that I didn't want to go out with him anymore and the reason why. He tried to explain but I told him that I had made my decision and I hung up. A few minutes later he called back very upset and told me that he had swallowed half a bottle of Aspirin tablets.

To this day he is surprised that nothing happened and that he did not get sick with the amount of pills that he swallowed. Then later that evening, his friend that introduced us the first time we met called me and explained his point of view as well as Tony's. He added that my reason for break up was not good enough. My friends from Montreal also told me that Tony had climbed the stairs of St. Joseph Church kneeling and praying that I would go out with him and eventually marry him. St. Joseph Church in Montreal, Canada is a tourist area because this Church is famous until now to be a miraculous Church. So many prayer request and healing happened and were reported. Knowing this, I thought I never met a man that loved me this much and I remembered what my mother told me, to make sure to marry a person that really loved me. So, I decided to go out with him again. After few months passed we got engaged and in six months we got married.

The fact that Tony was a Hindu and me a Catholic did not even enter my mind. This is how I realized how weak my faith was at this time. Age was a more important issue to me than religion to base my marriage upon. Because Tony is a Hindu, the Catholic priest will not marry us unless Tony took 6 weeks of classes about Catholic religion. The priest who gave the classes seemed surprised because Tony was quite knowledgeable about the Catholic religion. It was because Tony used to be in a Catholic boarding school in his elementary years in India.

The first time I met Tony's family, his grandmother (Bhabiji Indian language for grandmother) told me in broken English, "Elma in my family no divorce okay?" I told her that that was great because Filipinos don't like divorce either.

We got married on June 8, 1968. The period of adjustment that most married couples have was tough for both of us. We had many disagreements and fights. Tony thought that it was because he did not keep his promise to climb, kneeling, all the stairs of St Joseph Church, he only went half way up. So one night he climbed, kneeling, the remainder of the stairs of St. Joseph Church. This Church is built on top of a mountain (Mount Royal) so there are over three hundred stairs to reach the Church.

Coming from a less advantaged, or poor family, I tend to be materialistic and selfish, besides, very temperamental and controlling as well. Tony's lay-back type of personality (he loves to sleep and watch TV) made our disagreements and arguments worst. Also, never miss a time when I'm having PMS (pre-menstrual syndrome,) we used to have big fights. Somehow, Tony and I never believed in this, we both thought it was because of the situation. However, the PMS is the big contributory factor. I realized it later because no matter how I tried to control it, especially if there were other people around, I still felt cranky and got angry easily.

When we got married Tony was still finishing his Bachelors in Business and I went back to school to get my

Bachelors in Nursing, in McGill University. Then I became pregnant during the last year of my studies. I was told by our Director of Nurses that I was putting too many eggs in one basket because I was working, going to school and keeping a home while I was pregnant. I also worked extra every now and then (part time,) if I needed to send money to the Philippines to help my family.

In 1970 we had our son, Devin. Most of our friends, 6 couples altogether, got married and had one child at around almost the same time as us. We hung out almost every weekend, for parties or going to picnics. We got caught up with daily routine. Because of our busy lifestyle, we never had time to pray or go to church for that matter. Tony used to go with me to church every Sunday a few months after we got married. After that he refused to come with me so I did not go to church either.

When I was single, back in the Philippines, in the U.S. and in Canada, I was very religious. I loved to go to church every Sunday, if I missed one Sunday I would have to go for confession. I was also a devotee of Virgin Mary (Our Lady of Perpetual Help) so I never missed any Wednesday novenas. In St. Anne de Bellevue Veterans Hospital, I used to attend mass in our Chapel every single day. There were times that it was only me, another nurse and the priest during the entire mass. I was so afraid that one day no one might show up to mass except for me so I had to make sure that I had someone with me to attend the mass. Somehow, no one seemed to attend mass unless it was a holiday of obligation. I think this also happens at the present time. It is so hard to get a seat in Church during Christmas and Easter.

In Montreal with both of us working, we didn't have much money or material things, but we were comfortable. We had a house in the Town of Mt. Royal, a posh town at that time and until now as well. But because of Tony's dream to make a million before he turns 40, we had to move to the U.S., Tony thought he could only make it big in America.

While waiting for our immigration papers, we moved to Toronto Canada. I remember it very well, we seldom fought. Until now, Tony still thinks it was the best time we ever had. Maybe it is because I did not work. I did not have the pressure of work. I stayed at home not by choice but because at that time in Toronto there was no job for nurses. Unbelievable as it seems, but the only nurses' position available advertised in the paper was "ear-piercing nurse," we don't even need a registered nurse to do this job anymore. We had a small condominium place, but comfortable. Since we had less income without me working, we did not aspire for a house. We lived within our means.

We moved to California in July of 1977. We drove from Toronto and it took us four days, stopping three nights in a motel. It was in this journey that Tony told me that since we are starting in a new place, we should start a new life by getting closer to God.

I worked in Downey as a staff nurse in Rancho Los Amigos Hospital, a county hospital. Tony worked as an accountant. When we moved, we already had a house in the city of Downey which was vacant for almost a year. We bought this house a year before we moved, when I took my California license exam.

The plan to get closer to God was soon forgotten. Tony went to church with me and Devin for a while, but after a few months he stopped. I continued to go without Tony. Devin as a little boy watching our neighbors going to Church as a family was somewhat bothered. He kept on asking me why his Dad was not going to church. My response was always "He is tired." How can I explain to a young boy the real reason?

During this time God was so distant from me. Yes, I went to church with or without Tony when I was not working on Sunday. I did not remember that God was my priority, number one in my life. The worst thing was that I didn't even know that I was a sinner. I was bad tempered, selfish, envious, prideful and a very stubborn person. I thought that they were inborn traits that I inherited from my parents who had one-fourth percent of Hispanic in their blood (my great-great grandfather used to be a soldier from Barcelona.) Our parents used to tell us that they inherited their bad temper from their Hispanic forefathers. Tony was not a saint either, therefore we used to have a fights that once even sent our son Devin into hiding.

In the first year in my new work place, in California, I worked night shifts. Our nurse in-charge always came to work with her Bible and during down time she used to read it. My exposure to Bible was nothing except what the priest read during mass but never a close look. In my childhood I was told that it is sin to read the Bible, only the priests were allowed to read as they were the only one who were allowed to interpret it. Later, I learned that our charge nurse was a wife of a Baptist pastor. I used to wonder why our charge nurse was full of peace even during our emergency code blue. She remained calm and was full of joy as well.

The first Christmas in my new workplace, our Head-nurse asked us where to hold our Christmas party. I volunteered to hold it in our house. In this gathering, Tony met the husband of our charge nurse and they had an unusually warm acquaintance. A week after the party, I learned (once the pastor was already in the house,) that a

Bible study had been scheduled. Because Tony did not tell me about it, I was very angry with him and because of my anger I did not come out from my room. Every week, the pastor would come to give a Bible study to Tony but I refused to participate. All the time I stayed in my room. Then Tony confronted me and tried to convince me to attend the Bible study. The result was a big argument and a fight. I guess Tony was embarrassed towards the Pastor because I would not participate but he never gave up. He kept trying to convince me. I told him I didn't want to be converted and become a Protestant. During my childhood days, we were discouraged to hang out with denominations other than Catholics.

I remember that during my high school years, there was a very nice third year student. She sung "Rock of Ages" during our convocation program in our school. My Catholic friends right away labeled her as Protestant and told me not to hang out with her. I had no idea why they are called Protestant because I had no knowledge about the Church history. I did not like the meaning and the word Protestant. It was the main reason why I did not want to attend the Bible study, besides, what would my family say? I was really worried about my very religious, die-hard Catholic grandmother, what would she do to me when she learned that I became a Protestant.

I was getting tired of the many arguments with Tony so I talked to my co-worker who was also a Catholic and told her about my problem. She told me that time has changed, nowadays they are not even called Protestants but Christians. She told me to think about God's main commandments, to love God and your neighbor. They were my neighbors therefore I should love them. Then, that Sunday the priest that gave the sermon said there is more than one pipeline to get to God. I really did not quite understand what he meant but then he said we all should read the Bible. He also said to get a Bible that is easy to understand. With a statement like that and coming from a priest, I decided to attend the Bible study.

Our progress with the study was very slow. The pastor was patient in explaining everything word for word and verse by verse. In spite of his explanations I still had problems understanding. I had so many questions. Later, did I understand that we have to receive Jesus as our savior first, and then the Holy Spirit would help us understand the Scriptures.

I cannot explain the struggle that I had deep inside me. One of my questions was, "Why place so much importance on Jesus?" The importance and emphasis of our faith should be on God the heavenly Father. Many weeks of Bible study and I still did not get saved. Maybe because our pastor was hesitant because of my previous negative behavior and the cold shoulder I gave him, or he was waiting for the upcoming weekend retreat in the mountain that was being planned by his congregation. He was planning to invite all of us to this particular retreat.

The family weekend retreat came. I did not remember paying for it so it was a free complement by our pastor and his friends who organized this spiritual retreat. I never saw so many happy and friendly people in my life. People made jokes in every social gatherings, some are dirty, but I noticed their jokes were all clean jokes. One joke I heard that I thought was funny; One Christian asked another Christian, 'When did you get saved? Before he could give an answer a Catholic person asked, "Why? Did you drown? "When?" You see, we Catholics don't know what getting saved means. It was my first religious retreat, so I had no idea what to expect. I only knew a few people there, so I was quiet, observant and was content just watching everyone. Tony, being a sociable person and one who loved to talk, had already made friends with so many, and he told me that they were all Christians.

In the evening a renowned speaker was scheduled to talk, I made sure to go there early to get a good seat. As expected, it was a great sermon, of course Christian preachers are known for this. When the preacher asked for those who wanted to receive Jesus to come forward, Tony and I went forward. I did not feel anything to begin with in fact I was questioning myself about why I went forward. I did not realize it then but later I knew my heart was not in it. I was still full of pride and it was not a real repentance. At this point, to be honest, I still didn't know that selfishness, pride and a bad temper are sins. As I compared myself to others, I knew that I was not that bad. I considered myself a good person. I know now why in Billy Graham's crusade, a follow-up to those who receive the altar call is a must. Most probably they knew that some folks like me, without real repentance and real understanding just go forward with the crowd.

Later that evening, one Christian lady gave me a hug and said, "I saw you went forward during the altar call. Congratulations! Now you are saved! You are now my sister in Christ!" I felt anger and resentment inside me with her statement. I thought, "Why?" I was already saved. I believed in Jesus!

We went home after the retreat. The next day was still my day off. I remembered what the main speaker said that we must read our Bible to grow in our faith and to know more of Jesus. I picked up my Bible and started reading. I started reading from the beginning; in the book of Genesis. I had trouble understanding in some areas but I kept on reading until my mental absorption gave out. I looked at our clock and realized that I had been reading for more than three hours. I stopped reading, my mind wondered off and I was thinking about the retreat. A few minutes later, still thinking about something, unconsciously I was flipping my Bible. I was about to stand to start my housework, when I just happened to glance at the page of the Bible and it was in Revelation 20:6, it says, "And He said to me, 'It is done! I am the Alpha and the Omega, the Beginning and the End I will give of the fountain of the water of life freely to him who thirsts.' I just knew Jesus was talking to me and I started to cry uncontrollably. Somehow the word "Alpha" and "Omega," "Beginning" and "End" touched me. I just knew Jesus gave me this verse in the Bible because He knew that I doubted Him. I doubted that He is God and I doubted His resurrection. Right there I repented for my prideful heart and unbelief. I knew, that I had then understood, that I honestly repented and asked Jesus to come into my heart and to change me.

My sister-in-law, Tina, forwarded this story which I think everyone should read, because this story will increase our faith.

DOES EVIL EXIST? DID GOD CREATE EVIL?

The University professor challenged his students with this question.

"Did God create everything that exists?

A student bravely replied, "Yes he did!"

God created everything?" The professor asked.

"Yes sir," the student replied.

The professor answered, "If God created everything, then God created evil, since evil exists, and according to

My Life Before Knowing Jesus

the principal that our works define who we are, the God is evil."

The student became quiet before such an answer. The professor quite pleased with himself, boasted to the students that he had proven once more that the Christian faith was a myth.

Another student raised his hand and said, "Can I ask you a question professor?

"Of course," replied the professor.

The student stood up and asked," Professor does cold exist?"

"What kind of question is this?" Of course it exists. " " Have you never been cold?" The students snickered at the young man's question.

The young man replied, "In fact sir, cold does not exist.

According to the laws of physics, what we consider cold is in reality the absence of heat. Every body or object is susceptible to study when it has or transmits energy, and heat is what makes a body or matter have or transmit energy. Absolute zero [- 460? F] is the total absence of heat; all matter becomes inert and incapable of reaction at that temperature. We have created this word to describe how we feel if we have no heat."

The student continued, "Professor, does darkness exist?"

The professor responded, "Of course it does."

The professor responded, "Of course it does."

The student replied, "Once again you are wrong sir, darkness does not exist either. Darkness is in reality the absence of light. Light we can study, but not darkness. In fact we can use Newton's prism to break white light into many colors and study the various wavelengths of each color. You cannot measure darkness. A simple ray of light can break into a world of darkness and illuminate it. How can you know how dark a certain space is? You measure the amount of light present. Isn't this correct? Darkness is a term used by man to describe what happens when there is no light present."Finally the young man asked the professor, "Sir, does evil exist?"

Now uncertain, the professor responded, "Of course as I have already said. We see it everyday. It is in the daily example of man's inhumanity to man. It is in the multitude of crime and violence everywhere in the world. These manifestations are nothing else than evil."

To this the student replied, "Evil does not exist sir at least it does not exist unto itself. Evil is simply the absence of God. It is just like darkness and cold, a word that man has created to describe the absence of God. God did not create evil. Evil is the result of what happens when man does not have God's love present in his heart. It's like the cold that comes when there is no heat or the darkness when there is no light." The professor sat down.

The young man's name --- Albert Einstein

After reading this story, I wondered if my own faith would have become stronger had I read it before, when I was in doubt of my Christian faith. But then I thought, maybe not. Because when I made a decision to believe and accept Jesus as my Savior, then only my faith changed and my life was transformed. When the life of the risen Christ dominates in me, only then did I begin to understand what He taught while here on earth. I grew and developed the right condition inward, in my spirit, and the words that

Jesus spoke became so clear. I am amazed at why I did not grasp it before. I was not able to understand them because I had not yet developed in me the proper spiritual condition to deal with them. Now, I realize that what they said was true. As soon as I believed and put my trust in Jesus, the Holy Spirit testified to God's truth and He opened my eyes. God cannot reveal anything to us if we don't have His Spirit. The supernatural miracle happened, and I received the gift of faith that came only from God.

Oswald Chambers in his book, <u>My Outmost for His Highest</u>, said: Faith is the entire person in the right relationship with God through the power of the Spirit of Jesus Christ.

In the natural world we always ask for a miracle first in order to believe. Always, "To see is to believe," but in God's kingdom it doesn't work that way. We have to believe first, and then we see. That is why we need to make a decision to receive Jesus as our personal Savior.

"Now He who establishes us with you in Christ and has anointed us is God, who also has sealed us and given us the Spirit in our hearts as a deposit." (2 Corinthian 1:21-22.) Billy Graham explains this comprehensively in his book, <u>Hope For Each Day</u>, he writes: As we trust in Christ, God gives us the Spirit as a pledge, or, as some translations read, earnest or guarantee. "He... put His Spirit in our hearts as a deposit, guaranteeing what is to come."

In the Apostle Paul's day, a deposit or pledge did three things; it was a down payment that sealed a bargain, it represented an obligation to buy, and it was a sample of what was to come. As an illustration, suppose you decided to make a down payment on a new car. What does your deposit represent? First, it seals the transaction; from now on, both you and the seller are committed. Also, it shows that you have committed yourself to pay the rest of the purchase price. Finally, it enables you to take possession of the car right now (even though it still belongs to the bank!)

In the same way, the Holy Spirit in our hearts is God's pledge or deposit to us—sealing His commitment to save us, guaranteeing that some day our salvation will be complete, and enabling us to experience its joys right now.

Little by little the Holy Spirit is changing us to be like Jesus. 1

Chapter 2

LIVING WITH JESUS AS MY PERSONAL SAVIOR

The following morning after I got saved, on my way to work, I noticed the grass and the trees were greener and the sky was blue and beautiful. Somehow I felt great and more peaceful. Later I saw a police car a few blocks from our hospital. The police was guiding a handcuffed, black young man to get into the police car. All of a sudden I started to cry and said, "Poor him! God please save and help him!" Later I asked myself, "What happened to me? Before, when I saw a person get arrested I used to say, "Well! " It is about time to pay-back for crime baby!" Sometimes feeling pleased that they got caught.

I heard from one Evangelical preacher on TV a few years later that the first sign of a "Born Again" Christian is love. Like Jesus; He loved the sinner but hated the sin. By receiving and accepting Jesus as my savior, and in repenting sincerely for my sins, it was the beginning of my new, changed life. Little by little I grew in my faith; however I did still have doubts. I read my Bible everyday. This was also the beginning of my quest of trying to know the Lord Jesus more. It seemed as though I could not get enough of God's word.

At work, if I saw any writing in magazines or books that pertained to God, I read it regardless of what denomination. Also, when I used to hear or attend mass on

Sundays, during the sermon or homily I used to keep watch of the time as to when it would be over. It seemed too long and boring. After I was saved, I wanted to hear everything. I paid full attention and the sermon seemed short. I could not get enough of God's Word. Now everything was meaningful to me including the hymns that were sung in church, it moved and touched me.

The hunger for God's word and the desire to know more about Jesus, made me listen to any Christian broadcast. My favorites until now are, "Through the Bible Radio" and "For Every Man an Answer," it is recently called "Pastor's Perspectives." I also loved to listen to different pastors' preaching at Calvary Chapel. I read books that helped me know God more as well. I read the book of J.I. Packer, <u>Knowing God</u> and Colson's book, <u>Born Again;</u> these two books had a great impact on my Christian walk.

Every now and then doubts and questions would creep in. It must have been because my faith was not strong or it could be what St. Paul talked about in his letter to the Corinthians, "And I, brethren, could not speak to you as to spiritual people but as to carnal, as to babes in Christ. I fed you with milk and not with solid food; for until now you were not able to receive it, even now you are still not able; for you are still carnal. For where there are envy, strife, and divisions among you, are you not carnal and behaving like mere men?" (2 Cor.3: 1-3.) It could also be that I got converted just in my head and not from my heart.

I always thought that I had to earn my salvation. I had to be good, otherwise God wouldn't love me or I would go to hell. It was hard for me to accept that there is nothing I can do to win my salvation. I used to read Novenas or prayers that give big points of indulgences to get merit of forgiveness. But salvation is free! Actually it is not free because Jesus had to die for my sins.

My faith was really tested during Easter time a few months after I was saved. I heard one of our nursing attendant say, "I have to go to church Sunday! It's Jesus resurrection day! That is why Jesus is alive today."

All of a sudden I made this comment, "Do you really believe that Corina?" I remember she was really upset with me and told me, "Shame on you! And you call yourself a Christian?" Then she left, leaving me stunned. One of the nurses who were there told me, "Are you going to take that from her? That was very disrespectful of her talking like that to her nurse in charge." I said, "That's okay, I must have angered her that much." I thought, 'Out of your mouth your heart speaks. Was it me or the devil?' I asked myself. Then I prayed, "Oh God help my unbelief. Give me faith like Corina!" Later in one of my Bible study times I learned that even our faith is a gift from God. My Christian friend told me to pray to Jesus because He is the author and the finisher of our faith.

I also had a question about the Bible. Is this really the word of God? It was written by men! This question was answered when I heard Pastor McGee's broadcast in "Thru the Bible Radio." Since I only heard part of the sermon I called and ordered his book. Pastor Vernon McGee was a renowned Christian preacher in our time. Although he passed away a few years ago his radio program still exists, in fact it is broadcasted all over the world. This question is so common to all; how much more to a baby Christian like me. It should be asked and answered. In Pastor McGee's book he gave 5 reasons to this question:

How Do You Know the Bible is from God?

1. Preservation- One of the objective proofs, one of the external proofs, has been the marvelous preservation of the Bible. There was a king of old – we read about him in Jeremiah – who, when the Word was sent to him, took a penknife and cut it into pieces. But it was rewritten, and we have that Word today. Down through the centuries there have been a great many Bible burnings. Today there's a great deal of antagonism towards the Bible. In our country today it is not being burned because we think that we are too civilized for such behavior. Many "enemies of God's Word" try to get rid of it in our schools and in many other places. (Yet we talk about our freedom of religion and freedom of speech.) In spite of all the attacks that have been made upon the Bible, it still exists today – and of course, it's one of the best sellers. For many years it was the best seller, but it's not today. I regret to have to say that, but it's true. And that is certainly a commentary on our contemporary society. It reveals that the Bible is not really occupying the place that it once did in the history and in the life of this nation. Yet I think that the amazing preservation of the word of God is worthy of consideration.

2. Archaeology – Another way in which we know the Bible is the Word of God is through archaeology. The spade of the archaeologists has turned up many things that have proven that this book is the Word of God. For instance, critics for many years denied the Mosaic authorship of the Pentateuch on the basis that writing was not in existence in Moses' day. You haven't heard anybody advance that theory recently, have you? Well of course not. For years the spade of

the archaeologists has turned up again and again more evidence of the validity of the Bible. The city of Jericho and the walls that fell down are one example. Now there has been some argument between Miss Kathleen Kenyon and Sir Charles Marsdon relative to specifics, but it's well established that the walls did fall down and I'll let them debate about the time and all that sort of thing. The Word of God has been substantiated there, and in many other ways archaeology has demonstrated the accuracy of the Bible. Many of the manuscripts that have been found do that as well. It's quite interesting that when the Isaiah Scrolls, the Dead Sea Scrolls, were found, the liberal leaped because he thought he had found an argument that would discredit the Bible. However the scrolls have not discredited the Bible, and it seems that the liberal has lost a great deal of what has been getting them interested. This is a field into which you might do some research, as I cannot go to any great length in this brief study.

3. Fulfilled Prophecy – If I were asked today whether I had just one thing to suggest as a conclusive proof that the Bible is the Word of God, do you know what I would suggest? I would suggest fulfilled prophecy. Fulfilled prophecy is the one proof that you cannot escape, the one that you cannot move around. And the Bible is full of fulfilled prophecies. One–fourth of the Scripture, when it was written, announced things that were to take place in the future. A great deal of that - in fact, a great more than people imagine – has already been fulfilled. We could turn to many places where prophecy has been fulfilled exactly. We find that there were many local situations that were fulfilled even in the day of the prophet. For example,

Micaiah was the prophet who told Ahab if he went out to battle as he planned, he would lose the battle and would be killed. However, Ahab's false prophets had told him he would have victory and would return as a victorious king. Because he didn't like what Micaiah said, Ahab ordered him to be locked up and fed bread and water, and said he would take care of him when he got back. But Micaiah shot back the last word, "If you come back at all, the Lord hasn't spoken by me." Well, evidently the Lord had spoken to him because Ahab didn't come back. He was killed in the battle, and his army was defeated. He had even disguised himself so that there would be no danger of losing his life.

But an enemy soldier, the Scripture says, pulled his bow at a venture; that is, when the battle was about to be over, he had just one arrow left in his quiver; he put it in place and shot, not really aiming at anything. But you know, that arrow must have had Ahab's name on it and it found him. It went out to its mark. Why? Because Micaiah made an accurate prophecy. (1 Kings 22)

On another occasion, the prophet Isaiah said that the invading Assyrian army wouldn't shoot an arrow into the city of Jerusalem (2 Kings 19:32.) Well now, that's interesting. Micaiah's prophecy was fulfilled because a soldier shot an arrow by chance; pulled his bow at a venture. Wouldn't you think that among two hundred thousand soldiers – that "great host" – perhaps one might trigger-happy and would pull his bow at a venture and let an arrow fly over Jerusalem? Well, no one did. If the enemy had shot an arrow inside that city, they could be sure that Isaiah was not God's prophet. But he was, as was proven by this local fulfillment of his prophecy.

But Isaiah also said a virgin would bring forth a child, and that was seven hundred years before it was literally fulfilled. If you want a final proof, there were over three hundred prophecies concerning the first coming of Christ, which were all literally fulfilled. As Jesus Christ was there, hanging on the cross and dying, there was one prophecy recorded in the Old Testament that had not been fulfilled. It was, "They gave me vinegar to drink" (Ps.69:21.) Jesus said, "I thirst," and the enemy himself went and fulfilled the prophecy (John 19:28-30.) It's a most amazing thing.

Men can't guess like that. I have given very few examples of fulfilled prophecy, but in the Word of God there is prophecy after prophecy, and they have been fulfilled, literally fulfilled. By the way, I would think that that indicates the method by which prophecy for the future is yet to be fulfilled.

4. Transformed Lives – I offer two final reasons as proof that the Bible is the word of God. One is the transformed lives of believers today. I have seen what the Word of God can do in the lives of men and women. I'm thinking right now of a man in Oakland, California, who listened to my Bible teaching program. He probably had as many problems, as many hang-ups, and was in as much sin as any man that I know anything about. And this man began by listening to the radio program. I know of people who just hear the Gospel once and are converted. I think it's possible and that it is wonderful. But this man listened to it week after week and he became antagonistic. He became angry. Later he said to me, "If I could have gotten to you when you were teaching the Epistle to the Romans and you told me that I was a sinner, I would have hit you in the nose,"

and frankly, I think he could have done it. He's bigger and much younger than I am. I'm glad he couldn't get to me. Finally, this man turned to Christ. It has been wonderful to see what God has done to his life. Again and again and again this testimony could be multiplied. Young and old have found purpose and fulfillment in life, marriages have been saved, families reunited, individuals have been freed from alcoholism and drug addiction. Folk have had their lives transformed by coming to Christ. When I finished seminary, I was a preacher who majored in the realm of the defense of the Gospel, and I attempted to defend the Bible. In fact, I think every message I gave entered into that area. I felt that if I could just get enough answers to the questions that the people raised for not believing the Bible, they would believe. But I found out that the worst thing I could do is to whip a man down intellectually. The minute I did that, I made an enemy and that I could never win for the Lord. So I moved out of the realm of apologetics and into another area of just giving out God's Word as simply as I could. Only the Bible can turn a sinner into a saint.

5. Spirit of God Made it Real – Another reason that I've moved out of the realm of apologetics is because there has been a certain development in my own life. I have reached the place today where I not only believe that the Bible is the Word of God; I know it's the Word of God. I know it's the Word of God because the Spirit of God has made it real to my own heart and my own life. That is the thing Paul talked about to the Colossians. He prayed that they "might be filled with the knowledge of His will in all wisdom and spiritual understanding." I also want this

because I found out that the Spirit of God can confirm these things to your heart, and you don't need archaeology or anything else to prove that the Bible is God's Word. A young preacher said to me sometime ago "Dr. McGee isn't wonderful that they have discovered this?" He mentioned a recent discovery in particular. And I said, "Well, I don't see anything to be exited about." He was greatly disappointed and even chagrined that I did not respond enthusiastically.

"Why, what do you mean?" he asked. "Is it possible that this hasn't impressed you?" I answered him in this way, "I already knew it was the word of God before the spade of archaeologists turned that up." He asked how I knew it, and I said, "The Spirit of God has been making it real to my own heart." I trust that the spirit of God is going to make the Word of God not only real to you, to incorporate it into your living, but that He is also going to give that assurance that you can say, "I know that it's the Word of God." 1

Whence but from heaven, could men unskilled in arts,
    In several ages born, in several parts,
    Weave such agreeing truths, or how, or why,
    Should all conspire to cheat us with a lie?
    Unasked their pains, ungrateful their advice,
    Starving their gain and martyrdom their price.
                    --Dryden

Dr. McGee also explained in his book why the Bible is a unique book. He states, "In many ways the Bible is a most unusual Book. For instance, it has a dual authorship.

In other words, God is the author of the Bible, and in another sense man is the author of the Bible. Actually, the Bible was written by about 40 authors over a period of approximately fifteen hundred years. Some of these men never even heard of the others, and there was no collusion among the forty.

Two or three of them could have gotten together, but the others could not have known each other. And yet they have presented a book that has the most marvelous continuity, of any book that has ever written. Also, it is without error. Each author expressed his own feelings in his own generation. Each has limitations, and made his mistakes – poor old Moses made mistakes, but when he was writing the Pentateuch, somehow or other no mistakes got in there. You see, it is a human Book and yet it is a God Book."

It is a very human Book, written by men from all walks of life, prince and pauper; the highly intellectual and the very simple. For example, Dr. Luke writes almost classical Greek in a period when the Koine Greek was popular. His Greek was marvelous! But Simon Peter, the fisherman, wrote some Greek also. He was not so good, but God, the Holy Spirit, used both of these men. He let them express their thoughts and feelings exactly, and yet through that method the Spirit of God was able to overrule in such a way that God said exactly what He wanted to say. That's the wonder of the Book; the Bible.

It is a God-Book. In the Bible God says twenty-five hundred times, "God said...the Lord has said...thus saith the Lord," and so on. God has made it clear that He is speaking through this Book. It is a Book that can communicate life to you. You can even become a child of God, begotten "not by corruptible seed, but by incorruptible, by the Word of God that liveth and abideth forever." It is God's communication to man. And if God spoke out of heaven right now, He would just repeat Himself because He has said all that He wants to say to this generation. And, by the way, He didn't learn anything when He read the morning paper. When men went to the moon, he didn't discover anything that God didn't already know when He gave us the Bible. He is the same God who created this universe that we are in today.

The Bible is both divine and human. In a way it is like my Lord who walked down here and grew weary and sat down at the well. Although He was God, He was man. He talked with people down here and communicated with them. This is a Book that communicates. It speaks to mankind today. The Bible is for men as they are. 2

The Bible is a corridor between two eternities down which walks

The Christ of God; His invisible steps echo through the Old Testament,

 But we meet Him face to face in the throne room of the New; and it is

Through that Christ alone, crucified for me, that I have found forgiveness

For sins and life eternal. The Old Testament is summed in the word Christ;

The New Testament is summed up in the word Jesus; and the summary of the whole Bible is that Jesus is the Christ.

- Bishop Pollock

Psalm 33:11 says, "The counsel of the Lord stands forever, the plans of His heart to all generation." The Bible, the Word of God is absolute necessity for every person because it contains God's principles, rules and regulations on how to live. The counsel of God is through His word, the Bible. God gave His Word to us, His church. His Word contains His solution to all human problems, spiritual, physical, emotional, financial, family, marriage and etc. The Bible is the answer to our problem. If we find the Word we will have our answer. Jesus said, "If you abide in My Word, you are My disciples indeed. And you shall know the truth, and the truth shall set you free." (John 8:31-32) In order to abide in His Word we need to study and meditate the Bible. During my adversity; which I will mention in great length later, God's Word set me free from mental oppression, strengthened and comforted me and encouraged me to go on. In a letter to a friend Abraham Lincoln said, "I am profitably engaged in reading the Bible. Take all of this Book upon reason that you can and the balance upon faith, and you will live and die a better man." 3 ("One Sure Guide" from Hope For Each Day)

Chapter 3

LIFE'S JOURNEY WITH JESUS: THE CHANGED LIFE

Before I proceed to mention the major changes in my life after being "Born Again."

I have to tell you why we need to be "Born Again." You see, I had been following and doing what I was brought up to do as a good Catholic is supposed to do. I followed the rituals and prayers, without understanding the main reasons for them. There was no change in my life pertaining to my relationship with my Lord and Master Jesus Christ. Not until I gained the understanding of what salvation really meant, did I experience a changed life.

It is not enough to believe in Jesus, one Pastor said, even the devil believes in Jesus. We have to receive this gift of salvation by accepting Jesus as our savior. I used to think that it was automatic; if we believe in Jesus alone, we get our salvation. Like any gift, we have to receive and accept the gift to be ours. Salvation means to enter into the kingdom of God." For there is one God and one Mediator between God and men, the man Christ Jesus." (1 Timothy 2:5).

Our salvation comes in different stages:

Justification – We are justified by the death of Jesus alone, because he is without sin. That is why we cannot save ourselves; because we are sinful. The Bible said, "If we say we don't sin we are a liar." I am made right with God because, prior to all of that, Christ died. When I turn to God and by belief accept what God reveals, the miraculous atonement by the Cross of Christ instantly places me into a right relationship with God. And as a result of the supernatural miracle of God's grace, I stand justified, not because I am sorry for my sin, or because I have repented, but because of what Jesus has done. The Spirit of God brings justification with shattering, radiant light, and I know that I am saved, even though I don't know how it was accomplished. "Therefore, if anyone is in Christ, he is a new creation; old things have passed away; behold, all things have become new. Now all things are of God, who has reconciled us to Himself through Jesus Christ, and has given us the ministry of reconciliation, that is, that God was in Christ reconciling the world to Himself, not imputing their trespasses to them, and has committed to us the word of reconciliation."   (2 Cor. 6: 17-19).

This stage happens instantly. Because we are justified by the death of Jesus on the cross, we now officially become the children of God. "But as many as received Him, to them He gave the right to become children of God, to those who believe in His name: who were born not of blood, nor of the will of the flesh, nor of the will of man, but of God." (John 1: 12-13.) We now have many privileges as a child of God. I am now a child of the King of Kings, the God of the universe.

Sanctification – Holiness or sanctification starts as justification finishes. Sanctification means that as a believer we are now set apart from sin and are made holy. Because we are now His children, He fills us with His Holy Spirit. We are now identified with Him. When Paul said in Galatians 2:20, "I have been crucified with Christ...." He meant, "I have been identified with Him in His death." Our total commitment of ourselves to God gives the Holy Spirit the opportunity to grant to us the holiness of Christ.

"...it is no longer I who live...." My individuality remains, but my primary motivation for living and the nature that rules me are radically changed. I have the same body but the old satanic right to myself has been destroyed.

" ...and the life which I now live in the flesh," not the life which I long to live or even pray that I live, but the life I now live in my mortal flesh – the life which others can see, " I live by faith in the son of God...." This faith was not Paul's own faith in Jesus Christ, but the faith that the Son of God had given to Him, (see Ephesians 2:8.) It is no longer faith in faith, but a faith that transcends all imaginable limits – a faith that comes only from the Son of God." 1

Because of my position in Christ, with Him as my savior, I am now sinless and righteous in the eyes of our heavenly Father. We are beginning to change little by little until we are completely changed. In my case, the sin that I was not bothered with before, the Holy Spirit is now convicting me for. For example, if I lost my temper, I immediately ask for God's forgiveness and apologize to that person. To ask for apology is much easier to do, which previously was very hard because of my pride or ego. In the past, during a family argument, when I knew I was right I refused to apologize, now it does not matter who is right or who is wrong. If I don't apologize I won't be able to sleep. It is not that I am sinless because I'm born again but now I sin less and if I do sin, immediately I ask for God's forgiveness and try not to do it again.

I noticed I did not like to go to any "dance parties" anymore. I used to party a lot and I loved to dance as most Filipinos do, but somehow I lost the desire to dance. I do not even participate in group dancing. It is true that God changes our desires as well. I stopped watching T.V. shows that have fowl language, sex or violence. I only watch TBN programs and CBN. Lately I had been watching Korean soap, those with English subtitles because their shows were mostly clean. My son, Faustin, told me, "Mom, you only watch G-rated shows now. Which means God - rated, right?" I also stopped using profanity and uncouth words. Now, it bothers me a lot, when I listen to people swearing, especially using God's name in vain. At work, I try not to participate in listening to my co-workers when they are telling dirty jokes. After a while, I noticed my co-workers tried not to tell dirty jokes when I was around.

To build my faith, I desired to know more about Jesus. Since my understanding of the Bible was very little and I had so many questions that I wanted to ask, we decided to have a Bible study in our house. In our parish Church, Bible study was only offered in the morning. Since I worked during daytime, I was unable to attend any of the Bible studies being offered. One time, during our Bible study at home, Tony, my husband, asked this question, "How can we know that Jesus is God?" I think Tony was not satisfied with the answer because he said, "I suppose we just have to believe by blind faith?"

Years later, after I had received Jesus as my personal savior, I recalled Tony's question to our pastor, during a Bible Study. I remembered this clearly because of his comment earlier. I asked Tony this question: "Are you fully convinced now, that Jesus is God?" Then I shared with him what I had just read in Hope For Each Day, meditation book by Billy Graham. I will mention it here because like Tony, and me, many asked this particular question.

Jesus is God because of the following reason:

First, there was the proof of His perfect life. He could ask, "Which of you convicts me of sin?" (John 8:46.) – and no one can answer.

Second, there was evidence of His miraculous power. His power was the power of God Almighty. The Bible has many stories of the miracles that Jesus performed.

Third, there was evidence of fulfilled prophecy. Hundreds of years before His birth the prophets of the Old Testament spoke precisely of His death and resurrection.

Fourth, there was evidence of His resurrection from the dead. Fifth, there is the proof of changed lives. Christ alone, the divine Son of God, has the power to change the human heart, and He does. 2

Looking at my own life, knowing Jesus really changed me completely. I used to be religious and devoted to God, but there was no real transformation in my life. When I gave my life to Jesus as my Lord and Savior, my life was totally changed.

Faith in Christ is not a "blind faith" or "leap in the dark," it is based on the solid facts of Christ's life, death, and resurrection. We need a daily study of God's Word, the Bible, to have a relational knowledge of God. Jesus said, "And this is eternal life, that they may know You the only true God, and Jesus Christ whom you have sent. (John 17:3) Eternal life is the divine life with special function, and it is to know the Triune God, the Father, the Son and the Holy Spirit.

J.I. Packer, the famous author of the book <u>Knowing God</u>, when asked what he found helpful in experiencing the reality of knowing God, answered, "For me, the stewing over the Bible has been a really formative thing." Soaking yourself in Scripture is another way of putting it. Reading and re-reading and thinking about what I've read in Scripture, frankly, just enriches me more as I get older. As I do this, I'm able to see each bit of Scripture that I read more clearly in relation both to the rest of what's in the Bible and to the moral, practical realities of human life, both for my life and for the life of people around me. 3

When we are "Born Again" the Holy Spirit begins to work His new creation in us, and there will come a time when there is nothing remaining of the old life. Our old gloomy outlook disappears, as does our old attitude toward things, and "all things are of God" (2 Cor. 5:18.) How are we going to get a life that has no lust, no self-interest, and is sensitive to the ridicule of others? How will we have the type of love that "is kind...is not provoked, (and) thinks no evil? (1 Cor. 13:4-5) The only way is by allowing nothing of the old life to remain, and by having only simple, perfect trust in God—such a trust that we no longer want God's blessings, but only want God himself. St. Paul said in his letter to the Thessalonians, "For this is the will of God, your sanctification: that you should abstain from sexual immorality; that each of you should know to possess his own vessel, in sanctification and honor, not in passion of lust like the Gentiles who do not know God; that no one should take advantage of and defraud his brother in this matter, because the Lord is the avenger of all such, as we also forewarned you and testified. For God did not call us to uncleanness, but in holiness. Therefore he who rejects this does not reject man, but God who has also given us His Holy Spirit." (1 Thess. 4: 3-8)

The key to the right relationship with God and our fellow men is the work of the Holy Spirit. The Holy Spirit continuously will work with us until we die. The Holy Spirit is a living God, a part of the Holy Trinity. The works or the gifts of the Holy Spirit are: salvation, sanctification, piety, fortitude, charity and the fear of God, He keeps us dependent on Jesus, encourages us to do service for God, He makes our witness powerful and He gives us discernment in situations and circumstances (counsel, understanding and wisdom.) "But the fruit of the Holy Spirit is love, joy peace, longsuffering, kindness, faithfulness, gentleness, self-control. Against that there is no law." (Galatians 5: 22-23) Our part is to make sure not to grieve and quench the Holy Spirit. (1 Thessalonians 5:19) "not lagging in diligence, fervent in spirit, serving the Lord." (Romans 12: 11)

The Holy Spirit's work of sanctification makes us one with Jesus Christ, and in Him, one with God our heavenly Father, and it is accomplished only through the magnificent atonement of Christ. The effect in me is trust, obedience, service, and prayer, and this is the outcome of inexpressible thanks and adoration for the miraculous sanctification that has been brought about in me because of the atonement through the Cross of Christ.

This stage of sanctification is a process though; God saved us from being in sin from moment to moment because Jesus is continuously interceding for us. As I study and meditate in His word every single day, I wanted to please Him and follow his ways. At this point, I read the Bible and go to Church not because I feel obligated but because I want to. Because of my love for Him, I want to please Him and I want to worship and obey Him.

If we really mean the prayer of salvation in our heart, mind and soul, for sure we will have a new transformed life. Some signs of a transformed life are immediate and some signs come in a process. As you mature in your walk, the evidence of a mature spiritual person will start to show. You will love God and His Word and you will love others. This is because you are born of God, because you are now a child of God. As a child of God you are now living in His grace and you become a kind and forgiving person. It will be easier for you to keep His commandments and practice righteousness. "For this is the love of God, that we keep his commandments. And His commandments are not burdensome." (John 5:3) Of course our human nature will make us slip and fall and sin, but we don't habitually practice sin. Besides, if we do sin the Holy Spirit will convict us and we have to repent and confess our sins immediately. If we do habitually practice sin, we are not born of God or we are not a "born again" person. "Whoever has been of God does not sin, for His seed remains in him; and he cannot sin, because he has been born of God." (1 John 3:9) As a child of God we want to practice Christianity and apply God's Word in our life.

Lastly, we will be victorious Christians, (not wimpy) and we will be able to overcome the world. "For whatever is born of God overcomes the world. And this is the victory that has overcome the world – our faith. Who is he who overcomes the world, but he who believes that Jesus is the Son of God?" (1 John 5:4-5)

Chapter 4

MY PRAYER LIFE

Every religion has a concept and tradition of prayer. In general, there is reference to the human being seeking or having contact with God the Creator, or the Supreme Being, or at least a superior being. For a Christian, prayer is the raising of one's mind and heart to God. The praying soul, out of the depths of a humble and contrite heart, seeks to appear in God's presence, begging for the gift of contact with God. Prayer can be expressed through words, gestures, aspirations, or just elevations of the soul without being articulated in words. As one of the highest acts of a human being, prayer comes from the soul, the spirit, or, as graphically put, from the heart. Those whose hearts are far from God, do not offer the best of prayers. The Bible says: "The prayer of the upright is His delight" and "He hears the prayer of the righteous" (Proverbs 15:8, 29)

God knows our heart before we pray; yet it is useful for us to open our hearts to God. The heart is the place of desires, of decision, of truth, of encounter with God. It is in the heart that a person chooses life or death, chooses to say yes to God and obey His commandments, or to forsake God, the fountain of living water and to dig to oneself leaky cisterns that hold no water. It is in the heart that a person chooses to love the neighbor and seek reconciliation and peace, or to do otherwise. [1]

Christian prayer is moreover understood as communion with God, as a covenant relationship between men and God, who is Father, Son and Holy Spirit. God takes the initiative and the Holy Spirit guides us on how to pray. Christian prayer is generally offered to God the Father, through Jesus Christ His Son, in the unity of the Holy Spirit, (although one can also pray to Christ or to the Holy Spirit.) The intentions encompassed by prayer are as wide as the acts of the virtue of religion, namely: adoration, praise, thanksgiving, and propitiation for our offenses and petitions. For a Christian, the model prayer is the "Our Father," taught by Jesus himself and including seven invocations, which contain all that we can ask of God.

There are many forms of Christian prayer: liturgical prayer, that is, official prayer in the name of the Church (made up of sacraments, other public rites, and the Divine Office,) then devotional prayers of individuals or communities, meditative prayer, contemplation, silent adoration and intercessory prayer. [2]

"Devotional time or quiet time with God is one of the habits of a disciplined Christian. Why have devotional lives? Why take time to read God's Word, worship God and pray?

We don't do it because it is an obligation, but because it is an opportunity. If you think your devotional time is an obligation you will not get the promised blessings. Instead, it will turn out to be a burden. More Christians go on guilt trips over their undisciplined prayer life than perhaps any other personal problem. "Spending time daily with Christ in the Word and prayer should be an experience to enjoy and not an event to endure. Imagine a newly engaged fellow saying with a groan, 'Well, I have a date this evening with Lucy!' Or picture a child lamenting that Grandma and Grandpa are coming for a visit!"

Two words have rescued me from devotional doldrums: reality and relationship. The material world around us appears to be the real world, but it is not. In 1 John 2:17 John wrote, "The world is passing away." Paul reminded the Corinthians that "the things which are seen are temporary, but the things which are not seen are eternal"(2 Cor.4:18) A.W. Tozer used to remind us that the Bible world is the real world. When you spend time with the Lord you are in contact with reality, the things that matter most, the things that will last.

But you are also building a relationship, and in building this relationship you are building your own character and ministry. Jesus warned us, "Without Me, you can do nothing"(John 15:5.) If we abide in Christ, then we can bear fruit for His glory. "Your relationship with Jesus Christ is the single most important relationship in your life. Everything else flows out from it." [3]

Before I became a "Born Again" Christian, I did not have a regular time of prayer. Sometimes, when I was not tired, I would pray before going to sleep, the memorized prayer like the "Our Father," "Hail Mary" and then end it with "Glory be to the Father, to the Son, and to the Holy Spirit." When I became "Born Again," I was told that I should spend time with God regularly and read God's word so I would grow in my relationship with Him. Ever since I began spending time with the Lord regularly in prayer and in reading His Word, I have realized that my day goes smoothly at work and at home. My day is peaceful and if I encounter a problem, I seem to manage it well. Not only that, but if I miss my prayer time my day is chaotic. I dare everyone to try it and to see the difference for your selves. If we keep in mind what our devotional time means to our Lord, it will encourage us. God longs for our fellowship. That is why He created us.

Our devotional time should also mean something to us personally. We all need it. In my reading of God's word, God has many times given me guidance, confirmed decisions, issued warnings and granted promises just when I needed them. Our Father knows what we need, and if we allow Him, He will speak to us day after day through His Word.

Bible studying, if it takes time, like needing a Concordance, it should be done during a separate time, and not during your quiet time. We should simply be reading God's Word and receive it as though our Father is speaking to us. Usually, I prayed to the Holy Spirit to lead me into the truth that He wants me to receive for that day. I also pray for Him to help me understand if I have problem understanding the Bible. Sometimes the answer is immediate and other times it will become clear to me after a few days of spending time in His Word. If during my devotional time I received a personal message, a lesson learned, a nod of

My Prayer Life

encouragement or a promise to claim, I note it in my journal.

"David's heart thirsted for God as panting deer thirsted for water in the desert. Jacob would not let the Lord go until he had blessed him. Moses prayed to be privileged to see the glory of God. Even our Lord Jesus Christ rose up early in the morning that he might spend time with the Father in prayer. If the perfect Son of God needed to meet the Father each day, how much more do we need to meet Him!

The devotional time is a wonderful opportunity for us to please the Lord, grow in character, and be of greater help to those who need us. When, like Mary of Bethany, we spend time at the feet of Jesus, we are choosing that good part which can never be taken from us."[4]

As I matured in my walk as a "Born Again" Christian my prayer life was changed tremendously. My best time to pray was in the morning before I got ready for work. I made sure I spend 15 to 20 minutes. During this time I read my favorite praise and worship found in Psalms, thanking God for the favors from the previous day and for His protection during the night. Then I read "My Daily Bread," my meditation booklet for that day. After a few years I started to read Oswald Chambers', <u>My Utmost for His Highest</u> and Billy Graham's, <u>Hope for Each Day.</u> Then I prayed for traveling mercies, for guidance and protection, for a peaceful day at work and a prayer petition for that day. Every now and then I kept a journal of prayer and scriptures that touched my heart.

In the evening before I go to sleep I read and meditate on my "One Year Bible," the new international version. There is reading from the Old Testament, New Testament, Psalms and a few verses from Proverbs. I feel that this combination of readings communicates the truth and I always receive a lesson or two as well as encouragement from them. Then I pray for our government leaders especially our president, different ministries, especially the ministries that I support and partner with, for peace in the Middle East, especially Jerusalem and the nation of Israel, for my family's health and welfare, for the persecuted Christians all over the World and my regular intercessory prayers.

Oswald Chambers said, "Prayer is not a normal part of the life of the natural man," (not born again Christian). "We hear it said that a person's life suffers if he doesn't pray, but I question that. What will suffer is the life of the Son of God in him, which is nourished not by food, but by prayer. When a person is "Born Again" from above, the life of the Son of God is born in him and he can either starve or nourish that life. Prayer is the way that the life of God inside of us is nourished. Our common ideas regarding prayer are not found in the New Testament. We look upon prayer as simply as a means of getting things for ourselves, but the biblical purpose is that we may get to know God Himself." [5]

This is very true with my prayer life, before, I accepted the Lord. It used to be only "gimmie, gimmie" and a few intercessory prayers that my friends and family asked me to pray for them.

I found this old prayer of mine, which I wrote in the front page of my journal book. At this time I was a few months old believer.

My Prayer Life

Thank you heavenly Father for being so close to me

Thank you for drawing me to your Son Jesus

Thank you for Pastor Ed and Nellie Lacaba who helped me become "born again"

Thank you for giving me an open and a willing heart and the desire to know You.

Thank you for making me love Your Word and love You

Thank you for all Your teachings, and Your Holy Spirit's guidance.

Thank you for giving me clear understanding and for allowing me to listen

To Your Word, most of all thank you for talking to me.

Thank you for all the messages and lessons you give me each day

Thank you for Your workers, missionaries, evangelistic ministers, priests

Different ministries – all Your workers that diligently serve You.

In reading this prayer after many years, over 25 years, it amazes me that I did not pray for anything else besides just thanking Him. I am sure that the Holy Spirit was moving with me during this time.

I feel that our prayer is the most important work as a believer. Like Moses, God calls us to "hold up the staff of God"- to pray. "God was looking for a man who would build up the wall and stand before Him in the gap on behalf of the land so He would not have to destroy it, but He found none." (Ezekiel 22:30) We need to take our part in the plan and program of God seriously, developing the attitude that Samuel had toward Israel when he said, "As for me, far be it from me that I should sin against the Lord by failing to pray for you." (1 Samuel 12:2)

Prayer is work and prayer is hard work. But prayer is a holy work as well -vital and indispensable. God has a more difficult time finding people for prayer than for any other assignment.

Prayer includes meditating and studying God's Word. The Words of the Scripture are living Words. They are inexhaustible. They are eternal wisdom within the shell of human words. God wants us to "break open" His Word and for us to begin to discover the rich wealth of personal application and understanding which are in it. This is done through meditation and the teaching ministry of the Holy Spirit in us. "Do not let this book of the law depart from your mouth; meditate on it day and night, so that you may be careful to do everything written in it. Then you will be prosperous and successful." (Joshua 1:8) Meditation is a communion with God in the language of His own Word. Meditation is talking with the King's own Words. "My hand also will I lift up unto thy commandments, which I loved; and I will meditate in thy statutes." (Psalm 119:48) Meditation is a prayerful reviewing of the Scriptures. St. Paul told Timothy to "meditate upon these things."(1 Timothy 4:15)

My Prayer Life

Our Lord Jesus set such a glowing example to His disciples in prayer that they plead with Him to teach them how to pray. (Luke 11:1) As they had heard Him pray, a yearning had sprung up in their hearts to know a similar intimacy with the Father.

To the maturing Christian God's interests will always be important. The prayers of an immature Christian usually evolve around self. In response to the disciples' request to be taught how to pray Jesus said, "This then is how you should pray," and He gave them a pattern by which to model their prayers. "Our Father, Who art in heaven, Hallowed be thy Name: Thy kingdom come, Thy will be done on earth as it is in heaven. Give us this day our daily bread and forgive us our trespasses as we forgive those who trespass against us and led us not into temptation but deliver us from evil. Amen." It is noteworthy that in this prayer recorded in Mathew 6:9-13, the first half of the prayer is totally occupied with God and His interests. Only after that, do personal petitions find a place.

In reading and meditating God's Word, I think about the passage that touches me and make an application if it relates to my life. Then I ask questions; whether it is a command to obey or a promise to claim, or if there is sin that God wants me to avoid, or a new truth for me to learn, or an example for me to follow.

One thing I have to reiterate; we have to be watchful and be careful because prayer can become a mechanical routine, praying just for prayer's sake. We have to, "Think communication," you have to commune with the Holt Spirit, you have to communicate with the heavenly Father. Like regular conversation, this includes a great deal of listening. This needs practice and discipline.

Psalm 25 is my favorite prayer Psalm:

"To You Lord, I lift up my soul.

O my God, I trust in You;

Let me not be ashamed;

Let not my enemies triumph over me.

Indeed, let no one who waits on You be ashamed;

Let those be ashamed who deal treacherously without cause.

Show me Your ways O Lord;

Teach me Your paths.

Lead me in Your truth and teach me,

For You are the God of my salvation;

On You I wait all the day.

Remember, O Lord, Your tender mercies and Your loving kindnesses,

For they have been from of old.

Do not remember the sins of my youth, nor my transgressions;

According to Your mercy remember me,

For Your goodness sake O Lord.

Good and upright is the Lord;

Therefore He teaches sinners in the way.

The humble He guides in justice,

And the humble He teaches His way.

All the paths of the Lord are mercy and truth,

To such as keep His covenant and His testimonies.

For Your name's sake, O Lord, pardon my iniquity, for they are great.

Who is the man that fears the Lord?

Him shall He teach in the way He chooses.

He himself shall dwell in prosperity,

And His descendants shall inherit the earth.

The secret of the Lord is with those who fear Him,

And He will show them His covenant."

(Psalm 25: 1- 14)

This Psalm is my favorite prayer Psalm because I am asking for the deliverance of shame; forgiveness of my iniquities and for the sins of my youth, (which I have plenty of); it reminds God of His promises, His goodness, His mercies, His love and His ways; instruction of sinners of His ways; He reminds me to be humble so that He can guide me and He teaches me His ways, most of all, if I fear Him I will spend my days in prosperity, and my children and their children will inherit the land.

Linda Schubert author of a booklet called "Miracle Hour"- A method of prayer that will change your life; is a lay leader in the Catholic Charismatic renewal in San Jose, California. In 1997, she fell to her knees and prayed a prayer of surrender with Pat Robertson on the 700 Club television program. At that moment she knew, in the depth of her soul that "Jesus loves me." A whole new love for the Christian community and the Catholic Church began to blossom. She knew she would never again have to fight her personal battle again. The Lord gave her a scripture that was her special verse: "I set before you life and death, blessings and curses. Now choose life..." (Deut. 30:19). She came to know the Holy Spirit as her comforter, counselor, and best friend, and the one who would bring her into that abundant life in which she chose to live. She discovered that with Him she didn't need to hide or build walls. Linda is involved in writing, teaching workshops and prayer ministry.

Linda is actually one of my Christian heroes. She gave me the courage and the inspiration not only to pray at least one hour, but also to remain in the Catholic faith after being "Born Again".

In this booklet "Miracle Hour," Linda discussed the importance of prayer in every person's life. She encourages us to commit one hour to prayer each day. Linda received the inspiration from God who showed her a simple format for a daily hour that would not only draw us into deeper intimacy with God, but also empower us in our Christian walk. She divided the hour into twelve five-minute segments:

First segment –Praise

Second segment –Sing to the Lord

Third segment—Spiritual warfare

Fourth segment –Release of Holy Spirit

Sixth segment –Repentance

Seventh segment –Forgiveness

Eight segment – Scripture reflection

Ninth segment – Wait for the Lord to speak

Tenth segment – Intercessions

Eleventh segment – Petitions

Twelve segment – Thanksgiving

In each segment, Linda has suggested prayer and reflection as your guide to get you started. Between the five-minute segments, she suggested to add the "Our Father" and another prayer of your choice. For Catholics and others who are devoted to the mother of Jesus, to include a "Hail Mary." For those who pray in the charismatic gift of tongues, she encouraged that form of prayer language at various times throughout the hour.

I already mentioned earlier my routine system of prayer every day, but I used the same format of Linda's "Miracle Hour." With regards to time, sometimes I spend a little less than one hour and sometimes I can go for more than two hours depending on the Holy Spirit's leading.

There is such a desperate need for people of prayer in this world of Atheism and anti-Christian practices. I believe that God is calling His people to prayer more intensely than ever before. If we could only understand the immensity of God's plan and the importance of our prayers, we would stop in our tracks and reevaluate our priorities immediately. Life is just too short and too precious to waste on empty things.

Pray the following as you start your prayer hour: "Loving heavenly Father, we ask for a spirit of prayer to come upon us now. Increase our longing for You and our longing for the salvation of people around the world. I pray with the Psalmist, "As the deer pants for streams of water, so my soul pants for You, O God. My soul thirsts for God, for the living God. When can I go and meet with God?" (Psalm 42:1-2) Come Holy Spirit, I want to meet with God. Please teach me how to pray. Amen." [6]

Father God, I thank You for the Lord Jesus. He is Your Son and my Savior, my healer, my deliverer. He is the Apostle of my faith and the High Priest of my confession. It is in Him, Father, that I lift myself up on this day before You, giving You thanks for your directions; for Your guidance and for Your power to perform the Word of God in my life today.

Because of Christ being alive in my life I have power and ability. He has come into my life to make me successful and to put me over all things that pertain to life and godliness.

According to Matthew 16:19 and 18:18 "whatsoever I shall bind on earth shall be bound in heaven, and whatever I shall loose on earth shall be loosed in heaven." Therefore, I bind the spirits of fear, doubt, and timidity, in the name of Jesus; and I loose the Holy Spirit of faith, of love, of power and of a sound mind.

Father, You have blessed me with the blessings of the Lord, I am blessed when I go out and I am blessed when I come in. I am blessed in the field and I am blessed in the store. Everything I put my hands to is blessed. Now I don't run after these blessings; these blessings are running after me and overtaking me because You have made me the head and not the tail. I am born from above and not from beneath. My enemies come against me one way and seven flee. Goodness and mercy follow me all the days of my life.

In Jesus' name, Amen!

(Matthew 3:17; 2Timothy 1:10; Exodus 15:26; Genesis 22:14; Romans 14:17; Romans 2:26; Hebrews 3:1; Jeremiah 1:12; 2 Peter 1:3; Matthew 16:19; & 18:18; 2Timothy1:7; Deuteronomy 28:1-14; Psalm 23:6)

The Conqueror's Prayer

I arise today

Through God's strength to pilot me,

God's might to uphold me,

God's wisdom to guide me,

God's eye to look before me,

God's ears to hear me,

God's word to speak for me,

God's hand to guard me,

God's way to lie before me,

God's shield to protect me,

God's host to save me

From snares of devils,

From temptations of vices,

From everyone who shall wish me ill,

Afar and a near,

Alone and in multitude.

I summon today all these powers between me and those evils,

> Against every cruel, merciless power that may oppose my body and soul
>
> Against incantations of false prophets,
>
> Against black laws of pagandom,
>
> Against false laws of heretics,
>
> Against crafts of idolatry,
>
> Against spells of witches and smiths and wizards,
>
> Against every knowledge that corrupts man's body and soul.
>
> Christ shield me today
>
> Against poison, against burning,
>
> Against drowning, against wounding,
>
> So that there may come to me abundance of reward.
>
> Christ with me, Christ before me, Christ behind me,
>
> Christ in me, Christ beneath me, Christ above me,
>
> Christ on my right, Christ on my left,
>
> Christ when I lie down, Christ when I sit down,
>
> Christ when I arise,
>
> Christ in every man who thinks of me,
>
> Christ in the mouth of everyone who speaks of me,

Christ in every eye that sees me,

Christ in every ear that hears me.

I arise today

Through a mighty strength, the invocation of the Trinity

Through belief in the threeness,

Through confession of the oneness,

Of the Creator of Creation.

From Marilyn Hickey Ministries

Excerpt from "How The Irish Saved Civilization" by Thomas Cahill

Litany of Humility:

O Jesus, Meek and humble of heart, hear me

From the desire of being esteemed,

From the desire of being loved,

From the desire of being extolled,

From the desire of being honored,

From the desire of being praised,

From the desire of being preferred,

From the desire of being consulted,

From the desire of being approved,

Deliver me, Jesus,

From the fear of being humiliated,

From the fear of being despised,

From the fear of suffering rebukes,

From the fear of being calumniated,

From the fear of being forgotten,

From the fear of being ridiculed,

From the fear of being wronged,

From the fear of being suspected,

Deliver me, Jesus.

That others may be loved more than I,

That others may be esteemed more than I,

That in the opinion of the world, others may increase,

And I may decrease,

That others may be chosen and set aside,

That others may be praised and I unnoticed,

That others may be preferred to me in everything,

That others become holier than I, provided that

I may become as holy as I should,

Jesus grant me the grace to desire it.

Imprimatur: James A. Mcnulty – Bishop of Patterson N.J. (Taken from Pieta Prayer Booklet.)

Chapter 5

ANSWERED PRAYERS

Prayer is the speaking part of our relationship with God. Our relationship with Him depends upon our birth, while our fellowship—the quality of our relationship—depends upon our behavior. We must be born of God—"Born Again"—to be able to talk to God as His children in the first place, just as like with our own children. Our blood runs in their veins. Our relationship with our children depends upon their birth. If they mess up, our fellowship may be disrupted, but they will always be our children—our estranged children perhaps, but still our children.[1]

Jill Briscoe, author of <u>Prayer That Works</u> writes:

"To be effective in our prayer life we need to have the following:

First, We Need to Have Been Forgiven by God."Notice that it is the righteous man who has power with God. The Bible says, "The prayer of a righteous man is effective." (James 5:16 NIV.) Another way of looking at that word "righteous" is to realize that it means, among other things, that a person has been forgiven. Praying a simple prayer of repentance is to ask Jesus to enter into your life. Also, because the Holy Spirit helps us pray the right prayers we must confess anything that grieves the Holy Spirit.

What does the Scripture specifically say about the things that grieve the Holy Spirit? Ruth Paxson in her book, <u>Life on the Highest Plane,</u> says it well:

"To grieve the Holy Spirit means that we are causing pain to someone who loves us." What, then, in us causes the divine One grief?

He is the Spirit of Truth (John 14:17) so anything false, deceitful, or hypocritical, grieves Him.

He is the Spirit of Faith (2 Cor.14:13) so doubt, unbelief, distrust, worry and anxiety grieve Him.

He is the Spirit of Grace (Heb.10:29) so that which is hard, bitter, ungracious, unthankful, malicious, unforgiving or unloving grieves Him.

He is the Spirit of Holiness (Rom.1:4) so anything unclean, defiling, or degrading, grieves Him.

He is the Spirit of Wisdom and Revelation (Eph.1:17) so ignorance, conceit, arrogance and folly grieves Him.

He is the Spirit of Power, Love and Self-discipline (2 Tim.1:7) so that which is barren, fruitless, disorderly, confused or uncontrolled grieves Him.

He is the Spirit of Life (Rom.8:2) so anything that savors of indifference, spiritual dullness, deadness and that is lukewarm grieves Him.

He is the Spirit of Glory (1 Pet.4:14) so anything worldly, earthly, or fleshly grieves Him.

As long as we are indulging known sin, we are living in the same abode with a grieved Spirit who is thereby hindered from manifesting Himself fully and through us.

Second, We Have to Learn to Be Passionate in our Praying.

Elizah "prayed earnestly that it would not rain, and it did not rain" (James 5:17 NIV.) Elizah's heart was in his work. Many times we kneel to pray and we really don't care if God hears and answers us or not. Fervency is a condition of the heart that is developed through our growing relationship with God. As we grow to love Him, we find ourselves caring about the things He cares about. Prayers turns our thoughts away from our selfish concerns because we are putting ourselves into the presence of a selfless Being—and a little of that rubs off.

Third, We Need to Be a Persistent Prayer if We Are to See Our Prayers Work.

Elizah prayed continually about the work of God. He climbed a mountain and got to work. He set himself to watch and pray until the rain came. (Kings 18:42-46) Most of us give up far too soon when we are praying. We hit an obstacle such as unanswered prayer and stop dead in our tracks. When Elizah set himself to pray on the top of Mount Carmel, one gets the impression that he settled down until the answer came. God likes us to be persistent. Jesus told a story about a woman who persistently asked a judge to grant her request (Luke 18:1-8.) And Jesus commended the persistent, blind beggar (Luke 18:35-43.)

"I think that prayer is a bit like jogging. Everyone in my family was into the sport in a big way, and I didn't want to be left out. They talked enthusiastically about 'going through the wall.' I wondered what they meant. They explained that if you persisted when you felt you just had to give up, then you went through an invisible wall and got the second wind. It only happened to me once, but I do recall the sense of exultation and the sudden belief that I could run on forever. 2

I think that there is a wall as we engage in prayer as well. It's my belief that when many Christians practice prayer they live on this side of the wall. They get to what I call the point of push, and they stop instead of pressing on. Next time this happens to you, press on; be persistent and you will find yourself in a new country, a land of joy and freedom, with new hope and expectations. Persistence takes your prayer into a whole new orbit." "Are any among you suffering? They should keep on praying about it," (James 5:3.) Since I became a believer I have noticed that most of my prayers have been answered. I will mention only a few answered prayers that I sincerely believe was God's doing and I consider miracles.

I prayed that my son Devin would become a doctor. It has been my long time dream, (I was still single) to have one of my children become a doctor. As a nurse I always admired the hard work of a medical student. The process in becoming a doctor is long and hard, the dedication and sacrifice the doctors go through to practice medicine is indescribable. I always think it is a great, well-respected and noble profession. Working closely with them as a nurse, I sometimes wish that I was one of them. When my son was only two years old, his toys were mostly doctor's tools like a stethoscope, reflex hammer, syringes and needles, (without a sharp point.) His time playing with me was about patient and doctor, him the doctor and I his patient. I used to say "paging Doctor Chopra" and even when he was in another room, he would run where I was and say "Dr. Chopra." Some might call this "brain washing," but this is just to tell you how much I wanted him to become a doctor.

I used to attend a prayer meeting with Charismatic Catholics in Dominic Savio Church. One evening, an older man was sharing the importance of prayer and how God answered his prayers. He said that he prayed when both of his sons were under the age of five years old, he prayed that one of them would become a priest and the other would become a doctor, and just that happened. One became a priest and the other became a doctor. Since that time, after hearing that man's story, I started praying that my son would become a doctor.

At this time my son was in the fourth grade in "Our Lady of Perpetual Help" Catholic parish school. During his high school, a few months before his graduation, it seemed competition was tough and I was not sure if his grades would be high enough to enter the medical program, I told him to just take Pharmacy or Physical Therapist because it seemed he had a slim chance to get admitted to a medical school. But he told me that he would still go ahead and try as planned. I prayed that Devin would get accepted into any medical school. When he got accepted into one of the Podiatry schools in New York, Devin was very happy. I heard it from my neighbor that he was running in the street trying to tell everyone that he was accepted into medical school, even to people who he hardly knew. I prayed that he would maintain a good grade, get into a residency program and pass the board exam. The process over all was overwhelming, and Devin and me were always on our knees praying most of the time. God answered our prayers; he is a now, a practicing doctor and has two offices, one in Pico Rivera California and another in Whittier California.

The other answered prayer was for me to work as a school nurse. I always wanted to become a school nurse, when I realized that to work in nursing administration in any hospital was not my cup of tea. As a mother with a young child, I got attracted to work as a school nurse because the work schedule was great. When working in a school atmosphere, naturally you are off every weekend and holiday and have many vacation days.

In order for me to get ahead in my profession, I went back to school to get my Bachelor's in Nursing Degree. I specialized in administration and graduated in 1970. In 1977 we moved to Los Angeles California and I worked in Rancho Los Amigos Hospital. After many years of working as a hospital nurse, I felt burned out and needed a change. Then I remembered to try school nursing. When I answered an ad from Downey School District, they told me that I had to have a school teaching credential in order for me to be interviewed for the position. At that time I was unable to attend evening school because my son was still in Elementary school so I forgot all about my dream of becoming a school nurse. I continued to work in Rancho Los Amigos for about twelve years, then finally I decided to quit Rancho altogether to have my early retirement. The uncertainty of my future brought me on my knees to pray one evening. I was praying and at the same time complaining. I remember literally crying and telling God, "God! I thought you said in Your word that as Your child all my steps are directed by You! Why did You allow me to get my nursing degree and never let me use it? I don't need a nursing degree to be doing what I am doing now!" The next day a miracle happened. While working in my part time work in a nursing home, I met a new Filipino part time nurse for the first time. During our endorsement, I asked her where she regularly works and she told me that she was a school nurse trying to make extra money to pay for her tuition fees because she was taking her school nurse credentials. She then told me that with a Bachelor's in Nursing Degree, Los Angeles School Districts would hire me and allow me to work as a school nurse while taking classes towards getting my credentials in the evening. To make this story short, I was hired and worked as a school nurse, and in two and a half years I received my school nurse credentials.

  The following incident is an even greater miracle than the above story. It looks like the enemy tried to stop me from enjoying the best job that I had ever had. But thanks to God; He stopped the enemy from making that happen.

  Three months after I started to work as a school nurse, Los Angeles unified School District Personnel Department received a letter from Sacramento, telling them that my Bachelors Degree did not have enough credit to equal the Bachelors in the U.S. Shocked and puzzled I immediately went downtown to see the supervisor of personnel department. She reviewed my transcript and the evaluators' report and came to the conclusion that I needed four more units. She told me to take these courses and when I finished it to come back to see her. She also told me that I was going to be terminated from work in four days. She gave me the name and address of the school where I was to take my courses. Going home from the personnel's office I was quiet but not upset. I was still surprised and wondering how this could be. I totaled the number of years which I took my nursing school altogether, I had seven years total of nursing education. Four years of basic Nursing, including the preparatory nursing, and three years Bachelors of Nursing Accelerated program. The current nursing Bachelor's Program was only five years. I wondered why McGill University, one of the leading schools in Canada had a different Bachelors program than the U.S. Why was the Bachelors in the Philippines acceptable by the Los Angeles School District and not the Bachelors program of Canada? These questions kept popping in my mind.

Previously, when I had problems like this, I used to get upset, worried, angry, I would cry and carry it on me for a long time. This time I was not. Tony said, "Now I know that you are really, a changed person. You are so calm in spite of your problem." I was at peace and confident that God would deliver me from this problem because I knew that He had given me that job in the first place.

Everyone in my family wanted me to give up. Tony told me to work part time because I was closed to retiring anyway. Most educators I spoke to said, "Maybe Canada has a different system" and "Maybe it is because you graduated a long time ago; the system must have changed." Deep inside my spirit I felt the Holy Spirit's leading to pursue and find out more explanation that I could understand. I had my records evaluated from an agency in Long Beach and I was told that I had enough credit. When I told the personnel about it though, they told me that they didn't recognize or accept this particular evaluator. They recognized only three evaluators in the U.S. and she gave me the address of the evaluator in Sacramento. A few days after I sent my transcript to Sacramento, the evaluator called me. She told me that in order for her to evaluate my records properly she needed the course description of all my courses taken in McGill University. I made a few calls to the department of records and they told me that they couldn't help me because I had graduated a long time ago. They didn't have my records there anymore. The following day I called again and asked to be transferred to the supervisor of the School of Graduate Nurses Office. A very nice lady answered the phone; I just knew that she was an angel from God.

    She was very kind and helpful. She told me that she didn't have my records there either but that I could get them in the school library and to make sure to ask for the Archives Department. Luckily I had my niece, Aileen, studying nursing in Montreal and she was able to obtain these records for me. To make this long story short, I received the evaluators' report, and sure enough my Bachelors have more than enough credit, but the District did not accept it because it only stated "equivalent to U.S. Bachelors Program" and The District wanted it to state, "equivalent to four years U.S. Bachelors Program" which the new evaluator from Sacramento complied. The miracle here is that once I was a very impatient, worrywart, anxious woman, and now, I was one that was full of hope and had the patience to go through this problem. I was reinstated to my previous position as a school nurse four and a half months later. I lost my house in the mean time because I was not able to maintain the payment without a full time job. I was unable to refinance it either. Tony and my son told me to sue the first evaluator because I lost the house during the process. The first evaluator did not bother to ask for the course description, maybe because of the many number of years ago that I had graduated. I did not bother to file a lawsuit because while I was going through this entire problem, I made a promise to God; that if God would give me back my school nurse job, I would forget everything.

    Another miracle happened when I was forty years old and I had pain in my left knee. There were days that I limped because of the pain. Kaiser Hospital (where my health insurance from work was accepted) x-rayed my left knee and I was told that I had an early stage of Arthritis. I took a copy of my x-ray to show to one of the orthopedic surgeons that I worked with in Rancho Los Amigos Hospital. He confirmed my arthritis diagnosis and also told me that the space of my left knee joint was widening and that I might need a surgery in the near future.

During this time, I was attending a class, "Old Testament" in the Community Chapel Church in Norwalk, California. One evening during our class they announced that one guest pastor would be doing a healing service after class. I had never seen anyone laying hands or had ever had the experience of attending a healing service before. Deep in my heart I knew that I needed this for my knee problem, but as a new believer I hesitated and did not line up until there were only three people left to receive prayer for healing.

First off, as a nurse, I doubted. In my mind I thought, this will not work, medical problem needs medical treatment or management." Secondly, I hesitated because I was shy. I thought, "What will these people say? I am a nurse and believe in faith healing?" I was especially shy of my lady doctor friend who was in the same class with me. When there was only one person left in the line I jumped from my seat and ran to the line. The person laid her hand on my head without even asking about my problem. I thought she would lay her hand on my left knee and pray but she did not. Then I felt warmth all over my body, starting from my head down to my toes. Then I felt the warmth again this time starting from my toes and up to my head. A few years later I learned that the warmth I experienced in my body was the manifestation of healing. I am glad that I followed my heart and not my mind. I would have missed the miracle experience of my lifetime. I am 64 years old now, and I never had severe pain from that day.

Another answered prayer was about my brother Gilbert. For a long time I had been praying for him to accept the Lord as his savior in order to have a changed life. Two years after I became "Born Again" Gilbert and I went home to the Philippines for a family re-union. In the hotel where we stayed, I told him that I had accepted Jesus as my savior and I asked him if he would do the same. He told me, "I am not ready, maybe in the near future." I continued to pray for him and every time I sent him a letter I included an acceptance, a prayer of salvation. I remember quoting this scripture in my letter, "Draw near to God and He will draw near to you." (James 4:8.) The first time I visited him in Virginia, I gave him my Bible.

I remember seeing Pastor Shambach in one of his programs on the Trinity Broadcasting Network; he said that we could accept salvation for another person. So I did. I prayed with him and said Lord I am doing this for Gilbert.

In 1993 I requested a transfer to work in another District within LAUSD so that I would be closer to home. The staff of 116th St. Elementary School where I worked was so kind and so nice as to give me a wonderful farewell party. I was really overwhelmed because the day before the party they surprised me with flowers during our school assembly. Each class from Kindergarten up to Grade 5 gave me a flower. The Health Office was full of flowers and smelled very nice; just like a Florist shop. During the party, they gave me a nice diamond wrist -watch and a plaque with a note of gratitude and appreciation for my work. It was very humbling and really too much for me to take. I did not expect such kindness and I know that I did not deserve such honor.

The following morning during my meditation and prayer, I was thanking God for the party, the gifts, the flowers, but mostly the kind words of gratitude and appreciation that they all gave me. Then I said "O God I wish I am doing something for You, it will be a greater honor for sure. I never shared You to anyone besides my family! I never lead one soul to salvation. Even my brothers and sisters are not saved!" I was crying during this time. The following year, I heard from sister Dione who was visiting her daughter in Virginia. She told me that Gilbert was a changed person. She said that she was really surprised because every time Gilbert talked, he would include something about God. She added, "And he often watches Christian T.V. programs" I told my sister that Gilbert must be "Born Again" now. I remembered an incident, when I had just accepted Jesus as my savior, I was watching a Christian program and I was told by Tony, "How could you watch this?" Gilbert related a story to me a few years ago during Christmas. In his card, he sent all of his friends a personalized, Godly note instead of a regular Christmas card. He said that they all e-mailed him back asking if he was now a "Born Again" Christian. After fifteen years of asking God to save him, my prayers were answered. It is the greatest miracle. As what Pastor Binny Hinn said, "Becoming 'Born Again' is a greater miracle than a miraculous healing." I agree because the change that happened in me is the greatest miracle indeed.

The most recent miracle was about my property lot in the Philippines. I had been trying to sell this property for the last ten years. Nothing happened until finally, three years ago, I decided to list it to a realtor who lived in the community where my property was located. We bought this property with the intention of building a nice house for our retirement. This lot is located in one of the most expensive areas in Cebu, Philippines. Thirty years ago, it was not expensive then. Now only foreigner's and multi-millionaires live in this area. Looking at the houses in this area a few years ago, I realized that there is no way we can afford to build a house. Our only option was to sell. Besides, the property taxes are now increased tripled, especially if you are late in your payment. For many years I was wishing that this lot would be sold, but I never prayed for it to be sold. Then two months before my retirement, when I prayed with Tony (we always prayed before I left for work) I remembered to pray for my lot and prayed like this, "Lord, please sell my lot in the Philippines, I will be retiring soon and I don't think I can afford to keep paying for the taxes and I also need money for my ministry that I started in the Philippines!" That same evening we received an e-mail from our Realtor stating that someone was interested in buying our property at our full asking prize. We closed the deal one month after I retired. I was able to go home to the Philippines without missing work to sign the closing deal. Was this a miracle or what! God was so faithful not only because He answered my prayer, but because it was in a timely manner as well. What the Bible said, "You have not because you ask not!" is really true. And, I am still praising Him until now.

As the children of God we have access to God in prayer. He will answer all our prayers. The answer could be yes, no, or wait. When the answer is no, it means that the thing you asked the heavenly Father for, is not good for you because our God is an all-knowing God, and God is a loving God. He loves you so much that He will not withhold anything that you need. He will give you what is best for you. The answer for your prayer may sometimes be to wait. God wants you to wait until you are mature enough to receive and enjoy what you asked for. God will not hear you if your prayer is accompanied with doubts or if your motives are selfish. If you pray "thy will be done," He will always answer your prayer and in looking back later you will see that it was the best-answered prayer that ever happened in your life.

Another exciting answered prayer I had was about my son Devin. I had been praying that Devin would marry a Christian woman. Learning from my mistakes of marrying someone of different faith, it was very important to me that Devin would not make the same mistake that I did. Especially knowing what the Bible said, "Do not be unequally yoked together with unbelievers. For what fellowship has righteousness with lawlessness? And what communion has light with darkness?" (2 Corinthians 6:14.) Just a reminder, a Christian, or a believer, became righteous because of their faith in Jesus Christ. Unequally yoked means diversely, implying a difference in kind. Believers and unbelievers are diverse people. Because of their divine nature and holy standing, the believers should not be yoked together with the unbelievers. This should be applied to all intimate relationships between believers and unbelievers, not only to marriage and business.

As soon as Devin finished medical school I started praying that he would marry a Christian, "Born Again" woman. It didn't matter what religious denomination. Other things like education, personal attitude or family background was not important to me as long as she was a Christian woman.

One time I asked him, "Why not try dating Filipino ladies also?" Flatly he told me, "No way! I will end up marrying a temperamental and nagging woman like you! "

Answered Prayers

(jokingly.) I did not make any comment because what he said was true. In my mind I thought, 'I guess Devin does not want to end up with a divorced marriage like mine. He must have thought my constant nagging to his Dad was the thing that finally broke the camel's back. That is why our marriage ended up in a divorce.

Meanwhile, Devin was dating different girls and I continued the same prayer everyday. He turned 29 years old and was still not married, so he asked his aunt Tina to find him a nice Indian woman. Tina arranged one of her friend's nieces to meet with Devin in Toronto. She was born and raised in Lechtershire, England and she studied and graduated Optometry in England as well. I asked Devin to pray about his plan. The lady's name that he was supposed to meet is Mala, meaning garland of flowers in Hindu. Mala is also a Biblical name but spelled Mahlah. Mahlah is one of the daughters of Zelophehad who came from Shemedia, and Shemedaite clans are descendants of Gilead from the tribe of Manassah.

After Devin and Mala met, they planned to get engaged. Again, I asked Devin to pray about his plan. In the morning of their engagement party, in my prayer time, I said, "Lord, it looks like my prayer for Devin to get married with a Christian woman is not answered, but your will be done." Since I prayed and Devin prayed, I had peace in my heart. I surrendered the situation to God.

After they got married, Devin and Mala seldom miss attending the Mass every Sunday. I guess it is because of Devin's religious upbringing. A few years after their marriage, Mala told Devin that she would like to become a Catholic. When I heard the news I did not jump out of joy even though I felt like doing so because I did not believe that it would really happen. She went through adult

Catholic catechism for 6 months and finally, she was baptized and confirmed. I was her sponsor. She reconfirmed the acceptance of the Lord as her savior, months later in Billy Graham's crusade in San Diego.

This is another miracle and shows God's faithfulness towards me as His child. Jesus said, "You have not because you ask not." I asked and I have the answers to my prayers. I received what I prayed for. How awesome is our God! How majestic is His name over all the earth! He proves His mercies and kindness and His unfailing love over and over and over again! Halleluiah! Praise His holy name!

We feel ecstatic when God answers our prayers, but we must not forget that the purpose of prayer is to get a hold of God. Sometimes we feel that we are only closer to God and only trust Him if we receive an answer to our prayers. We must also be careful of the pitfall of spiritual lust that causes us to demand an answer from God. We should seek God Himself because of who He is and trust Him whether He answers our prayer or not.

What does the Bible say about effective prayer?

Billy Graham, in one of his sermon series about prayer said the following:

First: Prayer is for God's children.

Jesus said, "When you pray, say, Our Father..." (See Mathew 6:9)

God has a particular responsibility to His children, and unless we have been born into the family of God through the new birth, we have no right to ask favors of God.

The Bible says, "But as many as received Him, to them He gave the right to become children of God, to those who believe in His name."(John 1:12, NKJV.) God invites you to the intimacy of spiritual childhood, "That you may become blameless and pure, children of God without fault in a crooked and depraved generation, in which you shine like stars in the universe." (Philippians 2:15.)

Second: Effectual prayer is offered in faith.

The Bible says, "Therefore I tell you, whatever you ask for in prayer, believe that you receive it, and it will be yours" (Mark 11:24.)

Maltbie Babcock said, "Our prayers are to mean something to us if they are to mean anything to God." It goes without saying that if our prayers are aimless, meaningless, and mingled with doubt, they will go unanswered. Prayer is more than a wish turned heavenward…it is the voice of faith directed God-ward.

Third: Dynamic prayer emanates from an obedient heart.

The Bible says, "And whatever we ask we receive from Him, because we keep His commandments and do those things that are pleasing in His sight."(1 John 3:22, NKJV.) I know a wealthy father who refused to get his son a bicycle because the boy's report card showed disgracefully low marks, a yard remained without raking, and other assignments had not been carried out. I am sure that the father would not have been wise to lavish gifts upon such a disobedient and ungrateful son.

The Bible says, "However, if you do not obey the voice of the Lord, but rebel against the commandment of the Lord, then the hand of the Lord will be against you" (1Samuel 12:15, NKJV.) If you want your prayers through to God, surrender your stubborn will to Him and He will hear your cry. Obedience is the master key to effectual prayer.

Fourth: We are to pray in Christ's name.

Jesus said, "And whatever you ask in My name, that I will do, that the Father may be glorified in the Son (John 14:13, NKJV.) We are not worthy to approach the holy throne of God except through our Advocate, Jesus Christ. The Bible says, "Seeing then that we have a great High Priest who has passed through the heavens, Jesus the Son of God…let us therefore come boldly to the throne of grace" (Hebrews 4:14,16, NKJV.) God, for Christ's sake, forgives our sins. God, for Christ's sake, supplies our needs. God, for Christ's sake, receives our prayers. The person who comes with confidence to the throne of grace has seen that his approach to God has been made possible because of Jesus Christ. Many may ask, "Is there no way to pray except through Jesus Christ?" You may pray, but according to the Bible, "There is…one mediator between God and men, the man Jesus Christ" (1 Timothy 2:5.)

Fifth: We must desire the will of God.

Even our Lord, contrary to His own disposition at the moment said, "O My Father, if this cup cannot pass away from Me unless I drink it, Your will be done" (Matthew 26:42, NKJB.) Prayer couples you with God's true purposes for you and the world. It not only brings the blessings of God's will to your own personal life, but it brings you added blessing of being in step with God's plan.

And last: Our prayer must be for God's glory.

The model prayer which Jesus has given us concludes with, "Yours is the kingdom and the power and the glory forever"(Mathew 6:13, NKJV.) If we are to have our prayers answered, we must give God the glory. Our Lord said to His disciples, "And whatever you ask in My name, that I will do, that the Father may be glorified, in the Son" (John 14:13, NKJV.)

What a privilege is ours: the privilege of prayer!

Christians, examine your heart, re-consecrate your life, yield yourself to God unreservedly, for He will only hear those who pray with a clean heart. The Bible says, "The prayer of a righteous man is powerful and effective." (James 5:16.) We are to pray in times of adversity, lest we become faithless and unbelieving. We are to pray in times of prosperity, lest we become boastful and proud. We are to pray in times of danger, lest we become fearful and doubting. We need to pray in times of security, lest we become self-sufficient. Sinners, pray to a merciful God for forgiveness! Christians pray for an outpouring of God's Spirit upon a willful, evil, unrepentant world. Parents, pray that God may crown your home with grace and mercy! Children, pray for the salvation of your parents!

Christians, saints of God, pray that the dew of Heaven may fall on earth's thirsty ground, and that righteousness may cover the earth as the waters cover the sea. Pray believing, with this promise of our Savior in mind, "Whatever you ask in prayer, believe that you have received it, and it will be yours" (Mark 11:24.)

"Satan trembles when he sees the weakest saint upon his knees" – so pray, Christian pray!

Chapter 6

WORSHIP

To worship is to quicken the conscience by the holiness of God, to feed the mind with the truth of God, to purge the imagination by the beauty of God, to open the heart to the love of God, to devote the will to the purpose of God.

William Temple

Webster defined Worship (n.) as reverence, adoration; an expression of love and adoration. God is seeking true worshipers. Jesus said, "The true worshipers will worship the Father in spirit and in truth, for such the Father seeks to worship Him" (Jn.4:23.) It is God who seeks, draws and persuades. Worship is a human response to a divine initiative. In Genesis, God walked in the Garden seeking out Adam and Eve. In the crucifixion Jesus drew men and women to himself (Jn.12:32.)

"We desperately need to see who God is: to read about His self-disclosure to His ancient people Israel, to meditate on His attributes, to gaze upon the revelation of His nature in Jesus Christ." When we see the Lord of hosts "high and lifted up," ponder His infinite wisdom and knowledge, wonder at His unfathomable mercy and love, we cannot help but move into doxology.

> Glad thine attributes confess,
>
> Glorious all and numberless.

To see who the Lord is brings us to confession. When Isaiah caught sight of the glory of God he cried, "Woe is me! For I am lost; for I am a man of unclean lips, and I dwell in the midst of a people of unclean lips; for my eyes have seen the king, the Lord of hosts!" (Isaiah 6:5.) The pervasive sinfulness of human beings becomes evident when contrasted with the radiant holiness of God. Our fickleness becomes extreme once we see God's faithfulness. To understand His grace is to understand our guilt.

We worship the Lord not only because of who He is but also because of what He has done. Above all, the God of the Bible is the God who acts. His goodness, faithfulness, justice and mercy, all can be seen in His dealings with His people. His gracious actions are not only etched into ancient history, but are engraved into our personal histories. As the apostle Paul said, "The only reasonable response is to worship Him" (Rom. 12:1.) "We praise God for who He is and thank Him for what He has done." [1]

If God is to be our God, worship must have priority in our lives. In Exodus Chapter 20, God gave us His ten commandments. The first two commandments are the following:
"I am the Lord your God, You shall have no other gods before Me. You shall not make for yourself any carved

image, or any likeness of anything that is in heaven above, or that is in the earth beneath, that is in the water under the earth; you shall not bow down to them nor serve them. For I, the Lord your God, am a jealous God, visiting the iniquity of the fathers on the children to the third and fourth generations of those who hate Me, but showing mercy to thousands, to those who love Me and keep my commandments. You shall not take the name of the Lord in vain." (Exodus 20:1-7, NKJV)

God wants us to worship, honor (reverence) and to love Him first and foremost. The first commandment of Jesus is "Love the Lord your God with all your heart, and with all your soul, and with all your mind, and with all your strength. (Mk. 12:30) The divine priority is worship first, service second. Our lives are to be punctuated with praise, thanksgiving, and adoration. Service flows out of worship. Service as a substitute for worship is idolatry. Activity may become the enemy of adoration.

God wants us to praise and worship Him. Psalm 103:1 says, "Praise the Lord O my soul, all my inmost being, praise His name". Also, "God inhabits in the praises of His people." (Psalm 22:3.) There is amazing power in worship. When we praise and worship our Lord, we are acknowledging His supremacy and authority in our lives. Through praise we are stating that we are weak and that He is strong. Praise makes room in our hearts for God's will to be done, and it recognizes the absurdity of any attempt to manipulate God in prayer. He is sovereign. This awesome Creator, who loves us so much that He sent His Son Jesus to die for us that we might have a place in His family, deserves our adoration and praise. People of praise are people of great faith.

The very "sacrifice" of praise –working at it when we don't feel like it –draws us into the presence of the Lord. People of praise discover that this action of the heart, the mind, and sometimes just the will, is very healthy for body, mind, and spirit. Praise draws us into a healthy mental attitude, praise increases our capacity to live and grow in love and holiness. Praise draws us into the abundant life in which God created us to live.

Linda Schubert, the author of <u>Miracle Hour</u> – A method of prayer that will change your life - in her booklet includes a Litany of Praise that she encourages us to read aloud:

I praise You Lord Jesus! (This can be said before each salutation)

    I praise You ....You are my life my Love.

    I praise You ....You are the Name above all names.

    I praise You ....You are Emmanuel, God with us.

    I praise You .... You are the King of Kings.

    I praise You .... You are the King of creation.

    I praise You ....You are the King of the universe.

    I praise You .... You are the Lords of Lords.

    I praise You .... You are the Almighty.

    I praise You ....You are the Christ.

    I praise You .... You are the Christ, the King.

    I praise You ....You are the Lamb of God.

    I praise You .... You are the Lion of Judah.

    I praise You ....You are the Bright Morning Star.

    I praise You ....You are our Champion and Shield.

Worship

I praise You ....You are our strength and our Song.

I praise You ....You are the Way for our life.

I praise You ....You are the only Truth.

I praise You ....You are the Real Life.

I praise You ....You are the Wonderful Counselor.

I praise You ....You are the Prince of Peace.

I praise You ....You are the Light of the World.

I praise You ....You are the Living Word.

I praise You ....You are our Redeemer.

I praise You ....You are the Messiah.

I praise You ....You are the Anointed One.

I praise You ....You are the Holy One of Israel.

I praise You ....You are the Good Shepherd.

I praise You ....You are the Sheep gate.

I praise You ....You are the Lord of hosts.

I praise You ....You are the Rock of all ages.

I praise You ....You are my Hiding Place.

I praise You....You are the Savior of the World.

I praise You ....You are the Strong Tower.

I praise You....You are the Mountain Refuge.

I praise You ....You are the Bread of Life.

I praise You ....You are the Font of all holiness.

I praise You ....You are the Living Water.

I praise You ....You are the True Vine.

I praise You ....You are my Spouse, my Maker.

I praise You ....You are our Fortress.

I praise You ....You are the Deliverer.

I praise You ....You are our Victory.

I praise You ....You are our Salvation.

I praise You....You are our Righteousness.

I praise You ....You are our Wisdom.

I praise You ....You are our Sanctification.

I praise You ....You are our Justification.

I praise You....You are the Door.

I praise You ....You are the Great I Am.

I praise You ....You are the great High Priest.

I praise You ....You are the Cornerstone.

I praise You ....You are the Sure Foundation.

I praise You ....You are our Joy.

I praise You ....You are our Portion and Cup.

I praise You ....You are my Healing and Wholeness.

I praise You ....You are our Covenant.

I praise You ....You are the Promise of the Father.

I praise You ....You are the Everlasting One.

I praise You ....You are the Most High God.

I praise You ....You are the Lamb that was slain.

I praise You ....You are the Just Judge.

I praise You ....You are the Balm of Gilead.

I praise You ....You are the Mighty Warrior.

I praise You ....You are my Defense.

I praise You ....You are the Bridegroom.

I praise You ....You are my Patience.

I praise You ....You are the Solid Reality.

I praise You ....You are my Provider.

I praise You ....You are the Resurrection and the Life.

I praise You ....You are the Alpha and the Omega.

I praise You ....You are the beginning and the End.

I praise You ....You are the Source, Guide and Goal of all.

I praise You ....You are my Everything. [my own addition]

I praise You ....You are all that I need.

I praise You ....You are all that I want.

I praise You ....You are worthy of all praise!

If you read this litany of praise with complete concentration, you are allowing your spirit to open to the Holy Spirit You are drawing yourself into the realm of the miraculous. Just forget about yourself and focus your concentration on God. In my own experience, I could feel the awesomeness of God and feel His presence. Most often, I am overcome by emotions and start crying at this time while praising and feeling God's glory. 2

God declared that the primary function of the Leviticus priests was to "come near to me" (Exek.44:15.) For the Old Testament priesthood, ministry to him was to precede all other work. And that is no less true of the universal priesthood of the New Testament. One grave temptation we all face is to run around answering the call to service without ministering to the Lord himself.

"Another feature of worship in the Bible is that people gathered in what we could call only a "holy expectancy." They believed that they would actually hear the Kohl Yahweh, the voice of God. When Moses went into the tabernacle, he knew that he was entering the Presence of God. The same was true in the early church. It was not surprising to them that the building shook with the power of God, it had happened before (Acts 2:2; 4:31.) When some dropped dead and others were raised from the dead by the word of the Lord, the people knew that God was in their midst. (Acts 5:11; 9:36-43; 20:7-10) When more people come to worship with a "holy expectancy," it can change the atmosphere of the room and miracles happen. " [3]

In Binny Hinn's healing crusade service, many people were healed because they were expecting that Jesus would heal them in that particular service. Besides, in corporate worship like in Mass celebration, God always shows up, (His presence,) because He wants to show His glory and power to His people. The worship part of Binny Hinn's healing service is full of power and adoration to our God Almighty. People were drawn into a sense of God's presence. Their hearts and minds were lifted upward. Many people feeling the presence of God in this service got saved. Some became filled with the Holy Spirit and others got healed. Coming to God with holy expectancy shows a great deal of faith and God will surely honor it.

I tried this "holy expectancy" in our church. Before the Mass celebration started, I prayed my worship and adoration prayer and I prayed that God's presence would manifest to all of us in the church. Then I prayed for the priest that would be celebrating the Mass; that he would speak the truth boldly in the power of the Lord and most of all that the Holy Spirit would be with him during the entire Mass. I also prayed that the people would apply in their lives what they would hear in the liturgy. Many times these prayers were answered; the priest gave a sermon that taught, encouraged, and lifted up the congregation. In appreciation of the priest's sermon, the congregation applauded after his sermon, (this is not common in Catholic Mass).

One vital feature of the early church community was their sense of being "gathered" together in worship. First, they were gathered in the sense that they actually met as a group, and second, as they met they were gathered into a unity of spirit that transcended their individualism. In contrast to the religions of the East, the Christian faith has strongly emphasized corporate worship. Even under dangerous circumstances the early community was urged not toforsake assembling themselves together. (Heb.10:25.)

"The epistles speak frequently of the believing community as the 'body of Christ.' As human life is unthinkable without head, arms and legs, it was also unthinkable for those Christians to live in isolation from one another. Martin Luther witnessed to the fact that 'at home, in my own house there is no warmth and vigor in me, but in the church when the multitude is gathered together, a fire is kindled in my heart and it breaks its way through.' In the power of the one Spirit we become 'wrapped in a sense of unity and of Presence such as quiets all words and enfolds us an unspeakable calm and interknittedness within a vaster life.'" [4]

Here I should add my feelings to some of our co-parishioners that seemed not to respect and honor the house of God, especially during the Mass celebration on Sundays. It really bothers me when they come in the middle of the Mass or when they are converse during the Mass. Sometimes I wonder why they bother coming to church late when there are other Masses scheduled. Sometimes in spite of the reminder before the service to turn off their cell phone, there are a few phones that still ring during the Mass service. I bet you that they were the people that came late and missed the reminder before the service. Most parishioners really don't know the meaning of when we say that the second part of the Mass, the liturgy of the Eucharist, is a representation or perpetuation of Jesus' one sacrifice of Himself on Calvary for the sins of all people. In reverence for His sacrifice, the Mass should bring about a conscious, active, and full participation of the people, motivated by faith, hope and charity.

James Pittman, author of, <u>What is Worship</u>, discussed why we worship God and to whom we worship. He writes:

Whom do we worship?

The answer that we give to this question reveals whether or not our worship contains the first and most essential ingredient to the kind of worship that God is looking for. Our worship is right, only when we worship God as He is described in the Bible. False gods or inadequate views of the one true God can nullify even the most sincere efforts to worship. Jesus said, "You shall worship the Lord your God, and Him only you shall serve." (Mathew 4:10, NKJB) God has the right to be the only object of our worship because He alone is worthy, and that worthiness can be seen clearly as we reflect on His character and His works.

Worship

God is eternal. His inestimable value is seen in the mind-boggling fact that He is from everlasting to everlasting. (Psalm 90:2) Unlike any other being, He never had a beginning and He will never have an end.

God is all knowing. He is unlimited in His knowledge. (Psalm147:4-5) He knows everything there is to know about us, our world, and the universe.

God is all-powerful. He can do anything that He chooses to do. (Matthew19:26) No good thing is beyond His ability. No army, government or civilization can frustrate His purposes.

God is everywhere present. There is no hiding or escaping—no way to avoid the all-powerful One. No matter where you go in the universe, God is there. (Psalm 139:7-8)

God is sovereign. Regardless of the apparent turmoil, confusion or chaos in our world, the God we worship is One who does all things according to His will and purpose. (Isaiah 46:10-11) He is, has been, and always will be in control of all history.

God is unchanging. In His character, in His purpose and in His ability, God never changes. He has never been nor will be less good, less loving, less true or less powerful.

God is good. "Oh taste and see that the Lord is good."(Psalm 34: 8, NKJB) Because of His goodness He gives blessings and joy to His creatures. His goodness to us should cause us to offer our praise to Him.

We worship God because of who He is! He alone is worthy of praise and honor. He alone is worthy of our worship. 5

When crisis and troubles come into our lives, we still need to worship. In Acts, Paul and Silas were arrested for preaching the Gospel. Their backs were ripped open with Roman whips. Instead of groaning and complaining though, they worshipped the Lord. At about midnight, Paul and Silas were praying and singing hymns to God while the other prisoners were listening to them. They prayed and praised God. Because of Silas and Paul's praise and worship, there was an earthquake, and the prison doors flew open. (Acts 16: 19-25) "Suddenly there was a great earthquake, so that the foundations of the prison were shaken; and immediately all the doors were opened, and everyone's chains were loosed. And the keeper of the prison, awaking from sleep and seeing the prison doors open, supposing the prisoners had fled, drew his sword and was about to kill himself. But Paul called with a loud voice, saying, 'Do yourself no harm, for we are all here.' Then he called for a light, ran in, and fell down trembling before Paul and Silas. And he brought them out and said, 'Sirs, what must I do to be saved?' So they said, 'Believe on the Lord Jesus Christ, and will be saved, you and your household.'" (Acts 16:25-30) Paul and Silas led the jailer and his household to faith in Jesus Christ. The next morning they were released from jail. (Acts 16:31-40)

The Bible tells us to rejoice in the Lord always. Again, I will say rejoice! (Philippians 4:4) and also, "Be anxious for nothing, but in everything by prayer and supplication, with thanksgiving, let your requests be made known to God." (Philippians 4:6) I know with my own experience that it is very hard to rejoice and give thanks in the midst of our suffering and pain, in my case, the divorce. This was because I didn't know how to praise and worship during that time. Now I know that I can thank God not because of my suffering but because He is sovereign, He is still in the throne and He loves me and knows what is best for me. It is all right to be honest and tell God the truth; that you don't

Worship

like what you are going through. But just thank Him for His plan and purpose for this suffering and ask Him to give you strength to get through this problem. When we spend time in worship and praising the Lord, our problems, challenges and questions are often resolved. At least we gain a better insight on how to deal with them.

Chapter 7

THANKSGIVING

"O give thanks to the Lord; call upon His name: make known his deeds among the people. Sing unto Him, sing Psalms unto Him: talk ye all His wondrous works. Glory ye in His holy name: let the heart of them rejoice that seek the Lord." (Psalm 105:1-3)

As I mentioned earlier, before I became a believer of our Lord Jesus, or "Born Again," I did not have a regular time of prayer. I only prayed when I was in great need or under a great stress. My thanksgiving prayer only happened during the Mass celebration every Sunday. My prayers were often self-centered, full of "gimmie, gimmie" and full of requests. I didn't seem to notice God's goodness and kindness to me, or I seemed to forget the many blessings of God. In other words, I just took His blessings for granted, and I blame this on my ignorance of God's Word, the Bible. The Scriptures tell us to give thanks to God and in Psalm 92:1-2 says:

"It is good to give thanks to the Lord

And to sing praises to Your name, O Most High;

To declare Your loving-kindness in the morning,

And Your faithfulness every night."

Charles Stanley, a great Pastor and author of many books, in one of his "Life Principles Notes" titled, "It's Good to Give Thanks to God," He gave us eleven scriptural principles of why we give thanks to God:

1. Giving thanks to God honors Him.

Why is it so important for us to express gratitude to God? It is because He deserves the glory. When we bring hearts of thanksgiving to the Lord, we glorify and magnify His name. We act in obedience by giving the credit and praise to the One who should receive it. He is the author of every good thing, and should receive every honor.

2. Giving thanks to God refocus our attention.

Expressing gratitude to the Lord sets our sight on Him. What better way to bring our attention back to God than to think of the many blessings which He has given to us. What happens when we rise in the morning? We hurry and focus on the world. We should begin each day by setting our minds on eternal things, and realizing the many awesome things about Him prepares us for the day.

3. Giving thanks to God releases us from anxiety.

We live in an age of anxiety and worry. In Philippians 4:6-7, Paul urges us not to give in to worry. Instead, we should bring God our requests with thanksgiving. Then, the peace of God will guard our hearts and minds. Giving Thanks to God is the best way to be at peace in a time that has so much anxiety.

4. Giving thanks to God refreshes our relationship with Him.

Bringing our gratitude to the Lord has a wonderful effect on our personal relationship with Him. As we declare His loving-kindness in the morning and His faithfulness at night, our spirits are rejuvenated. We feel closer and closer to Him because He draws near to us when we thank Him and praise Him. You can't reflect on His blessings and continue to feel downhearted.

5. Giving thanks to God reinforces our faith.

The Israelites remembered the mighty works of God. They recalled how He crushed the Egyptians at the Red Sea, and how He fed them on manna in the wilderness. When they kept these memories alive, their faith grew stronger. When you remember the things God has done to you, your faith is reinforced.

6. Giving thanks to God causes our spirit to rejoice.

What else happens through thanking God? We get more joy out of life. Counting blessings can only make your heart soar. Do you sing when you are alone? It doesn't matter how your voice sounds, but only how your heart feels. Give thanks and praise by singing songs that express gratitude and worship.

7. We give thanks by expressing it in words.

Giving thanks to God is one of the greatest possible ways we could use our time. Thank Him in words even if all you can think to say at first is, "Thank you, God." Then begin saying thank you for every single blessing and fact about God that you can recall.

8. We give thanks by singing.

Another way to thank God is by singing. There is music all around us, from the birds and from the steams that make their own melodies. There is power in song, and God made that power so that we could use it to bring Him our thanks and our praise. There are so many kinds of music today, and we can use them to sing with hearts of joy about the wonderful things God has done for us.

9. We give thanks by living obediently.

We can, however, express our gratitude without ever saying or singing a word. Nothing pleases God more than an obedient life, because that says, "Lord you have done so much for me, now I will live for you." Sincere gratitude will come from an obedient heart, and will lead to obedient actions. We can devote our entire lives to thanksgiving by serving Him and following His will every day.

10. We give thanks through public worship.

One of the reasons why we gather for worship is to express our thanks to God. Most people attend church to receive something, whether it is teaching, fellowship, or just enjoying the choir. God's primary purpose for fellowship however, is that we might worship and express adoration and thanksgiving. As we hear the Gospel God is giving us something, when we sing our praises we are giving something back.

11. We give thanks by giving generously.

Finally, we offer our thanksgiving by giving our resources back to God. We owe every breath and everything we own to our Lord and Creator. When we understand this, we give naturally from hearts filled with joy and thanksgiving. He would not spare His only Son, so how can we be anything but generous by returning our gifts to Him." 1 (Charles Stanley, It's Good to Give Thanks to God" Life Principles Notes / LPO 61119)

In Linda Schubert's booklet, "Miracle Hour," a method of prayer that will change your life, her thanksgiving prayer guide seemed to cover everything that we can be thankful to God for. She suggested using this prayer guide as a jumping off point, where later on you can thank God on your own spontaneously.

Prayer of Thanksgiving:

"Giving thanks to the Father, who has qualified us to be partakers of the inheritance of the saints in the kingdom of light." (Col. 1:12)

Thank you, Father in heaven, for the amazing grace of this "Miracle Hour" with You. Thank you for drawing me to prayer and giving me hunger and thirst for you. Thank You for the joy of surrender, repentance and forgiveness. Thank You for sending the Holy Spirit to teach, guide and counsel me. Thank You for the infilling of the Holy Spirit today and for a release of the gifts of the Holy Spirit. Thank You for sending me people for ministry. Thank You for the fruit of the Spirit working in me: love, joy, peace, patience, kindness, goodness, faithfulness, gentleness, and self-control. Thank You for encouraging me to ask when I have a need, and helping me to understand the desires of my heart. Thank You for the wonderful gift of praise.

Thank You for breaking the power of old habit patterns and bringing me to deeper conversion. Thank You for the grace to listen to You, believe in You and come to You. Thank You for all the ways in which You have helped me and intervened on my behalf. Thank You for the plan for my life, for creating me with high purpose in mind, for giving me a sense of worth. Thank You for loving me unconditionally and never leaving or forsaking me, no matter what I do. Thank You for being there all the moments of my life, the rough and smooth, and bringing me through those moments to a place of maturity and deeper faith.

Thank You for Your living Word that strengthens and empowers me. Thank You for enabling me to rise out of discouragement and walk in joy. Thank You for lifting me up when I fall. Thank You for keeping me in perfect peace as my mind is stayed on You. Thank You for making all things work together for good as I place my trust in You. Thank You for enabling me to dwell in safety, and protecting me from the snares of the fowler. Thank You for giving Your angels charge over me, to guide me in all ways. Thank You for blessing me as I come in and go out. Thank You for guiding me and giving me wisdom.

Thank You for Your goodness and mercy that follow me wherever I go. Thank You for the grace to lean on Your understanding, not my own. Thank You for enabling me to forsake all negative thoughts today, and only think those thoughts that are healing and uplifting. Thank You for giving me a tongue that speaks healing and life. Thank You for the abundance of Your love that casts out all fear. Thank You for fighting for me against my enemies, and even making my enemies at peace with me. Thank You for the grace to choose life today. Thank You for enabling me to keep my heart fixed on You.

Thank You for giving me a spirit of power, love, and of a sound mind. Thank You for always causing me to triumph in Christ Jesus and for turning curses into blessings. In You I am more than a conqueror. Thank You for giving me the ability to think Your thoughts and walk steadfastly in Your ways. Thank You for opening the gates of heaven and pouring out blessings. Thank You for supplying all my needs in accordance with Your riches in glory. Thank You for giving me favor with You and my fellow men. Thank You for freeing me from sickness in body, mind and spirit, and bringing good out of the times when trouble came.

Thank You for giving me a spirit of wisdom and revelation to know the great hope to which I have been called. Thank You for flooding my heart and mind with the light of heaven. Thank You for revealing the immeasurable and unlimited power of God available in me. Thank You for the grace to walk in forgiveness, faithfulness and love. Thank You for my exceedingly increasing faith. Thank You for opening my hands to give to the needy, opening my eyes to see the needs of my brothers and sisters, opening my ears to their cry, opening my heart to love the wounded and lost, opening my lips to speak of Your love, and opening my arms to receive others in love. I especially thank You for ___ (here, I usually thank God for my family, my job, my health, for America and God's guidance, protection, provision and for the favor that He showed the day before.)

Thank You for all the blessings of life: godly ancestors, family, friends, teachers, professional people, clergy and church. Thank You for all who have helped me along the way. Bless them, Lord. Thank You for faith, freedom, health and work. Thank You for science and art and medicine, bicycles and satellites and all the material advancements that improve the quality of life. Thank You for the wonderful gift of life, exactly the way it is. I embrace it as a priceless gift from You. And I thank You for the greatest gift of all Your Son Jesus. Thanks be to God for this indescribable gift." [(2 Cor.9:15.) 2 Linda Schubert " Miracle Hour"]

(Ps. 100:4, 2 Cor. 3:18, Lk.8:39, Acts 13:47, Dan. 12:3, Ps. 126:3, Jn.1:16, 2 Cor. 9:8, 2 Pet.1:2, 2 Pet. 3:18, Philemon. 7, Ps 91:11, Ps 90:17, Ps 29:11, Deut. 23:5, Ps 107:22, Thess. 5:18)

" You are the God who performs miracles; You display Your power among the Peoples." (Psalm 77:14)

Amen!

Chapter 8

WORK ETHICS

"Being filled with the fruit of righteousness, which is through Jesus Christ, to the glory and praise of God." (Philippians 1:11) "The fruit of righteousness is the living product of the believers living a proper life by the element of righteousness, with a righteous standing before God and man. Such a life could be lived not by the believer's natural man for their boast but through Jesus Christ as the believer's life, experienced by them to the glory and praise of God." 1

This righteousness is a testimony of a "Born Again" Christian, and he or she should take it to their work place. You can tell that a person is a Christian because they are diligent, industrious, hard working and their work ethics are tremendous. I have not encountered a lazy, "easy go lucky" Christian. In my work place, hospitals, clinics and schools, you can spot them easily. That is, if they are truly a "Born Again" and not the professed only. They are the one that walk the talk.

"Some decide to follow Christ on impulse, making their decision on the crest of a wave of enthusiasm that too often proves short-lived. It was with such person in mind that our Lord stressed the importance of first counting the cost before making a decision with such far-reaching implications. An impulsive decision often lacks the element of intelligent commitment, with the result that when its implications become clearer, the cost proves too great and they fail to 'continue in the Word of Christ.' 2

The Bible also states, "Remind the people to be subject to rulers and authorities, to be obedient, to be ready to do whatever is good, to slander no one, to be peaceable and considerate, and to show true humility toward all men." (Titus 3:1-2) The very first thing that St. Paul mentioned in this Epistle is the fact that as a Christian we should be law abiding. A believer should obey the rules and regulations of his employer. He should follow his job description carefully. He should be obedient to his superiors and the authority that his superior represents unless these laws conflict or contradict his duty and relationship to God. In Hebrews 13:17 it states, "Obey your leaders and submit to their authority. They keep watch over you as men who must give an account. Obey them so that their work will be a joy, not a burden, for that would be of no advantage to you."

Jesus also said, "Let your light shine before men, that they may see your good works, and glorify your Father which is in heaven," (Mathew 5:16) Certainly in God's kingdom the believers are going to be the light of the world. This is a tremendous principle for us to follow. We need to be a light in our neighborhood and wherever we go. In the present age, in this lost world in which you and I live in today, our prime motivation should be to bring glory to God. This is something that every Christian should consider very seriously. The aim and purpose of our lives should be to glorify our God through our good works. "Born Again" Believers are friendly, happy and helpful people. They help you beyond and above their call of duty.

Work Ethics

They usually go out of their way to accommodate you. They hardly miss work.

In my personal reflection I, noticed that after I became "Born Again" the Holy Spirit took over and equipped me with enthusiasm, zeal, consideration, love, super charged energy and a compulsion to give my very best in my work and service to others.

In comparison to my previous life I realized ever since I have known the Lord I wanted to glorify Him through my work. I don't mind difficult assignments and I respect and honor my superiors. I always go to work early and leave 30 minutes after I am supposed to leave. This is a big change for me because I used to get annoyed when I had to work 10 to 20 minutes over time especially if I didn't get paid. Hospitals will only pay for 30 minutes or more overtime. I never miss work except when I am unable to stand up. I never call in sick for minor colds, although this creates problem at times because some people don't want to be exposed even if I am following the universal precautions. I don't even miss work because of a doctor's appointment. I schedule my doctor's appointment after work or on my days off. We nurses used to call in sick when we expected short staff or when we knew that we were getting hard, difficult or different assignments. We called sick when we were in a bind with our home obligations or when we had a very important appointment and our request for day off was denied. We often called it "mental health" sick leave, and this is expected and accepted by all except of course by our superiors. As a believer, I can't call sick like this anymore because I don't want to lie and displease my Lord.

Catholics and some Christians believe that there are minor sins, (venial sin,) and big sin, (mortal sin.) Some might say that to call in sick at work is just a small sin. But in knowing God's word, the Bible, I know now that in the eyes of God there is no such thing as small or big sin. Sin is sin. However, there are small, and big or grave consequences for sin.

Another thing, a good worker should not take anything from their work, like ball pens, paper clips, tapes etc. However small the item may be, it matters because it will add up. Just imagine if 1000 employees from a big hospital take one ball pen a day. I remember my hospital supervisor, Bettye, when she became born again, the first change we noticed from her was one Christmas when she gave each department under her 5 lbs. of sugar. I asked her, "Why? You used to give us chocolate or cookies, why sugar?" She told me that it was not good to use the hospital's sugar. She added, "We should buy our own sugar for our own use starting today." The following Christmas she gave us ball pens that hung on our neck so we wouldn't lose our pen, and she told us not to take pens that belonged to the hospital. She also told us to check our pockets before leaving work for pens, tapes and other things that belonged to the hospital.

Since that time, if by chance I took the pens or tape unconsciously, I made sure that I took it back. We also take something from our work place by how we spend our time at work. It really bothers me how someone can spend so much time socializing and talking so much at work, and they call it "shop talk" They can also look busy but their productivity is poor. I can always tell when our superior is out for some kind of meeting because our work place becomes chaotic. The saying, "When the cat is away the mouse will play," is very true. Some workers take extra 5 to 10 minutes from their breaks and lunchtime without consideration of their employer. The mark of a true

Work Ethics

Christian is to work hard even if the supervisor is not watching, because God is watching. The believers' ultimate boss is God. Ever since my conversion, I don't mind working extra time without pay because I want to compensate my inadequacies, just in case I am slow in my pace. I feel that by working a few minutes extra, I will compensate for the time when my productivity was inadequate.

One day, in the school where I worked as a nurse, one of the clerks asked me, "Elma, I hope you don't mind my asking this, what is your religion?" I told her that I was a "Born Again" Christian Catholic. She said, "I thought so, because you are really different."

"What is the profit my brothers, if anyone says he has faith but does not have good works? Can that faith save him?" (James 2:14) In other words St. James said, "Show me your faith by showing your good works." Faith without good works is dead.

I have a concern that has been bothering me for a while. I am really concerned that more and more people have been working too hard to the extent of having two full time jobs which means two 8 hours shift jobs. They hop from one hospital to another or from one work place to another. It is alright if they are doing it temporarily for some emergency reason, but it is because they over commit themselves by buying big and luxurious home or cars; expensive "toys" and material things. Some buy two or three houses.

Twenty years ago I received a call from my sister in the Philippines telling me to come home by means of my father's request because he was sick. This time I was recently divorced and was struggling financially. To pay for my ticket the only way to get money was to work extra.

So, I decided to work double for three days. Since only night shift was available, I was forced to work night shift from one hospital then day shift from my regular work place. The first day was fine but the following days were horrible. I was like a "zombie," I ate my lunch during my morning break and slept during my lunch break. I was very touchy, grouchy and was not a nice person to be with. Neither was I a nice person towards my patients.

On top of it all, I made our nursing assistant, Isabel, cry. To offend her, there was for sure something wrong with me. Isabel was the nicest person I had ever known and the best worker. She was always there to help or to offer help to everyone. Everyone loved her, even until now she is a dear friend of mine. She told one of our co-workers that I snapped at her or that I had made unkind remarks. Honestly, I did not even know that I had made her cry. The only reason to explain my behavior was my lack of rest and sleep from working double shift. That was the last double shift I worked, and I said that I would never again work a double shift. I was surprised that I did not quit after the second night but I was determined to get my plane ticket so I could see my sick father in the Philippines. Of course I worked extra, but not double shifts. I worked only when I was off from my regular job, and even then, that was very hard for me to do, and how I wished I did not have to do it.

I realized that it is not really good for you because you jeopardize your health, not good to your patients or customer because you are not in good shape physically or mentally to take care of them, not good to your employer because you cannot give one hundred percent of what is expected of you, and lastly, it is detrimental to your family. I have heard of a few who have suffered and have ruined their family relationship. Their children were on drugs because of the lack of supervision, lack of care and follow up, and lack of discipline. I even heard of one woman who after working double shift for three consecutive months was all of a sudden unable to get up one morning. I don't know how others are able to do this for a long time. There are consequences that are bound to happen; it has to give way somewhere, somehow.

I will include a few scriptures hoping that we can all learn a lesson from these verses:

"For the love of money is the root of all evils, because of which some, aspiring after money, have been led away from the faith and pierced themselves with many gains. (1 Timothy 6:10) I heard one preacher say that we become the slave of money instead of making the money our slave.

"He who is greedy for gain troubles his own home." (Proverbs 15:27)

"So are the ways of everyone who is greedy for gain: It takes away the life of its owners." (Proverbs 1:19)

As a nurse myself, I would like to share what Pope John Paul 11 said of health care workers. He writes:

"The 'word of the cross' has a message for you health-care workers, who at various levels and with varying responsibilities do your jobs in hospitals.

"It is Jesus Christ who hides and is revealed in the face and in the flesh, in the heart and in the soul of those whom you are called to help and to care for. He considers done to Himself what is done to the least of these brothers, who are ill and often alone and marginalized by society.

This requires of your words, gestures, and inner attitudes inspired not only by a profound and rich humanity but also by a genuine spirit of faith and charity.

"I therefore ask you, and through you, all those who work in health-care facilities, to overcome the temptation to indifference and selfishness and to do your utmost above all to humanize these health-care environments and make them more livable, in such a way that the sick may be cured in the totality of their body and soul. Do your utmost so that all the fundamental rights and values of the human being may be recognized and supported, and above all the right to life, from its beginning to its natural end. That requires attention to different situations, respectful and patient dialogue, generous love for every man and woman considered as the image of God and, for those who are believers, an 'icon' of Christ who suffers."[3]

"I wish to express to the doctors, nurses, and health-care aides my deep appreciation and respect for the skill and attention they bring to the practice of their professions. This is a true vocation, undertaken for the care of our brothers and sisters who suffer. Few other professions are so worthy and honorable as that of the doctor who works with commitment and has strong ethical and humanitarian feelings. It approaches a sort of priesthood whose mission consists in healing the body and also in comforting the soul.

Thus, I urge these professionals to be aware of the value of their mission, always to serve life and never death, to be completely honest in the choice of treatments and surgical interventions, not to yield to the temptation for money, not to abandon their country for purely material gains, and to see in their patients – even the poorest, who at times cannot pay for their services – human beings and children of God.

I commend to the Lord all those who work on behalf of the sick in hospitals, clinics, and hospices. I wish to repeat to all, doctors, nurses, chaplains, and hospital personnel: yours is a noble vocation. Remember that you serve Christ in the sufferings of your brothers and sisters."4

Pope Paul 11 said all of what is needed to be told about health –care workers. This letter needs to be posted in all health-care facilities and mailed to all health-care workers to remind us of our mission every now and then. We should remember that we are serving Jesus, our Lord, when giving care to our patients. Speaking of myself, I know I have failed to give my best occasionally and therefore I failed my patients, my mission, and most of all I failed my God, and I truly repented for what I have failed to do.

Chapter 9

GIVING

Another change that I noticed after my encounter with the living Lord was my way of giving. Before, my mentality was, "Why should I give, when the Catholic Church is a very rich Church? I have heard they have lots of properties and they are exempted from taxes." I also said, "I don't know where and how they will allocate their funds" or I would say, "I could certainly use this money for something more useful," or "the rich people should be the only ones who should give." With this kind of reasoning, you can easily tell that I was an unbeliever. In growing up and attending Catholic church all of my life, the priest hardly gave us a sermon in tithing or in giving except when they were in dire need, or when they were raising money for some project. I have the feeling that they tried to avoid it because they were afraid that they would get a letter of complaint from the congregation.

During one of our bible study sessions, many years ago one of the Christian men made a joke about us Catholics, of the way we give tithe in our church. The joke went like this: A twenty-dollar bill asked the one-dollar bill, "Where have you been these past months?" The dollar bill answered, "O same old thing, you know, just going from one Catholic Church to another's collection baskets every Sunday." The twenty-dollar bill responded, "Man, do you know where I have been?" I have been to night clubs, entertainment shows, expensive hotels and casinos." I will never forget this joke because this is how I used to give, one or two dollars. It is because I was ignorant of what God said about giving or tithing. As I previously mentioned, I had never heard the word tithe until I read the Bible.

In the Old Testament the scripture says, "Will a man rob God? Yet ye have robbed me. But ye say wherein have I robbed thee? In tithes and offerings." (Malachi 3:8)

(Tithe is one-tenth of our income, which God wants us to give it back to Him through His Church.) God is not trying to get something away from us. What God was doing was actually blessing them and saying, "I am going to let you have nine-tenths and you return to me one-tenth." Catholics are not really requiring this. Some Parish Churches are only suggesting 5% of our weekly income.

"The offerings in Israel were the first fruits, not less than one-sixtieth of the corn, wine and oil."(Deuteronomy 18:4) "There were several kinds of tithes: (1) Tenth of the remainder after the first fruits were taken, this amount went to the Levites for their livelihood. (Leviticus 2: 30-33) (2) Tenth paid by the Levites to the priest. (Numbers: 26-28) (3) The second tenth paid by the congregation for the needs of the Levites and their own families at the tabernacle. (Deuteronomy 12: 18) (4) Another tithe every third year for the poor. (Deuteronomy 14:28-29) 1

Our government has done much in an effort to help the poor, however the Church, ought to have more emphasis on helping the poor. God gave instruction to Israel: "At the end of three years thou shall bring forth all the tithe of the increase the same year, and shall lay it up within thy gates: And the Levites (because he hath no part nor inheritance with thee,) and the strangers, and the fatherless, and the widows, which are within thy gates, shall come, and shall eat and be satisfied; that the Lord thy God may bless thee in all the work of thine hand which thou doest." (Deuteronomy 14:28-29)

When St. Paul wrote to the Corinthians, he used the Macedonians to be an example: "How that in great trial of affliction the abundance of their joy and their deep poverty abounded unto the riches of their liberality." (2 Cor. 8:2) Though they were very poor they gave generously. This answers my saying, or complaint, which I stated in the beginning, that only the rich should give, and not the poor. "For the power, I bear record, yea, and beyond their power, they were willing of themselves." (2 Cor. 8: 3) They gave beyond their tenth. They simply gave because of their love for the Lord.

Giving is a fellowship. It is a part of fellowship and part of the worship of God's people, the Church. Now I have the understanding why in our Catholic mass, we offer the host, (bread) wine, and the collection of money to the altar as a worship offering before we partake in the communion.

The Bible teaches that blessings follow those who give liberally. Proverbs 11:25 says, "The generous soul will be made rich, and he who waters will also be watered himself."

Generous giving is a kind of thanksgiving sacrifice. We give for what we are grateful for. It is a genuine expression of our heartfelt gratitude of what God has done for us. It is also the responsibility of every believer to support their local church where they go for fellowship and to receive God's Word. Not only do we give the tenth percent as our tithe, we should also give an offering by giving or supporting different ministries that are doing excellent jobs in helping the poor and for evangelization. If a believer does not support God's work and their Church, who will? Each one of us should ask this question of ourselves.

The concern I had of whether or not the church or organization might mishandle their funds has been cleared as well. Every Church or individual is accountable to God alone. I should be concerned only on what God told me, and that is to give. Of course we are also told to be wise and to ask for discernment from the Holy Spirit as to which ministries to give towards.

"Ye are cursed with a curse; for you have robbed me, even this whole nation." (Malachi 3:9) This is one of the reasons why we don't see the blessing that attend God's work. God made it clear in His Word that our giving is something that He looks at. If a church or an individual is not giving, God has not promised to bless them at all.

"Bring ye all the tithes into the storehouse, that there may be meat in mine house, and prove me now herewith, saith the Lord of hosts, if I will not open the windows of heaven, and pour out a blessing, that there should not be room enough to receive it" (Malachi 3:10) There are many humble believers with very little income for whom a tenth would be too much to give. They should only give what they can comfortably afford, as long as it comes from their heart. God loves a cheerful giver. Those on welfare and on fixed Social Security income should not feel guilty if they cannot give because this is not an income that requires a tenth or tithe, only an allowance.

Giving

"And I will rebuke the devourer for your sakes, he shall not destroy the fruits of your ground; neither shall your vine cast their fruit before the time in the field saith the Lord of hosts. (Malachi 3: 11) When we are generous to God He says, "I'll open up heavens and pour you out a blessing, and I'll rebuke the devourer." In other words, your vineyards will produce abundantly, and judgment comes from God upon a nation and individual that will reject and disobey Him. This explains my situation when I failed to give my tithe or offering for some reasons, all of a sudden my washing machine, other appliances or my car would break down, or some unexpected bills came up, or my family got minor illness that required medication. Now, I can't afford not to give my tithes. I make sure that I give weekly and monthly for my offerings in order for God to bless my income and my household. Aside from my weekly contribution to my Parish Church, I try to support other evangelic ministries. I believe they do excellent job in evangelization and in helping the poor. I believe these ministries are a good ground where you can put your seed in (donation,) and in turn get their share of blessings from God.

In Luke 6: 28, Jesus said "Give and it will be given to you: good measure, pressed down, shaken together, and running over will be put in your bosom. For with the same measure you use, it will be measured back to you." With this instruction, I don't think anyone can afford not to give. The tithe that I give does not belong to me anyway. All I have belongs to God, including my health. If it weren't for Gods love and grace, I wouldn't have anything. The many blessings that I receive surpass the little that I give. I am blessed financially, spiritually, and physically, and I am praising and thanking God for it every single day. I have discovered what countless others have known across ages: We can't out-give God.

One believer told me, "There was a man who became "Born Again", when he knew someone needed a kidney; he volunteered to give his kidney. When he told his wife about his plan of giving his kidney, she was amazed. Her response, 'What happened to you? You of all people, you never even give a chewing gum to anyone.'"

Right after I learned the principle of giving, I soon realized that I was not giving enough for our tithe. So, I decided to volunteer for two hours in the nursing home close to my home. I helped taking patient or residents to the bathroom, answered call lights, and helped feed the Residents during supper. I thought this would compensate for my inadequate tithing for the past years.

Knowledge of the scripture is so important in our Christian walk. I wonder how many Christians and Catholics out there don't have the knowledge of God's principle of giving. For churches that are having problem collecting offerings or tithes, they should give Bible studies about giving and see what happens. It is worth a try and you are helping the congregation receive their blessing through giving. This reminds me of the cartoon I saw posted on the bulletin of a Baptist Church many years ago. The background or setting; a certain church just finished their service. A man came out from the Church with out his shoes, without his pants or shirt, (only with his underwear on.) He was talking to another man saying; "My! " What a sermon in giving!" He gave away all he had except his underwear. We sure need a good sermon on giving more often than what we are having these days, so that we can receive God's blessing as He promised in return for our generosity.

Giving

One day as I was talking to my Catholic friend, she told me that she had contributed $1000 dollars to her Church because they had to build additional parking lot. She added, "I felt obligated to give a reasonable amount this time because as you know I only give a dollar here and there every Sunday." I smiled because I remembered the joke of the dollar bill story that only circulates in Catholic Churches. I guess there is some truth in this and I wondered how our Catholic Church survived to keep up with their expenses.

Finally, everyone should give with a good attitude, expecting nothing in return because it will remind us that what we have is not really ours. God gave us everything that we have, and it actually belongs to Him. King David said a prayer to God, "All things come from You, and of Your own we have given You." (1 Chronicles 29:14) Also, when we give we help meet the needs of others whom God loves as well. By giving to others we testify to God's love for them, and we point them to the greatest gift of all – God's gift of His Son, Jesus, for our salvation.

Chapter 10

FACING ADVERSITY

The adversity or trial of my Christian walk happened a few months after we moved to our new house in Downey, California. As I mentioned previously, my character flaws consisted of me losing my temper easily, being selfish, complaining and stubborn person. A few years after accepting Jesus as my savior, I was really trying to follow the scripture to submit to my husband. In doing this I let him make the major decisions, like selling our big house without even asking the detail why and to buy another house without me seeing the house before closing the deal. Tony rented our big house with an option to buy a kind of deal without even discussing it with me. He bought another house without my knowledge. He told me that this two-story house was also custom-built with a beautiful garden. I did not know that he had been experiencing problems with his business. He never shared his problems with me. He told me much later after the divorce, that he did not want me to worry. One person in the family was enough to worry, and that would be him.

I really didn't like the idea of moving but I had no choice, he had already rented the house. In this house we used to hold bible studies and had a church service once a week under Ed Lacaba, the pastor who was responsible for Tony and I to become "Born Again". The big house was my dream house and the envy of my friends.

This house was a custom built house, built by the previous owner who was a well known architect. The house was built around a good-sized rectangular pool. Every area of the house opened or pointed to the pool except the dining room and the guest room. The pool was the central focus of this house. The long hallway from the entrance to where our bedrooms were was quite impressive because of the terrazzo-tiled floor. The landscaping around the pool, the greeneries, and the few palm trees was a delight to everyone that came to our house. This house was like a Hollywood type of house except smaller. I am sure the house was built for entertaining. It had built-in double oven and a huge built in fridge. There was another fridge in the washer and dryer area. It had a piped-in music and intercom system. From the outside the house looked smaller, but it was huge inside.

As you entered the house there was an indoor garden to the right and the entertainment room to the left with custom built cabinets and a wet bar. The plants received natural sunshine through the skylight. We changed that garden and placed three big Benjamina plants in a big barrel type of pot. The entertainment room had a wet bar with fancy built-in cabinets and a guest bathroom. Then there was a long marble hallway towards the inside of the house with sliding glass doors all around that lead to the pool. To the right was the high ceiling living room, and formal dining room, then the kitchen. Past the kitchen was the dinette, then the den with the study room and another guest bathroom. At the end of the hallway was the master bedroom to the left, the two bedrooms to the right and the family bathroom. If you ask me what part of the house was my favorite, I would say everything, but I fancy most our master bedroom and our den. Lying down in my bed I could see the water from the pool and its surrounding garden. The master bathroom had two closets and two sinks. The huge shower was sunken, with three steps going down. The walls of the master bathroom were with white tiles up to the ceiling except one with clear glass that opened to the atrium. The atrium had plants and flowers enclosed with a wooden fence but open to the sky. I could see the birds and the garden while taking my shower.

The part of the house I missed the most was the den because I used to spend my meditation time there, also praying and reading my bible in this area. The scenery was awesome and conducive for meditation because I could see the water from the pool and enjoy the plants as well. We had many bird of paradise plants with other ornamental plants, in all the planter areas in the pool deck, where every morning the humming birds would come to feed on the nectar of the flowers. These birds were close enough for me to see them through the sliding glass doors without them noticing me. I was so close to these birds, yet I did not disturb them.

I remember one day during my meditation hour, I was enjoying the scenery and at the same time felt the glory of God so close to me. I was also enjoying God's presence, meditating on His goodness and delighting in the beauty of His creation. I remember saying, "Lord You must have known how I love this house because You know everything. I thank you for all this, but if You want to take this away from me it is all right." A few months after this communing with God, Tony's financial problem started to go from bad to worse. His financial problem started when we decided to add a second story to our already big house. His main reason to build an add-on to our house was because he wanted his parents to live with us. We added another master bedroom with a walk-in closet and another good-sized bedroom. We also added a huge bathroom with a Jacuzzi tub and a shower. In the front area of the second floor of our house we added a large room for our Bible study. In this room we used to hold a church service as well.

We had a few problems while in this house, but I can't call it trials, instead, discipline because of Tony's wrong choices. Tony was experiencing problems at his Real Estate brokers business but he never shared it with me, and he got upset when I asked him for the reason of his gloominess. He seldom attended our scheduled bible studies and seemed distant from God.

We moved to the smaller house in Downey. Devin, our son, was in college, so it was just Tony and I in the house except on holidays. I noticed Tony's behavior changed. He seemed cold and avoided to talk to me. I presumed that it was about his business, so I continued with my regular routine, hospital, work and housework. One day as I came home from work, Tony met me in the door and told me, "I already cooked rice and warmed the chicken why won't you come and eat? I was about to have some snacks anyway so I said okay. He said that he was not hungry so he would not eat with me. Right after I finished eating he said to me, "I already moved out to an apartment. I can't live with you any longer, I just came to say goodbye." You cannot imagine the shock I had. I felt so sick and felt like throwing up. I remember that I was screaming and crying from the shock of the devastating news. I had no idea that he would really do it this time except during our last fight a few weeks back, when out of my anger I mentioned, "Let's separate" and he said, "Okay I will move out now." He was quite serious so I immediately apologized so that he wouldn't move out.

After a few minutes I tried my best to calm down so that I could talk him out of it; I begged him to stay. I even knelt down begging him to change his mind. I told Tony that we could stop living as husband and wife and be separated but still live in the same house. He could stay in the guest room and I would give him all the freedom he wanted, (I heard of a couple with a similar arrangement.) This time I could only think of how to save myself from shame and embarrassment from my family and friends, nothing else. I am the first and the only person in our family that is divorced.

Right away I called our parish priest and he told me to come and see him the next day. He asked a few questions and most of the time he was just listening and I did all the talking. His advice was to see a psychiatrist and he gave me the name and the address. Then I called a few of our close friends and Tony's family to tell them about the divorce, and to my surprise they all seemed to know it already. I felt very bad that no one was kind enough to tell me. I could have prepared or at least I could have been spared from the horrible shock. I did not tell the people at work except my Christian friend who was also my supervisor. Although I did not tell my co-workers they all seemed to know all about it. Just leave it to the tele-woman it will spread for sure. Much better than telephone or telegram, when it comes to gossip the tele-woman works the surest and the fastest. A few times I caught my co-workers talking and when I passed by or entered the nurse's station they all became quiet. I just knew that they were talking about me.

This trial was the worst and the most traumatic experience ever in my life. The heartache or pain is different than the pain I experienced when I lost my mother at the age of 19. For three nights in a row I had no sleep but kept on working because it helped me a little; to keep my mind occupied. As a nurse I know the stages of loss or death in theory, and this time I experienced the practical side of it. I was experiencing loss because of a death in a relationship.

The first stage was anger. I was angry with Tony for leaving me, angry enough to plan a revenge to hurt him. I could not pray either because at this time I was very disappointed with God for allowing this to happen. I was angry with the ladies in Tony's office, particularly the one that Tony frequently mentioned in his conversations. I thought that they had an affair and that was why Tony left. I portrayed this anger so badly that it was infectious. My son, Devin who was 16 at this time got it too. Devin felt so sorry for me, and to make me feel better he asked his friend to go with him to throw stones at this woman's house. Looking back at this situation now I think that I must have been really crazy to allow my son and his friend to do this. I was so crazy that I even had thoughts of suicide. As I said, I never had heartache pain before. I could never sympathize to my patients and friends who experience loss because I never experienced it myself. This physical pain in my chest area would not go away. The numbing pain just stayed forever 24-7 while I was awake. I was fortunate if I could sleep a little, because then I wouldn't have to feel the pain for a little while.

I remember seeing an old movie a long time ago where the lead lady died of heartache because her boyfriend left her. I said, "No way!" " No one dies of broken heart!" Now I know that we can, out of emotional stress or mental breakdown. One time I was looking for old papers and I came across our old family photos. This day was one of my worst low bottom points; I had just finished one of my bouts of crying. All of a sudden I became hysterical and I was hyperventilating. I had difficulty breathing and was out or short of breath. I felt that my chest was about to burst. My heart was beating very fast; it was good that my niece was around. I told my niece to take me to the psychologist that our parish priest suggested for me to see. We got there in less than five minutes because her office was just a few blocks from our house. When she counted my pulse it was over 130 beats per minute. She talked to me for a while and then she told me to go to the emergency room stat in medical term, (means right away in layman's term.)

The Chinese doctor in Kaiser was very nice. He listened patiently as I poured out my feelings and overbearing emotions including my desire to die. He must have sensed the seriousness of my intent to kill myself because he only gave me 4 tablets of the smallest dose of Zanax. He told me to take ½ pill a day so it lasted only for 8 days. With a very short counseling I received, he told me to get over my depression because divorce happened to many people nowadays and not only to me. He also told me to enjoy my son and whatever family I had left because life is too short. "It is easier said than done," I said to myself as we left. When I asked for a prescription refill they told me to go without it. Thank God for over the counter mild allergy pills.

When we are facing a very painful adversity we can't help to think of ending it all. I wanted to quit my life. My brother –in-law shared the following story to me recently. How I wish I had this in my hand when I was going through my suffering. It would have helped me some.

Here's the story:

One day I decided to quit. I wanted to quit my life. I went to the woods to have one last talk with God.

"God," I said. "Can you give me one good reason not to quit?"

His answer surprised me...

"Look around," He said. "Do you see the fern and the bamboo?"

"Yes," I replied.

"When I planted the fern and the bamboo seeds, I took very good care of them. I gave them light. I gave them water. The fern quickly grew from the earth. Its brilliant green covered the floor .Yet nothing came from the bamboo seed. But I did not quit on the bamboo!" He said, "In the third year, there was still nothing from the bamboo seed. But I would not quit. In the fourth year, again, there was nothing from the bamboo seed. But I would not quit" He said. "Then in the fifth year a tiny sprout emerged from the earth. Compared to the fern it was seemingly small and insignificant. But just six months later the bamboo rose to over 100 feet tall. It had spent the five years growing roots. Those roots made strong and gave it what it needed to survive. "I WOULD NOT GIVE ANY OF MY CREATIONS A CHALLENGE IT COULD NOT HANDLE."

He said to me, "Did you know my child that all this time you have been struggling; you have actually been growing roots. I would not quit on the bamboo. I will never quit on you. Don't compare yourself to others."

He said, "The bamboo had a different purpose than the fern, yet, they both make the forest beautiful."

"Your time will come," God said to me. "You will rise high!"

"How high should I rise?" I asked.

"How high will the bamboo rise?" He asked in return.

"As high as it can?" I questioned.

"Yes." He said, "GIVE ME GLORY BY RISING AS HIGH AS YOU CAN."
I left the forest and brought back this story. I hope these words can help you see that God will never give up on you...

Never regret a day in your life.

Good days give you Happiness.

Bad days give you Experiences.

Both are essential to life.

Keep going....

Happiness keeps you Sweet,

Trials keep you Strong,

Sorrows keep you Human,

Failures keep you humble,

Success keeps you Glowing,

But only God can keep you Going!

I was so thankful for my Christian friends who supported and comforted me. They must have been tired of listening to my tireless complaints and grieving stories. I kept repeating it like a broken record. One of my Christian friends told me, "Don't be like one of the ladies I heard about, she literally went crazy and was running on the street naked! Think about it."

My friend and my supervisor, Bettye, took me to a weekend retreat hoping to help me get over my depression. I did not get anything from it because I was not able to listen and concentrate. How could I when my mind and body were preoccupied with my loss and my pain? This time I couldn't even pray! It is impossible to pray when your heart is full of anger and hatred because it is impossible for the Holy Spirit and anger to have fellowship together in spiritual realm. You can't expect God to hear you when you are with a sinful heart. Besides, self-absorption on our part can keep us from receiving God's words of encouragement, hope, correction, and love.

For those who have a friend or a family experiencing a divorce, make sure to comfort and stay with them as much as possible during Thanksgiving and Christmas seasons. I finally understood why suicide rates are in highest peak during this time. My first Thanksgiving Day by myself hit the lowest bottom pits of my life. Devin, my son, spend his thanksgiving holiday with his girlfriend's family, therefore I was alone. I purposely scheduled myself to work in one of the nursing homes where I worked a part time to keep myself busy. As I was having my shower to get ready for work, I was so overwhelmed with sorrow and depression that I screamed as loud as I could to get over the emotions. It must have been loud enough to scare my next- door neighbor; she came by to check on me after hearing my scream.

A few weeks after my divorce Ihad lost over 10 lbs. of my average weight due to lack of sleep and lack of food;

very unusual for a person who loves to eat to all of a sudden no longer have any appetite to eat. I used to think that losing a husband by physical death is much better than losing a husband through a divorce. At least, if your husband dies, your friends will send you sympathy cards or give you plants and many will stay and grieve with you a little longer. Most of my friends told me later that they could not call me because they felt uncomfortable. After all, Tony and I were both their friends and they didn't know what to say anyway.

I kept asking God, "Why God? I thought I was your child!" Then I asked myself, "Why now after 21 years of marriage?" I felt embarrassed and ashamed that my marriage failed. I also felt rejected. There were times that I felt so sorry for myself, (pity party) and there were times that I blamed myself. I told myself that it must be my behavior or my character that was causing this divorce. As the old saying goes, it takes two to tango. Later I learned that Tony was tired of our many fights. Most of the reason we fought was because Tony lied a lot. Then he told me that the reason he lied was because he was afraid I would get mad and we would have another fight. Sometimes I thought that maybe it was because of my sins that God allowed this to happen in my life.

I also experienced that I was unable to laugh since the divorce. I used to envy my co-workers when they were laughing for some silly jokes. I remember talking to God, "Lord when can I laugh again, I really miss that!"

The loneliness I felt was similar to what the Psalmist says in these few verses:

> "Because of my loud groaning
> I am reduced to skin and bones.
> I am like a dessert owl,
> Like an owl among the ruins.
> I lie awake; I have become
> Like a bird alone on a roof
> (Psalm 102:3-7)

The realization that I could be at fault as well was the beginning of my acceptance, and I started to live with my problem. However, the physical and the emotional pain in my chest were still there. I said to myself, "I can't go on with this pain any longer. Since I am not going to see a doctor for professional help, God has to help me." This is the problem for most people, Christian believers or not, we run to God as the last resort. I repented for my anger, for my sins, and for the things that I failed God. Then I asked God to help me not have any more hatred.

My friend told me about Trinity Broadcasting Network (TBN.) The preaching in TBN encouraged me and helped me get closer to God once again. Most of the time I left my T.V. on in this station for 24 hours just to keep me company, especially if I was feeling lonely.

As time passed by my prayer life was much better. My friends gave me Bible verses full of encouragement and God's promises, and I meditated on these verses:

"For the Lord will not cast off forever.
Though He causes grief,
Yet He will show compassion
According to the multitude of His mercies
(Lamentations 3:31-32)

"I called Your name, O Lord
From the lowest pit. You heard my voice:
From my sighing, from my cry for help.
You drew near on the day I called You,
And said, 'Do not fear!'
(Lamentation 3: 55-57)

"Then you will call upon Me,
and go and pray to Me,
and I will listen to you"
(Jeremiah 29:12)

"He shall call upon Me and
I will answer him
I will be with him in trouble;
I will deliver and honor him
With long life I will satisfy him,
And show him my salvation."

(Psalm 91:15-16)

"And not only that, but we also glory in tribulations, Knowing that tribulation produces perseverance; and perseverance, character, and character hope."
(Romans 5:3-4)

One Friday evening I felt the Holy Spirit's leading to ask God for my healing. Kneeling and crying I asked God to remove my pain. Out of desperation I made a vow; "Lord if you help me from now on I will devote my life to You, You will be my priority, number one in my life!" This time I was really serious about my petition, begging God for His help and promising a total surrender to Him. I don't know how long I was praying, but I fell asleep on the floor with my body and face down. When I woke up I felt great; I did not feel any pain. It was indescribable the ecstasy and joy that is felt when one is free of pain. I was jumping and praising God. I could only say, "Halleluiah! Praise the Lord! You are ever- faithful, Oh Lord Jesus! My God Almighty!"

I felt so good physically, emotionally and mentally. I felt like a new person. The closest thing I can describe this feeling to, is like the feeling felt after having a baby. Most women with children, who have gone through childbirth, will know what I mean. The only difference is that the labor pains last for 8 hours or so for first baby delivery and shorter for multiparas. (more than one pregnancy.) Relief of pain and discomfort after childbirth are mostly physical. The relief I experienced due to depression was physical, mental and emotional. Unlike childbirth, with pain that comes on and off, the pain of depression was longer in duration and continuous.

I am sure the unbeliever will say, " It is because time heals, that is how you got better, Everyone knows that!" But, I say, to this day that God visited me in His mercy and grace. It was the greatest miracle that I have ever encountered in my life. God healed me dramatically and instantly.

Jesus said, "For everyone who asks receives, and he who seeks findest and to him who knocks it will be opened." (Mathew 7:8) and in Proverbs 8:17 it says, "I love them who love me, and those who seek me diligently will find me."

I was so thankful for knowing the Lord, and that Ihad a personal relationship with Him before I had this adversity, otherwise I might have been dead already. I knew all along that God was with me for me to be able to go through it for many months without professional help. I won't go into it in great detail, but God delivered me from being very close to ending my life. As a nurse I had the knowledge and the access, it was very easy for me to do it. God promised, "No testing has overtaken you that is not common to every one. God is faithful, and He will not let you be tested beyond your strength, but with the testing He will provide the way out so that you may be able to endure it." (1Corinthians10:13)

In some instances we seek to know God out of desperation when there is no way out, like running into a wall with no where to go. In my case I was already a believer. I know now that it was a test and a purification time for me. Maybe God was testing me to see whether I would remain faithful to Him. Maybe the devil had something to do with it, but like in Joseph's life the devil meant to harm him but God turned it into good.

God tested whether my faith in Him would waver or not. Whether I would obey His will or disobey Him by continuing my anger, bitterness and complaining. It was also my time of purification to prepare me of my future service for Him as His servant. Not only that, but God knew that He needed to change my character. In this trial, I did not only feel that I had to have a close fellowship with Him, He also comforted me and I learned to trust Him in everything. This trial equipped me to share what I learned, and it can comfort others who are experiencing the similar problems that I had.

If we are not living in touch with God it is very easy to blame Him or pass judgment on Him. In going through my trial, I learned to know God better. Through it all, I felt that God was telling me, "Enter into fellowship with Me; arise and shine." God accomplished His purpose in me through a broken heart and now I am thanking Him for it. God will continue to work in us through the trials to reach His Highest goals until His purpose and our purpose become one. God is Almighty and all knowing, He knows not only what is good for us but also what is best for us.

When I experienced the crisis of my life, the crisis of divorce, I unfortunately was just a new believer. I wish I could have been mature enough, or had an intimate relationship with Jesus. I would not have wasted six months of living in emotional pain. I would not have tried to be distant from Him at that period of time. Instead, I should have stayed closer to God and spend my time praying more. I was not able to have a wholehearted prayer because of my emotional pain. I should have practiced and really believed in my favorite Psalm that I often shared with my family and friends. Psalm 46:10 says, "Be still and know that I am God." During my divorce, I knew little about God and His Word. I should have trusted God more, the One who manages the outcome of our crisis. Had I known God for all that He is and is able to do, I would have had the capacity to turn my trials and adversities over to Him, to let go, and just be still.

"The Hebrew word "be still" has nothing to do with rapt attention to God. Rather, it has everything to do with relaxing. In fact, the verse could be translated literally as "Relax, and know that I am God." The Hebrew word paints a vivid picture. It means to let go. When life takes us to the rugged edge, we always want to keep our hands on the problem, manipulate it, seek to control it, and force it to the outcome we want. We are like a little child who always wants to get involved in a project with his parent. (I don't know why it is that when kids are too young to help they want to help, but when they they're older and more capable they are no longer interested!) God says that when we get out to the rugged edge we have to let go. We need to give up controlling, manipulating, and striving to somehow make it work. If we don't we'll usually just make things worse.

The Hebrew word also means to let go, to put our hands down to our sides. In times of struggle we usually want to defend or protect ourselves. Putting our hands down at our sides makes us feel vulnerable. But that's what God is saying here. He's saying that we have to stop striving, let go, put our hands down, take a deep breath, and relax.

If that were all God told us to do, it would probably be impossible. But, thankfully, the psalm goes on to give us the process for doing this. The only way we can relax is to know something about God. As the verse says, "cease striving and know..." Normally we don't connect our responses to knowing but rather to feeling." 1

If I really know God, I have the assurance that there is order and meaning under the chaos, and that all things will work out for His glory and for my good in the end. Psalm 46:1 says: "God is our refuge and strength, a very present help in trouble." I should have stayed close to God because He is my refuge, my strength and help. Also, in verse 7 and 11 we are told that, "The Lord of hosts is with us." God is present with us by supplying His grace so that we can overcome our grief and be victorious. Had I known back then what I know now, I would have been praising and worshipping Him more. In Psalm 46:10 the psalmist focused on what they knew to be true about God, and their knowledge resulted in hearts full of praise. In 2 Chronicles 20:15 it says, "...for the battle is not yours but Gods." I should have given my troubles and anxieties to God and trusted Him more.

Another thing I had to do differently was to stay quiet and calm instead of constantly murmuring and complaining. I used to call my friends to pour out my feelings of suffering. I was so overwhelmed with my emotions that I used to call them regardless of time. Sometimes without realizing the time I woke them up from their precious sleep. In looking back at the way that I behaved, I am ashamed of how pathetic I was. Even my own son called me a "wimp." Devin used to tell me, "Mom! You are behaving as if you are not a Christian." I should have remained quiet, followed in obedience, and offered my sufferings to Him. I could have listened and understood more of what God's plan and purpose for my trials were.

Joseph M. Stowell in his book, <u>Coming Home</u>, discussed the four measurements we can use in measuring our spiritual blood pressure in the midst of our anxiety. He writes:

"How can we take a spiritual blood pressure test in the midst of anxiety? How do we know if we are spiritually relaxed? Psalm 46 and its historical background gives us at least four measurements we can use to track how well we're doing.

Number one is the Jehoshaphat response: turn our face to the Lord. We can either turn our faces to the Lord and put our arms down and acknowledge that He is in control, or we can turn our backs to Him and lean on our own capabilities—and finally give ourselves ulcers and high blood pressure and anxiety and despair and hopelessness. When we turn our faces to the Lord, it's a sign that we are beginning the process of relaxing. The longer we look at His face and His grand powers, the smaller our problems look. There isn't a problem in life that is bigger than God.

The second measure is that when we look to Him we must believe. Why would Jehoshaphat command the singers to have a worship service before they ever went to battle? Because he believed what he knew to be true about God. The prophet had said, "the battle is not yours but God's." Jehoshaphat believed that the outcome was safe in God's hands.

The third measure is that we praise God in the midst of our difficulties. This doesn't mean that tears aren't running down our cheeks or our hearts aren't broken or we're not feeling the pressures of our problems. God doesn't promise to release us from the symptoms of our problems, He promises to be there with us and see us all the way through. With quivering lips in the midst of the pain we praise Him.

We say that He is good, that we are trusting in Him, and that He will see us through. It's a worship service regardless, for we have turned our faces towards Him in belief.

Fourth, we will be faithful, faithful even in the tough assignments that God gives to us. God told Jehoshaphat to advance towards the enemy at daybreak. They faithfully obeyed even though it might have meant annihilation.

It is easy for us to be unfaithful in the time of trouble. If some enemy or other person has caused trouble in our lives, it's easy to respond with vengeance, hatred, and bitterness towards them. Faithfulness calls us to the tough task of forgiveness. When life takes us to the rugged edge it is easy to doubt, to be unfaithful to God, and to lose trust in His character. It's easy to doubt that He is good anymore. It's easy to believe that He doesn't care. It's easy to feel abandoned by Him. Yet staying connected means that we never stop clinging to Him regardless of our instincts to the contrary. Faithfulness means we are willing to suffer for God's sake if necessary, in the midst of trouble.

Being faithful means staying connected to God; clinging to Him in such a way that disloyalty never actualizes itself in our choices.

Turning to God…believing in Him…praising Him…being faithful to Him. This is how we can know if we have learned to be still and know that He is God.

I have to add a word of caution here. We need to remember that we are trusting God to manage the outcomes, and that means that He manages the timing. God wants us to be still and let Him manage the outcomes, not only in regard to timing, but also in regard to method. He's in charge of the way the problem is resolved. Usually we can think of specific things we want God to do. But we have to let go of the problem and relax in His power, presence, protection, and reputation. Let Him manage. Our job is to stay intimately and faithfully connected all the way through the end. We will see that there was good and glory and gain to the kingdom through our struggle." 2

Dr. Charles Stanley in his "Life's Principles Notes," explains that one of the most important and awesome ways of God is that He uses our suffering. Dr. Stanley enumerates fifteen Scriptural principles:

1. Suffering is the result of anything that causes us pain in some way. In such a sinful world, all of us suffer. Some of our suffering may take the form of persecution for our faith. There are other kinds of suffering we bring to ourselves, such as violating good health principles.

2. God uses our suffering to get our attention. In verses 67 and 71 of Psalm 119 we read that affliction helps us to learn God's ways. When He sees that we are moving toward sin and disobedience, the Lord allows suffering because our pain drives us back to Him.

3. God uses suffering to develop personal righteousness and maturity. As Christians, we are often unaware of sinful activities that remain in our lives. God is in the process of developing maturity through us, and suffering helps to reveal those issues that He wants us to resolve.

4. God uses suffering for the purpose of pruning. Pruning is God's process of cutting back the useless parts of your life that will never be productive for His kingdom. What does God prune? He "cuts away" our attitudes and our actions so that godly ones may

grow, thus maximizing our potential as children of God.

5. God uses suffering to teach us obedience. Even Jesus had to learn obedience. (Hebrews 5:8) He was always perfect, yet always learning obedience. Focus on what God is teaching you. Accept His discipline because it applies to those whom He loves.

6. God uses suffering to teach us to trust Him. In Peter 1:7, we read that our faith, when tested by fire, is more precious than gold, which is perishable. God makes no apology for sending us sufferings because He loves us so much.

7. God uses suffering to bring about continuous dependence upon His grace. Paul wrote about the incredible lesson he learned—when he was at his weakest in human strength, he was at his strongest in Christ. Only in our weakness is God glorified the most, because we must rely on the Lord.

8. God allows suffering to manifest Christ's life in each of us. When we speak of the body of Christ, we don't mean His physical body because He is now at the right hand of the Father. The body of Christ refers to all believers, the church. Christ uses all of us as His physical body on earth, to demonstrate His power to the world.

9. God allows suffering to purify the heart and to make us holy. We can share in the holiness of Christ, according to Hebrews 12:10. God's goal for us is that we be like Jesus. Through our suffering, God purifies our hearts, allowing His holiness to shine in our character.

10. God allows suffering to teach us to give thanks in everything. Being thankful for suffering isn't easy, is it? We read in 1 Thessalonians 5:18 to give thanks in everything, for this is God's will. We may not feel thankful, but we should have gratitude knowing that He uses our suffering.

11. God allows trials to build character. We learn perseverance and steadfastness in our trials. Even though we suffer, we know that the Creator is doing His awesome work in our lives. In Romans 5:1-5, we learn that suffering brings perseverance, the character, and finally hope; a hope that will never disappoint us.

12. God allows adversity to enable us to share the sufferings of Christ. In Philippians 3, Paul writes that he desires suffering because Jesus Christ is on his behalf. Since Christ and Paul suffered, we know that God calls us to endure trials as well. It is a false Gospel that claims our faith should only bring us health and prosperity.

13. God allows suffering to prevent pride and broaden our ministry. Paul knew that God allowed him to be tormented by a "thorn" of some kind (we don't know the specifics.) Paul prayed for the thorn's removal, but God told him that His grace is sufficient. In Philippians 1:12-13, Paul tells how his imprisonment was used for good by spreading the Gospel.

14. God allows suffering to reveal man's evil and God's righteousness. God's righteous judgment is the result of humanity's wickedness. The Creator is alive and active, and He punishes sinfulness.

15. How should we respond to suffering? We should always ask God what He wants us to do. Was this suffering caused by our own sin, or though some other influence? Ask God for strength and discernment during this time of testing."

Dr. Stanley concluded these notes: "If you are a Christian seeking to walk in faith, know that God has a purpose for your trials, even when you can't see what they are. Use this time to increase your understanding of Him. God is gracious even in the way He uses the most unpleasant things in life to ultimately bless us. There are so many reasons that He sends suffering, and every single one of them is for our best.

Be patient! Be steadfast and persevere, because you will ultimately know why God allowed every difficult time in our life. Then you will be able to say, 'Thank you Lord, for You knew best.'" [3] (Dr. Charles Stanley; "Life's Principles Notes / LP 060910 Part 7:" He uses Our Suffering)

Every one of us while in this world is bound to experience trials and adversity in this life. Intimate or close relationship with our Lord Jesus and moment by moment faithfulness with Him, will prepare us for being connected to Him in times of crisis. I did not have this close relationship. As I mentioned earlier, I was only a baby Christian, had just gotten saved. I was not walking a surrendered life completely. If I did, I could have managed my crisis differently and not suffered for quite a long time. Better yet, maybe I could have been spared from this particular trial. I look up with admiration to those Christians and non-Christians that remained with the same wife or husband until their death. If I had an intimate relationship with Jesus, I could have been victorious in my trials, as a Christian should be, and a good witness for Christ my Lord and savior.

Chapter 11

FORGIVENESS

Lewis B. Smedes, in his book <u>Forgive and Forget</u>, included a fable "The Magic Eyes," that I feel I need to include here because the message and the lesson in forgiveness is very helpful to anyone having difficulty in forgiving.

The Magic Eyes: A Little Fable

In the village of Faken in innermost Friesland there lived a long thin baker named Fouke, a righteous man, with a long thin chin and a long thin nose. Fouke was so upright that he seemed to spray righteousness from his thin lips over everyone who came near him; so the people of Faken preferred to stay away.

Fouke's wife, Hilda, was short and round, her arms were round, her bosom was round, her rump was round. Hilda did not keep people at bay with righteousness; her soft roundness seemed to invite them instead, to come close to her in order to share the warm cheer of her open heart.

Hilda respected her righteous husband, and loved him too, as much as he allowed her; but her heart ached for something more from him than his worthy righteousness.

And there, in the bed of her need, lay the seed of sadness.

One morning, having worked since dawn to knead his dough for the ovens, Fouke came home and found a stranger in his bedroom lying on Hilda's round bosom.

Hilda's adultery soon became the talk of the tavern and the scandal of the Faken congregation. Everyone assumed that Fouke would cast Hilda out of his house, so righteous was he. But he surprised everyone by keeping Hilda as his wife, saying he forgave her as the Good Book said he should.

In his heart, however, Fouke could not forgive Hilda for bringing shame to his name. Whenever he thought about her, his feelings toward her were angry and hard; he despised her as if she were a common whore. When it came right down to it, he hated her for betraying him after he had been so good and so faithful a husband to her.

He only pretended to forgive Hilda so that he could punish her with his righteous mercy.

But Fouke's fakery did not sit well in heaven.

So each time that Fouke would feel his secret hate toward Hilda, an angel came to him and dropped a small pebble, hardly the size of a shirt button, into Fouke's heart. Each time a pebble dropped, Fouke would feel a stab of pain like the pain he felt the moment he came on Hilda feeding her hungry heart from a stranger's larder.

Thus, he hated her the more; and his hate brought him pain and his pain made him hate.

The pebbles multiplied. And Fouke's heart grew very heavy with the weight of them, so heavy that the top half of his body bent forward so far that he had to strain his neck upward in order to see straight ahead. Weary with hurt, Fouke began to wish he were dead.

The angel who dropped the pebbles into his heart came to Fouke one night and told him how he could be healed of his hurt.

There was one remedy, he said, only one, for the hurt of the wounded heart. Fouke would need the miracle of the magic eyes. He would need eyes that could look back to the beginning of his hurt and see his Hilda, not as a wife that betrayed him, but as a weak woman who needed him. Only a new way of looking at things through the magic eyes could heal the hurt flowing from the wounds of yesterday.

Fouke protested, "Nothing can change the past," he said, "Hilda is guilty, a fact that not even an angel can change."

"Yes poor hurting man, you are right," the angel said. "You cannot change the past, you can only heal the hurt that comes to you from the past. And you can heal it only with the vision of the magic eyes."

"And how can I get your magic eyes?" pouted Fouke.

"Only ask, desiring as you ask, and they will be given you. And each time you see Hilda through your new eyes; one pebble will be lifted from your aching heart."

Fouke could not ask at once, for he had grown to love his hatred. But the pain of his heart finally drove him to want and ask for the magic eyes that the angel promised. So he asked. And the angel gave.

Soon Hilda began to change in front of Fouke's eyes, wonderfully and mysteriously. He began to see her as a needy woman who loved him instead of a wicked woman who betrayed him.

The angel kept his promise; he lifted the pebbles from Fouke's heart, one by one, though it took a long time to take them away. Fouke gradually felt his heart grow lighter; he began to walk straight again, and somehow his nose and his chin seemed less thin and sharp than before. He invited Hilda to come into his heart again, and she came, and together they began again, a journey into their second season of humble joy.

The effect of the divorce was very traumatic for me. I felt betrayed, I felt Tony left me cold, a sure sign of rejection. Most of all, he brought shame to my name and my family. The hurt of divorce does not heal with the coming of the sun. In fact it lingers on and on. How I wish I could reach back to that painful moment and cut it out of my life. I remember even wishing for a big earthquake so that the whole Los Angeles would slide to the ocean and that would be the end of me. During this time, there was a prediction that a big earthquake would come, and Los Angeles would disappear.

Some people are lucky; they seem to have the gift of forgetfulness. They never hold any grudges and never remember old hurts and sorrows. But for most of us, especially me, I find that the pains of my past keep rolling through my memories, and there is nothing I could do to stop them.

Forgiveness

Tony and his 4 year old son came back to live with me after his divorce from his second wife. I accepted him back because he was worth a lot to my son, Devin, and me. I accepted him because I felt committed to him and because of the good things that he brought my son, Devin, and me. I thought that accepting Tony back was forgiveness, but it was not. Accepting a person can feel a lot like forgiving, but it is not the same.

There is a difference between accepting and forgiving: We accept people because of the good people that they are towards us. We forgive people for the bad things that they did to us. We accept people for the good they are, and we forgive them for the bad they did.

The last time I saw my brother-in-law in the Philippines, I had my last conversation with him because he passed away four months later, his comments: "Tony was a lucky man Manang!"(Affectionate name for elder sister in Filipino dialect) "He left and divorced you, got married and had a child and came back to you as if nothing happened." My response: "It is not easy; I am still suffering from anger and bitterness. He must have suffered too because no matter how I tried to be civilized, my anger shows up at times. To be able to go through it all I can only say it is the grace of God. I know I can't do it on my own." During this time I accepted Tony and his child back and supported them because his income was not enough to support them. But I guess that I have not forgiven him because of the hurt and the bitterness that I was experiencing.

In order for me to continue a right relationship with God, I have to forgive Tony. I said to myself, "Okay, I took him back and I helped support him and his child; that is Godly love and forgiveness for sure." But it was not. My anger and bitterness to Tony for leaving me stayed for years. In my regular prayer time I asked for forgiveness, I felt good for a while but then when I remembered what I had gone through because of what he did, my anger and bitterness would come back.

As I mentioned in the previous chapter, 6 months after my divorce the physical pain was lifted, but I still had the bitterness that came every now and then. The relief of physical pain was an answered prayer from God Almighty and a big miracle for me. However, because of this feeling of anger and resentment, I didn't have the joy or the inner peace that I used to have after knowing Jesus. To have this feeling of anger and resentment, I thought, I must not have completely forgiven Tony. I knew that God had forgiven me, so I should also forgive him. One day I remember saying to myself, "But I am just human! I can't forgive like God."

I heard a TV preacher say that forgiveness, like love, is a choice. We can choose to forgive. The reason we refused to forgive is because we want to punish the one who hurt us. In forgiving, we are surrendering our right to hurt back. We demand an apology or admission of their fault, but demanding an apology is actually one way of punishing them. He also said that prolonged un-forgiveness can lead to bitterness. After a while of feeling angry and resentful we can become numb of this feeling and become a bitter person. Bitterness will hurt us and eventually destroy us through illness. I know this is true because our physical body is affected by our emotions.

When I was going through my severe episode of stress a few days after my divorce, my pulse went up to 130 beats per minute rate. Negative emotion can lead to physical symptoms. Anger, resentment and stress can weaken your

Forgiveness

immune systems and you are prone to all kinds of illnesses. In the Old Testament it says; " eye for eye, tooth for tooth, hand for hand, foot for foot" (Exodus 21:24,) this states the law of reciprocity. During this time, this law had to be enforced if there is to be law and order and protection for human life and property. When we are angry we want to hurt back. Sometimes we want to hurt more. In the New Testament, Jesus in the sermon of the mount said,

"But I say to you who hear:

Love your enemies, Do good to those who hate you,

bless those who curse you, and pray for those who

spitefully use you.

To him who strikes you on the one cheek,

offer the other also. And from him who takes away

your cloak, do not withhold your tunic either.

Give to everyone who asks of you. And from him who

takes away your goods do not take them back.

And just as you want men to do to you,

you also do to them likewise.

And if you do good to those who do good to you,

what credit is that to you? For even sinners do the same.

And if you lend to those from whom you

hope to receive back, what credit is that to you?

For even sinners lend to sinners to receive as much back.

But love your enemies, do good, and lend, hoping for nothing in return;

and your reward will be great, and you will be sons of the Highest.

For He is kind to the unthankful and evil.

Therefore be merciful, just as your Father also is merciful.

Judge not, and you shall not be judged. Condemn not, and you

shall not be condemned.

Forgive and you shall be forgiven."

(Luke 6:27-37)

Then Peter came and said to Him, "Lord, how often shall my brother sin against me, and I forgive him? "Up to seven times?"

Jesus said to him, "I do not say to you, up to seven times, but up to seventy times seven. Therefore the kingdom of heaven is like a certain king who wanted to settle accounts with his servants. And when he had begun to settle accounts, one was brought to him who owed him ten thousand talents. But as he was not able to pay, his master commanded that he be sold, with his wife and children and all that he had, and that payment be made. The servant therefore fell down before him, saying, 'Master, have patience with me and I will pay you all.' Then the master of that servant was moved with compassion, released him, and forgave him the debt. But that servant went out and found one of his fellow servants who owed him a hundred denar; and he laid hands on him by the throat, saying 'Pay me for what you owe!' So his fellow servant fell down at his feet and begged him saying, 'Have patience with me, and I will pay you all.' And he would not, but went and threw him into prison till he should pay the debt. So when his fellow servants saw what he had done, they were very grieved, and came and told their master all that had been done. Then the master, after he had called him said to him, 'You wicked servant! I forgave you all that debt because you begged me. Should you not also have had compassion on your fellow servant, just as I had pity on you?' And his master was angry, and delivered him to the torturers until he should pay all that was due to him. So my heavenly Father also will do to you if each of you, from his heart, does not forgive his brother his trespasses.

(Mathew 18: 21-35)

There is One who is prepared to extend His grace, and He is Jesus who wants us to follow His example. Galatians 5:22 calls love a "fruit of the spirit;" it is a characteristic of God, which He has placed in the heart of all believers. Every single person who is indwelt with the Holy Spirit has the capacity to love in a Godly fashion, although not every Christian is obedient. This Godly love has the power to forgive. An unforgiving spirit is one of life's great challenges, but love enables us to pardon others. Many people, like me, have been wronged in grievous ways – including physical, mental, verbal and so on. We struggle with the idea of forgiving our offenders, but we should also remember: While we each deserve death as penalty for our sins, Jesus paid your sin-debt and mine, in full on the cross. As a believer, I know we have been equipped with God's power to walk in the fruit of the Holy Spirit, to forgive those who have hurt us, to love the unlovely, and to remain stable in spite of our circumstances. With His help, I can make a choice to do what is right, and that is to forgive no matter what. I also know that my anger and resentment does not promote the righteousness that God desires, but controlling my emotions does.

My journal entry in 2/19/'99,"Still experiencing anger and resentment towards Tony. I prayed to the Holy Spirit to remove it from me. I hated how I felt inside. I think today the pain is worst than the pain of a broken heart. I wish it would go away. It is my day off today! I have a lot of time to think! It must be true idle mind can play a lot of bad tricks on us. My reading in "My Outmost for His Highest," says that sin can numb our senses. The sin of bitterness can numb my senses. Forgive me Lord and remove my hatred and bitterness. I know that only You and Your grace alone can help me." (End of my journal entry)

"Another principle we are taught in the Bible is that we are to be imitators of God. So however God is, that is the way we should be. Clarke's commentary describes God as holy, just, wise, good and perfect, and adds, "so must the soul be that sprung from Him." [1]

"The Lord is merciful and gracious,

Slow to anger and abounding in mercy.

He will not always strive with us,

Nor will He keep His anger forever.

He has not dealt with according to our sins,

Nor punished us according to our iniquities.

Forgiveness

> For as the heavens are high above the earth,
> So great is His mercy toward those who fear Him.
> As far as the east is from the west,
> So far has He removed our transgressions from us.
> (Psalm 103:8-12)

Verse 8 and 9 states, "The Lord is merciful and gracious, slow to anger and plenteous in mercy and lovingkindness. He will not always strive with us, nor will he keep His anger forever."

This means that God is forgiving us even if we don't deserve to receive forgiveness, and He will not keep His anger forever or hold any grudge. God wants us to be the same way. Since we receive forgiveness and mercy from Him He expects us to give it to others. One day in my prayer time I said, "Lord, You know I am willing to forgive Tony, but you have to help me. You have to help me and remove my anger and bitterness inside me. I will do my part to control these emotions." As I chose to forgive Tony and asked for God's help, this decision made me more conscious of all my thoughts. Every time I remember or hear things that trigger my anger, I tried to snap it out and change the negative thoughts with something different. I know that if I dwell on these negative thoughts, my resentment and anger will come back.

"Be anxious for nothing, but in everything by prayer and

supplication, with thanksgiving, let your requests be made known to God;

and the peace of God that passes understanding will guard your hearts

and minds through Christ Jesus.

Finally, brethren, whatever things are true, whatever things are noble,

whatever things are just, whatever things are lovely, whatever things are of good

report, if there is any virtue and if there is anything praiseworthy – meditate on these things

(Philippians 4:6-8)

Instead of thinking of what hurtful things Tony did to me, I replaced it with the good things that he did. Just like what St. Paul said in the last verse, "whatever is lovely, if there is any virtue and if there is anything praiseworthy, to think on these things." It was not easy in the beginning, but with continuous prayer and practice it prevailed. After a few weeks of my decision to forgive Tony, I was set free.

I had to forgive Tony for the following reasons.

- Jesus commanded me to love my brethren and my enemies
- As a Christian, I am supposed to follow Jesus' ways to be forgiving
- To forgive; it is the right thing to do – if I do right things, right things will happen to me.
- It is impossible to love without forgiveness

Forgiveness

Besides of the above that I mentioned, the most important reason is because of my own benefits and my own protection.

The benefits: Forgiveness has brought about the closest relationship that I have ever had with God, I have peace with my brethren and therefore I have peace and joy in my walk with God. If I don't forgive Tony or my brethren, my fellowship with God would be broken and He will not hear my prayer. If He won't hear me, my prayer will be empty and in vain. If I refuse to forgive, then I will limit my blessings from God. How can God bless a disobedient child?

The protection: I am protected from any ailment or illnesses that could happen because of resentment, bitterness and un-forgiveness.

In reading back my journal after many years of being set free, I can't help but cry. That pain of hurt and resentment was real and awful to experience. You can't imagine the great feeling that I am now experiencing after being set free. Most of all, I have the joy of the Lord and the peace of God back in my life.

How I dealt with my bitterness:

I chose to forgive for my own sake because I was the only one hurting. Looking at Tony, he seemed to be just fine. Worst of all, he didn't even know the pain that I was going through. One time I even prayed, "Lord, I wish he knows how I am feeling." The anger that I was feeling came out at times in my conversation with Tony, and as the result he became angry with me as well.

In choosing to forgive Tony, every time that I would feel hurt, or I would remember what I went through, I snapped it out and tried to remember other things. Then I forced myself to pray even if I didn't feel like praying. I took a deep breath and repeatedly mentioned Jesus name, because I know that there is power in His name. Then I said, "Holy Spirit please help me! Lord Jesus have mercy on me, remove and help me overcome this pain I am feeling." Then I encouraged myself with the following scriptures:

"Blessed are those who mourn.

They shall be comforted."

Mathew 5:4

"Come to me who are tired from carrying heavy loads, and I will give you rest"

Matthew 11:28

"I'm leaving you peace. I'm giving you peace. I don't give you the kind of peace that the world gives. So don't be troubled or cowardly."

John 14:27

"At the same time the Spirit also helps us in our weakness, because we don't know how to pray for what we need. But the Spirit intercedes along with our groans that cannot be expressed in words."

Romans 8:26

Forgiveness

"Trust in the Lord, and do good;

Dwell in the land, and feed on His faithfulness.

Delight yourself also in the Lord,

And He shall give you the desires of your heart.

Commit your way to the Lord,

Trust also in Him,

And He shall bring it to pass."

Psalm 37:3-5

It took almost seven years for the pain of resentment and bitterness to completely disappear. Literally, I can say it was a long and painful process. But praise God; it is gone. I started to remember it lesser and lesser each day until finally, even if I do remember those hurtful memories, it does not hurt or bother me anymore.

Lewes B. Smedes, in his book, <u>Forgive and Forget,</u> explained about forgiveness being love's ultimate power. He states:

"Forgiving is loves ultimate power:

Love is the power behind forgiveness.

But it does not work the way a lot of people suppose.

Love is not a soft and fuzzy sentiment that lets people get away with almost everything, no matter what they do to us. Love does not make us pushovers for people who hurt us unfairly.

Love forgives, because love is powerful.

Love has two ingredients that make it strong. One ingredient is respect. The other is commitment.

On the other hand, these two qualities make us vulnerable enough to need to forgive.

First, consider love's power to give you respect for yourself.

If you love yourself truly, you will respect yourself truly. And it is precisely your self-respect that gets you into situations where you are challenged to forgive.

When you respect yourself, you set limits to the abuse that you can accept from thoughtless or cruel people, even if you love them. Some pain will be unacceptable to you for the simple reason that you have too much dignity to deserve it. You will not accept disloyalty from friends you trust, or betrayals from a spouse you love, or abuse from children you care for. Such hurts go beyond the limits that a self-respecting person allows.

Love is too powerful to let you lump all the blame for your pain on yourself, as if it must always be your fault when your father deprives you of love, or your spouse has an affair, or your children throw away your values. Love does not let you blame yourself falsely for long. Sometimes it reaches down into the reservoir of your nobility and says: 'No more, I have too much self-respect to put up with anymore.'

When love gives you back your self-respect, and you refuse to take it anymore, you will have to make a decision about forgiveness.

Will you glue yourself to the painful memory of the hurt you didn't deserve? Will you roll it around your memories, savor its bitter taste, squeeze the last ounce of

Forgiveness

crazy-making pleasure you can get out of your pain? Or will you, in self-respect forgive and set yourself free?

The same self-respecting love that gets you into the crisis of forgiving has the power to move you into the place of forgiving.

Love will not let you lock yourself in the prison cell of your bitter memories. It will not permit you the demeaning misery of wallowing in yesterday's pain. Your love for yourself will generate enough energy, finally, to say: 'I have had enough; I am not going to put myself down by letting somebody's low blow keep hurting me forever.' And so you begin forgiving.

Now you can reverse your focus and point your love toward the people who hurt you. Love enables you to respect them too, no matters how mean, cruel, or terribly unfair they were.

Love respects people as genuine human beings, even after they have treated you like dirt. People who hurt you so badly are not just lumps of degenerate corruption; they are complex people with more to them than meanness and craziness. They have the potential to become better people, truer people, than they were when they stung you. Respect for them will help you to see the person behind the rat. And this respect can stimulate to move in the direction of forgiveness.

Now let us go on to the second ingredient in the power of love, love's power to risk a commitment.

True love dares to commit itself to someone, and therein lays both its vulnerability and its power.

When you commit yourself, you reach out into the future that you cannot control, and you make an appointment to be there with someone you love. You pledge yourself to be there with them no matter what the circumstances are. And in committing yourself to people, you expect them to commit themselves to you. But what a risk it is to trust anyone's commitment not least your own.

If you not dare to risk forgiving, all you have to do is avoid commitments. But anyone whose dares to commit him is a candidate for forgiving. 2

"When we forgive the one who hurt us, we are doing what is right, and lots of right things will happen in our life. Right action brings right fruit and wrong action brings wrong fruit.

We have seen the unpredictable, outrageous, and creative thing we do when we forgive another human being.

We reverse the flow of seemingly irreversible history…our own history…. of our own private history. We reverse the flow of pain that began in the past when someone hurt us, a flow that filters into our present to wound our memory and poison our future.

We heal ourselves.

It is utterly unpredictable; no one could suspect, in the nature of things, in the natural cause and effect of things that anyone should ever forgive.

We perform a miracle that hardly anyone notices.

We do it alone; other people can help us, but when we finally do it, we perform the miracle in the private place of our inner selves.

We do it silently; no one can record our miracle on tape.

Forgiveness

We do it invisibly; no one can record our miracle on film.

We do it freely; no one can ever trick us into forgiving someone.

It is outrageous: when we do it we commit an outrage against the strict morality that will not rest with anything short of an even score.

It is creative: when we forgive we come as close as any human being can to the essentially divine act of creation. For we create a new beginning out of past pain that never had a right to exist in the first place. We create healing for the future by changing a past that had no possibility in it for anything but sickness and death.

When we forgive we ride the crest of love's cosmic wave; we walk in stride with God.

And we heal the hurt we never deserved." 3

Dr. Charles Stanley, in one of his, In Touch T.V. programs said: "One of the steps to a clear and blameless conscience is to have a daily cleansing by confessing our sins and repenting of them." Un-forgiveness, is one of the sins we have to deal with. It is not all right to say, "I have forgiven her, but just don't want to have anything to do with her." Dr Stanley said; " Your conscience will not allow you to get by with it." Even those who hurt you have moved far away or have died already. If they are dead, Dr. Stanley suggested for you to get two chairs and put that person in front of you and ask for forgiveness of the way you responded to what they did. Even if you think the one who hurt you is pure evil, you still need to forgive to clear your conscience, because we will be judged by God if we don't. I know for myself that it is very difficult to do, but I personally agreed with Dr. Stanley because we have to assume responsibility in our part to have a clear, clean and blameless conscience.

A reflection happened in my own life recently that I feel I needed to include here. A conflict happened between the youngest of our family and me. Helen, my younger sister, misunderstood my letter to her. She thought I was upset with her because she canceled her trip with me to Jerusalem and Egypt last year. I don't know exactly what triggered her anger. The worst part was, I didn't even know that I had hurt her.

In response to my letter Helen wrote many unkind and hurtful words to me. In the last part of her letter she said that she was sorry but that she had to express all the misgivings that she had been keeping with her for many, many years. Apparently I refused to lend her some money many years ago, and she had now decided to tell me all her misgivings and disappointments.

I was shocked because of what she said to me. I did not expect it at all, especially coming from her. Her hurtful words literally penetrated my heart and soul. Her words kept coming back in my mind and the hurt that I felt emotionally became a physical pain that I felt in my chest. To be honest and to my amazement, the pain was similar to the time when I first heard from Tony that he wanted a divorce. Now I can empathize with my aunt when she said that her heart hurt when her son dishonored and disrespected her by not calling for months.

As soon as I read Helen's letter, my response was to of course write her back and lash out my anger on her. I thought that no matter how grave my fault was, I didn't deserve those rude and hurtful remarks. Besides, I am her older sister (over ten years difference). I did not have a decent sleep for two days because of this incident.

Before I was about to write my letter to pour out my anger on her, I stopped and said; "This is not right! I am behaving just like Helen and not as a Christian. I better pray about it." Then I prayed, "Lord! You said in Your Word that You direct the footsteps of Your children, if we acknowledge You. Why did You allow this to happen? What is Your purpose in all this?" Then I added, "I am sorry Lord for what I did that displeased You and I am sorry for hurting my sister." Then I composed this letter to Helen, (I will only mention a part of it.)

"I guess some truth are better left unsaid. I should not have sent that letter. You did a good job in using those mean and rude words to hurt me, I hope you felt better because you bruised my soul. I did not expect it coming from you of all people. Anyway, I hope there is no scar left from the hurt I caused you and the hurt you caused me. I forgive you Helen and I hope you forgive me too. No matter what I still love you.

I never get the chance to help you because you are well off and when you wanted to borrow money from me I did not believe that you earnestly needed it, as you are pretty well off. In fact, our family always comes to you for help in time of emergency.

I really tried hard not to be burdened and dragged down by your rude letter because of my blood pressure problem, so I offered it to God, I hope you will do the same of your disappointments."

The next day, my meditation reading was in Mathew 5:23-24, "Therefore if you are offering your gift at the altar and there remember that your brother has something against you, leave your gift there in front of the altar. First go and be reconciled to your brother and come and offer your gift." As a Christian and as a Jesus follower, I cannot stand in front of Jesus to pray with an angry spirit towards my sister. It is just like Jesus was telling me in this verse; "Don't come to me with prayer, be obedient first by making things right. First, be reconciled with your sister."

This scripture reading confirmed my action that what I did in apologizing to my sister was the right thing to do. I had to swallow my pride, even as the elder sister, and apologize first. After all, Helen is still a baby Christian. I know deep inside me that I would not have been able to do this if I didn't have a close relationship with Jesus.

As soon as I sent my apology letter I felt peace in my heart and the emotional pain was gone. What a relief!

What was God's purpose in this incident? In Helen's part, I am sure she knows it by now. In my part, God was teaching me humility. God was reminding me of two things: To be angry is easier than to forgive. The other, is to be obedient to God's principle at all time no matter what the consequence or cost.

Joyce Meyer, a famous author and teacher said, "Anger is a negative emotion that breathes death everywhere it is permitted to remain. But we can receive help from God through His Son Jesus and His word, and be totally set free. That is why we must read our Bible and fill ourselves with the Word. I know from personal experience that the word of God changes people because it changed me completely, and it will do the same for you. But it must be learned and applied. 4

Forgiveness

The love of Christ, by dying on the cross to save me compels me to love Him back. And because of my love for Him, I choose to forgive those who hurt me just like the way Jesus forgave me. I was able to forgive Tony and my sister because I felt and experienced Christ's forgiving love in my own life.

Chapter 12

REPENTANT HEART

"He who covers his sins will not prosper, but whoever confesses and forsakes them will have mercy."

Proverbs 28:13

Repentance is a biblical word. The Old Testament thunders, "Repent, and turn from all your transgressions, so that iniquity will not be your ruin" (Ezekiel 18:30, NKJV.) The New Testament also vigorously exhorts men and women to repent. "Unless you repent, you will all likewise perish," said Jesus (Luke 13:3, NKJB.) "Repent... and be converted, that your sins may be blotted out," said the apostle Peter (Acts 3:19, NKJB.) The apostle Paul said, "Now (God) commands all men everywhere to repent." (Acts 17:30, NKJB.)

The Bible commands it, our wickedness demands it, justice requires it, Christ preached it and God expects it. The divine unalterable edict is still valid: "God commands all men everywhere to repent." [1]

What is repentance? Billy Graham expounds this word in his message, "True Repentance, Real Change," He writes: It might be well to notice first what is not repentance.

First, repentance is not penance. Penance is the voluntary suffering of punishment of sin, and does not necessarily involve a change of character, or conduct. People who lie on a bed of spikes or throw themselves headlong on the ground are doing penance, but this act does not mean that their guilt had been absolved." (Billy Graham)

A good example of penance is what some Filipinos do during Lent; they beat themselves till their bodies are bleed. Some go the extent of crucifying themselves like Jesus and literally pierce their hands with nails. However, there is no change in character. They go back to their own selves after Lent. Some do this because they made a vow and some do this to get favor or for their requests to be answered by God.

"Second, repentance is not remorse. Judas was remorseful over his sin of betrayal of the Son of God, but his shallow regret led to suicide instead of to God, because remorse is not true repentance.

Third, repentance is not self-condemnation. You may hate yourself for your sinfulness, but self-condemnation only opens wider the wounds of guilt and despair. We should hate our sins, not ourselves. Hate your false ways, hate your vain thoughts, hate your evil passions, hate your lying, hate your covetousness, hate your greed, but do not hate yourself. Self-hatred leads to self-destruction, and it is wrong to destroy that which was created in God's image. Repentance is not self-condemnation.

Then what is repentance? Repentance is not a word of weakness but a word of power and action. It is not a self-effacing emotion, but a word of heroic resolve. It is an act that breaks the chains of captive sinners and sets heaven to singing." (Billy Graham)

The Bible says, "There will be more joy in heaven over one sinner, than over ninety-nine just persons who need no repentance. (Luke 15:7, NKJB.)

There are three elements in genuine repentance. First, there is conviction. You must know what is right before you can know what is wrong. If you get on the wrong road, you will never know it until you have some knowledge of the right road. You stray off the highway and first, you miss the familiar markings, the customary scenery, and then suddenly the conviction strikes you that you have lost your way. Spiritual conviction is like that. It is the signpost planted in the heart saying, "Stop. Look. Listen! Danger ahead!" The spirit of God, your conscience, and your better judgment all join to warn, "Detour! Change! You're on the wrong road!" If you have this conviction, be thankful. God is waving the red flag, directing you to a proper path. Before men and women can come to the cross of Christ and have their sins forgiven, they must be convicted of their sins, and the Holy Spirit upon the soul, does that convicting work.

The second element of true repentance is contrition. The Bible says, "The Lord is near to those who have a broken heart, and saves such as have a contrite spirit" (Psalm 34:18, NKJB.) Contrition or, "Godly sorrow," as it is called in 2 Corinthians 7:10, is neither a shallow sentiment nor an empty emotion. It is a sincere regret over past sins and an earnest desire to walk in a new path of righteousness. Peter, that rugged man who meant so well and erred so often, "went out and wept bitterly" (Matthew 26:75.) He was never more lovable nor more admirable than when he stood there alone, apart from the crowd, with his frame trembling as the hot tears of contrition ran down his cheeks. In his heart was a noble resolve to live for the One who would die for him. Brokenness, with godly sorrow for sin, is the second step toward true repentance.

Third, repentance carries with the idea of changing – changing your mind, changing your attitude, changing your ways. The Bible says, "For godly sorrow produces repentance leading to salvation" (2 Corinthians 7:10, NKJB.) If we are truly repentant, our will is brought into action and we will make a reversal of direction, and God, seeing that we are earnest, gives us the gift of eternal life.

God has given the Lord Jesus Christ to die on the cross and shed His blood for our sins. God has raised Him from the dead; that provides the ground of our salvation. The Holy Spirit acts upon our dead souls. That is God's first step of convicting. God even helps us repent. We become so contrite over our sins that we decide to change our way of living.

Have you repented? Have you changed? Is your life different from what it used to be? God's commands to repent are not capricious. It is not that He wants to see people groveling in subjection to Him. In His imperative call for people to repent, He has their welfare and happiness as His motive. "For godly sorrow produces repentance leading to salvation." Repentance is a necessary step to salvation. [2]

The more that we are open to the Holy Spirit, the more aware we will be of those areas in our lives where Jesus is not yet fully revealed in us. With that awareness should come a deep knowledge of the Lord's unconditional love. If you start feeling like a failure, remember the power of God's forgiving love as expressed on the cross at the Calvary. Sin has a power to hold us down and block the flow of God's love. We hide when we feel guilty. Repentance has the power to lift us up again and release the flow of God's love.

But if we walk in the light, as He is the light, we have fellowship with one another; and the blood of Jesus, His Son, purifies us from all sin." (1 John 1:7.) For Catholics (and those from other sacramental churches,) the sacrament of reconciliation is one of the greatest gifts they can give themselves when they are faced with sin and guilt, especially when it is deep and heart-felt, and not ritualistic or superficial. Many are healed, emotionally and even physically, through this powerful instrument of grace. So this is a brief period of self – examination, of asking the Lord to reveal areas of not confessed sin, and then making some positive choices. The Lord may be calling you to speak with a pastor or with a wise and trusted friend. He may call you to make amends to a person you have harmed. Be obedient to what the Holy Spirit tells you to do. God won't ask you to do anything without giving you the strength to succeed. [3]

Linda Schubert suggested the following prayer to stimulate an active conscience:

PRAYER OF REPENTANCE

" …return to me with all your heart…" (Joel 2:12)

Loving Father, I am sorry for all the ways I have offended You, knowingly or unknowingly. I have sinned in what I have done, and in what I have failed to do. I come before You and ask for the grace of a deeply repentant heart. You know my innermost secrets. I open my heart to You today and ask You to show me the ways I have blocked the flow of Your love. Forgive me Father, for all my sin, faults and failings. For all the times I have gone astray and not chosen life, I am deeply sorry. I repent of lack of faith, unbelief in Your goodness, or lack of truly believing in Your love for me.

I ask forgiveness for sins against purity: lust, fornication, adultery, unclean books, movies, and videos and sexual fantasies, especially --------------------------. I turn away from all those activities and I turn to You. I deeply repent of having an abortion or encouraging someone to have an abortion. Forgive me, Lord.

I repent of any compulsive, addictive behavior: drinking, drugs, gambling, sex, food, and all addictions, especially ------------------------. Thank You, Father, for setting me free. I repent for not taking care of my physical and emotional health: lack of balance in nutrition, rest and exercise, perhaps the unhealthy suppression of emotions. I make a commitment today to take care of myself.

I am sorry for the times I have hurt other people. I repent of any stealing, lying, deceiving and defrauding. I regret any lack of affirming others, brushing people off, coldness, and unloving and inconsiderate behavior. I am sorry for gossiping, betrayal of confidences and all breaches of faith. I repent of any envy, hatred, resentment, un-forgiveness, jealousy, criticizing or judging others, not receiving love in the way it is offered, and withholding expressions of love. I especially ask forgiveness for --------- --------------.

I bring before You now those areas that I have hidden, such as certain personal habits, secret guilt, dark areas about which I have previously refused to bring to You. I bring You all areas about which I am the most ashamed, especially ----------------------. Lord, I will no longer hide them to You, or from myself. Today is my day of healing and liberation.

Loving Father, what else should I bring to You? (Be still and listen.) For these offenses I beg pardon today. I accept Your forgiveness and now share Your forgiveness with others. Thank You, Lord. Amen.

(Ps 51:17, Ac 3:19, Pr 28:13, 1 Jn 1:9, 2 Ch 7:14, Is 55:7, Ac 2:38, Ps 51:17, Joel 2:13, Eph 5:11, 2 Cor7:10, Ps 103:3, Ac 13:38, Eph 1:7, Heb 9:14, Ro 12:2, Mic 7:18, Lam 3:22, Rev. 22:14, Is 43:25, Ro 8:1,34, 1 Co 14:25, 1 Pe 1:16, 1 Th 4:3, Heb 10:10, Eph 5:11) 4(Linda Schubert; <u>Miracle Hour</u>)

In my own experience as a Catholic, I used to read a written suggested prayer of "Act of Contrition" that says the following: "O my God, I am heartily sorry for having offended Thee, and I detest all my sins because I dread the loss of Heaven and the pains of Hell, but most of all because they offend thee, my God who art all good and deserving of all my love. I firmly resolve with the help of Thy grace, to confess my sins, to do penance and to amend my life. Amen." Then I confessed my specific sins and named them one by one. Then I prayed the suggested penance prayer.

I believe that I had the conviction but no godly sorrow, as result I did not have a change of mind, change of attitude and change of ways. I believe it is because I did not have the idea of what "sin" was as defined in the Bible and what true repentance meant. However, I know now that the reason I did not have the changed, or transformed life was because I did not go to the next step or level. I did not receive Jesus into my heart as my personal Lord and Savior. I did not know that God's purpose for my life was my salvation in order for me to have peace.

Part of the reason was, my lack of knowledge of what my infant baptism and my confirmation entailed. I am sure my parents didn't know either; otherwise they should have lived out, or shared their faith with us, their children. In my recent study of my Catholic faith, I learned:

At Baptism:
- Original Sin washed away
- Indwelling Presence of God – Father, Son and Holy Spirit
- Brought into the mystical body of Christ, Member of the Catholic Church
- Indelible character
- Given Supernatural Virtues and Gifts of the Holy Spirit

In confirmation we are:

- Filled with the fullness of the Holy Spirit – the God of love
- So that we can stand up for Jesus and His Church,
- For God the Father's greatest Honor and Glory!

"The reception of the Sacrament of Confirmation is necessary for the completion of Baptismal grace. For "by sacrament of Confirmation, (the baptized) are perfected to the Church and are enriched with a special strength of the Holy Spirit. Hence they are, as true witnesses of Christ, more strictly obliged to spread and defend the faith by word and deed." [4]

In my opinion, as Catholics aside from a yearly renewal of baptismal faith, we need a conscious (really meaning it from our heart) choice of giving our life to Jesus, which also means accepting Him as our personal savior and following Jesus' holy way of life and living with the gifts and the fruit of the Holy Spirit.

Steps to peace with God:

1. Recognize God's Plan---Peace And Life

God loves all of us, His creation, and He wants us to experience His peace and life. The Bible says... "For God so loved the world so much that He gave His only Son, so that everyone who believes in Him may not die but have eternal life." (John 3:16.)

2. Realize Our Problem---Separation

People choose to disobey God and go their own way. This results in separation from God. The Bible says… "Everyone has sinned and is far away from God's saving presence." (Romans 3:23.)

3. Respond to God's remedy---Cross of Christ

God sent His Son to bridge the Gap. Christ did this by paying the penalty of our sins when He died on the cross and rose from the grave. The Bible says… "But God has shown us how much He loves us—it was while we were still sinners that Christ died for us!" (Romans 5:8.)

4. Receive God's Son---Lord and Savior.

You cross the bridge into God's family when you ask Christ to come into your life. The Bible says… "Some, however, did receive Him and believed in Him; so He gave them the right to become God's children." (John 1:12)

The invitation is to:

REPENT (turn from your sins) and by faith RECEIVE Jesus Christ into our hearts and life and follow Him in obedience as your Lord and Savior. If you will receive Him, He will receive you and you will find that His Gospel, which tells of His death, burial, and resurrection for you, is the power of God unto eternal salvation.

PRAYER OF COMMITMENT

"Lord Jesus, I know I am a sinner. I believe You died for my sins. Right now, I turn from my sins and open the door of my heart and life. I receive you as my personal Lord and Savior. Thank You for saving me now." 5

To receive Jesus means you believe in Him completely. You will trust Him with your life. Then the greatest miracle will happen, you will be changed little by little.

"To become one with Jesus Christ, a person must be willing not only to give up sin, but also to surrender his whole way of looking at things. Being born again by the spirit of God' means that we must first be willing to let go before we can grasp something else. The first thing we must surrender is our pretense or deceit. What our Lord wants us to present to Him is not our goodness, honesty or our efforts to do better, but real solid sin. Actually, that is all He can take from us. And what He gave us in exchange for our sins is real solid righteousness. But we must surrender all pretenses that we are anything, and give up all our claims of even being worthy of God's consideration.

Once we have done that, the Spirit of God will show us what we need to surrender next. Along each step of the process we will have to give up our claims to our rights to ourselves. Are we willing to surrender our grasp on all that we possess our desires, and everything else in our lives? Are we ready to be identified with the death of Jesus Christ?

We will suffer a sharp painful disillusionment before we fully surrender. When people really see themselves as the Lord sees them, it is not the terribly offensive sins of the flesh that shock them, but the awful nature of the pride of their own hearts, opposing Jesus Christ. When they see themselves in the light of the Lord, the shame, horror and desperate conviction hit home for them.

If you are faced with the question of whether or not to surrender, make a determination to go on through the crisis, surrendering all that you have and all that you are to Him. And God will then equip you to do all He requires of you." 6

This surrendered life is what Paul meant when he said, "I have been crucified with Christ; it is no longer I who live, but Christ lives in me, and the life which I now live in the flesh I live by faith in the Son of God, who loved me and gave Himself for me." (Galatians 2:20)

> "Have mercy upon me, O God,
>
> According to Your loving kindness;
>
> According to the multitude of Your tender mercies,
>
> Blot out my transgressions.
>
> Wash me thoroughly from my iniquity,
>
> And cleanse me from my sin.
>
> For I acknowledge my transgressions,
>
> And my sins is always before me.
>
> Against You, You only, have I sinned,
>
> And done this evil in Your sight –
>
> That You may be found just when You speak,
>
> And blameless when You judge."
>
> Psalm 51:1-4

> "But if we walk in the light,
>
> As He is in the light, we have fellowship
>
> Of one another, and the blood of Jesus, His Son,
>
> Purifies us from all sin."
>
> 1 John 1:7

In Catholic religion we have a sacrament of reconciliation or penance. Jesus as the Son of God has the authority to forgive sins and He gives this authority to the apostles. To St. Peter Jesus said, whatever you bind in earth shall be bound in heaven, whatever you loose on earth shall be loosed in heaven (Mt 16:19.) Later, He told the other apostles the same thing (Mt 18:18.) Even more directly, in John's gospel, Jesus appeared to the apostles on Easter and said, "Receive the Holy Spirit. If you forgive the sins of any, they are forgiven them; if you retained the sins of any, they are retained. (Jn. 20:22-23, TNKJV) This follows a pattern that is consistent in the gospel. Jesus had special authority from His Father to establish the reign (or kingdom) of God on earth, and Jesus passed on this authority to His apostles so that they could continue His mission and ministry after He departed. He gave them the Holy Spirit as the source of their authority to forgive sins in Jesus' name. Following this pattern the apostles passed on their authority to forgive sins to the bishops. In the early church, formal forgiveness for sin, or absolution, was reserved for those who had committed very serious sins, such as murder, adultery and apostasy, and it was accompanied by a long period of severe public penance. [7]

Growing up in Catholic faith, we go regularly for confession for every sin we committed like lying, anger, fighting, saying bad words and other sins. As I grew older, we learned from our family and elders that we could confess only to our parish priest for serious sins, and for minor sins we could confess directly to God. The reason behind this change is because we don't want to miss out the sacrament of communion. (We are supposed to go for confession prior communion.)

Without the knowledge of the Word of God to reinforce what we learned in our catechism during our elementary years, we tend to have no true repentance for our sins. The sacrament of reconciliation or penance, and the sacrament of communion were taken for granted for many adults and children alike. We have the tendency of going through the motion of confessing sins and then taking communion without a true repentant heart. We keep committing the same sin over and over without even trying not to commit the same sin again. This is very important to mention here because before I accepted the Lord as my personal savior, bad words, using God's name in vain and swearing came easily in my mouth and I didn't feel bad about it.

When it was time for me to go for confession, I would remember a particular sin and confess it. Then after church, I would do it again without even a second thought. As I became a mature Christian, sin, regardless of how minor it is, like bad words, bother me more and more. I used to take God's name in vain openly. Now I can't stand people doing what I used to do. I tried to avoid and refused to be entertained by T.V., the very sin that Jesus my Lord and Savior had died for. We need to approach God with humility and a true repentant heart in order to obtain God's tender mercy and grace. Only then can we receive His unconditional forgiveness.

Webster defined repentance as: "repenting or being penitent; feeling of sorrow, of wrongdoing." Repentance is a change of mind resulting in a change of behavior.

"Two counterfeit forms of repentance are often passed off as the real thing. One of them goes like this: "Lord, I'm really sorry I got caught" The other sounds like this: "Lord I'm really sorry I sinned. I certainly hope I can do better next time." Both of these are prompted out of guilt or embarrassment, not a heartfelt sense of remorse over the fact that God has been grieved. Usually, these people have no intention of changing. They are attempting to get God off their backs. Genuine repentance involves several things. First of all, confession. Not just, "Lord, I'm sorry for my mistake," but "Lord I have sinned against you." Confession acknowledges guilt. Second, repentance involves the recognition that the sin was against God. Notice what David said in Psalm 51 verse 4 "Against You, You only have I sinned" That doesn't mean he failed to recognize that he had sinned against Bathsheba and her husband. David realized that his sin was primarily against God. " [8]

In August 1996 while talking to Tony, I reminded him of one of the things that happened because of our divorce. Then he told me, "Don't blame me for everything," I have heard our divorce happened because of your sin of having an abortion. I was saddened to hear that it was God's punishment or discipline that could be the cause of our divorce. I felt true guilt overwhelmed me. The worst part of it was that I did not repent with a true repentant heart.

This incident happened in Montreal, Canada. I was 24 years old then and was working in a Jewish Hospital. Based on my good work evaluation, I was given a scholarship award and this hospital allowed me to take a leave so I could go back to school to take my Bachelors of Nursing. When I graduated from Bachelors of Nursing, right away I was promoted from assistant head nurse to a head nurse in the Medical Floor. I was told to get a clearance from our Personnel Health Department. The nurse in charge in our Personnel health department told me that since I was in a childbearing age, I needed to be vaccinated with measles (MMR.) Since I would be working in a medical floor, I was going to be exposed to measles and it was dangerous to get the measles while being pregnant. She told me not to get pregnant within three months after vaccination because the baby that I would be having would have 96-98 percent chance of being a handicap.

After 6 weeks I missed my monthly period. Somehow, the contraceptives that we had been using for years failed this time. Then I notified the personnel health nurse and she told me to bring a urine sample for pregnancy test. Two days later I received a call to report to my OB/GYN doctor that same morning. My doctor asked me if I remembered having a fever after I received the measles vaccination. I told him, "yes" because I was at work at that time and I felt feverish so I checked my temperature and it was 100.8 F. He told me that my vaccination had certainly taken effect. Now my chance of getting an abnormal baby was 98 to 99 percent. We had to abort the baby as soon as possible. In Quebec, Canada, being a Catholic State, abortion was illegal at that time, so my doctor told me that we needed two other doctors to sign the abortion papers besides my husband's and my signature. Within a few days I had the abortion and as far as I can remember, I wasn't even sorry about what I did because I did not know that I had committed a sin. I thought I was doing the right thing since it was recommended by a few doctors to have it done. Every one I knew, medical and non-medical people said that I had made the right decision. You can tell that I was not a Christian because God was not included in this particular decision.

I had a co-worker from Rancho Los Amigos Hospital who was an LVN. She happened to mention her handicap daughter so I asked her what was wrong with her daughter. She told me that she is blind, has severe heart problems and needed a caretaker twenty- four hours a day. She added that her doctor told her that it was because she was exposed to measles during her first trimester of pregnancy. Her doctor said that her daughter's problem was typical of measles exposure, and added that it was too bad she did not know she was pregnant when she got the measles, she could have terminated the pregnancy. When I told her about my story, she told me, "At least you had the option I did not. Looking at my child's condition now, I wish I had an abortion too" I told her she was blessed, she was spared of the guilt feelings that I have been going through.

To get rid of my guilt feelings I kept reading and meditating in the following scriptures:

"For all have sinned and fall short

of the glory of God, being justified freely by His grace

through the redemption that is in Jesus Christ.

Whom God set forth to be a propitiation by His blood, through

faith, to demonstrate His righteousness, because in His

forbearance God had passed over the sins that were previously

committed."

Romans 3:23-25

"There is therefore now no condemnation to those

who are in Christ Jesus, who do not walk according to the flesh,

but according to the Holy Spirit.

For the law of the Spirit of life in Christ Jesus

Has made me free from the law of sin and death.

Romans 8:1-2

"For the wages of sin is death,

but the gift of God is eternal life in Christ Jesus our Lord."

Romans 6:23

"But God demonstrates His own love towards us, in that while we were still sinners, Christ died for us."

Romans 5:8

Repentant Heart

Psalm 51: The Miserere: Prayer of repentance:

"Have mercy on me, O God,
According to Your loving-kindness;
According to the multitude of Your tender mercies,
Blot out my transgressions.
Wash me thoroughly from my iniquity,
And cleanse me from my sin.
For I acknowledge my transgressions,
And my sin is ever before me.
Against You, You only, have I sinned,
And done this evil in Your sight—
That You may be found just when You speak,
And blameless when You judge.
Behold, I was brought forth in iniquity,
And in sin my mother conceived me.
Behold You desire truth in the inward parts,
And in the hidden part You will make me to know wisdom.

Purge me with hyssop, and I shall be clean;
Wash me, and I shall be whiter than snow.
Make me to hear joy and gladness,
That the bones which You have broken may rejoice.
Hide Your face from my sins,

And blot out all my iniquities.

Create in me a clean heart, O God,
And renew a steadfast spirit within me.
Do not cast me away from Your presence,
And do not take Your Holy Spirit from me.

Restore to me the joy of my salvation,
And uphold me with Your generous Spirit.
Then I will teach transgressors Your ways,
And sinners shall be converted to You.

Deliver me from blood-guiltiness, O God,
The God of my salvation,
And my tongue shall sing aloud Your righteousness.

O Lord, open my lips,
And my mouth shall show forth Your praise.
For You do not desire sacrifice, or else I would give it;
You do not delight in burnt offering.
The sacrifices of God are a broken spirit,
A broken and a contrite heart—
These O God, You will not despise.
Psalm 51: 1-17

I lost one baby but because of my experience I was able to save another one. Here is the story.

One young Catholic and a single nurse from my work became pregnant. The father of the baby had no profession and was unemployed. Since she was a registered nurse, her mother wanted her to marry a man with a profession. To make the story short, her mother wanted her to have an abortion. My co-worker asked for my advice. I told her, "Don't make a bad mistake like I did. I know your mother is wrong therefore it is all right for you to disobey her." I told her that God's commandment prevails in this situation and no one else. I told her to move out from her parents and not to tell her mother where she was moving. I told her to inform her mother only after the baby was born. She followed my advice and guess what? She is now reunited with her parents and she got married with the baby's father.

My true repentance included taking full responsibility for my sin. I stopped rationalizing by not saying, "Any way that baby would be handicapped" or "I was an unbeliever then"

All of us need to recognize that sin is primarily against God. I hold my sin up to the unconditional love and grace of God as expressed through the giving of His Son for my redemption. Knowing Jesus as my Lord and Savior, I know that I know that I have been forgiven because of what He did on the cross for me.

If I knew then, what I know now as a believer, I would never have had that abortion. I don't mind if my child was going to be a handicap. I cannot help telling myself, "I bet if I was obedient to God in the first place I am sure that God would not have allowed my child to be a handicap and He would have given me a normal child." For those unbelievers out there, think of what faith in Jesus Christ claims and provides, He can present us faultless before the throne of God, inexpressibly pure, and profoundly justified. Stand in absolute adoring faith "in Christ Jesus, who became for us wisdom from God and sanctification and redemption... (1 Corinthians 1:30) Whatever sacrifices we do for Him are beyond compare to what He did for us. He saved me from hell and total destruction.

Chapter 13

EVIDENCES OF DISCIPLESHIP

The initial call of Christ to every believer whom He planned to use in His purpose of world evangelization was a call of discipleship. Jesus, before He ascended to heaven, gave to His disciples a command, "Go and make disciples to all nations." The task of the church is not so much to make "Christians" or "Believers" but Disciples of Christ. A disciple must of course be a believer.

Jesus said, "If anyone comes to Me and does not hate his father and mother and children, brothers and sisters, yes and his own life also, he cannot be my disciple. And whoever does not bear his cross and come after me cannot be My disciple. For which of you, intending to build a tower, does not sit down first and count the cost, whether he has enough to finish it- lest, after he has laid the foundation, and is not able to finish it, all who see it begin to mock him, saying, 'This man began to build and was not able to finish.' Or what king, going to make war against another king, does not sit down first and consider whether he is able with ten thousand to meet him who comes against him with twenty thousand? Or else, while the other is still a great way off, he sends a delegation and asks conditions of peace. So likewise, whoever of you does not forsake all that he has cannot be my disciple." (Luke 14:26-33) Verse 26 simply means that if you love your family or things more than you love Jesus Christ you can't be His disciple. These conditions are extremely hard to follow unless you have a passionate love for Jesus. That is why not all believers are disciples basing the above standard.

The word disciple means "a learner or pupil" who accepts the teaching of Christ, not only in belief but also in lifestyle. This involves acceptance of the views and practice of the teacher. In other words, learning with a purpose to obey what is learned. It involves a deliberate choice, a definite denial, and a determined obedience. There is no such thing as easy and instant discipleship. One can begin a walk of discipleship in a moment, but the first step must lengthen into a life-long walk. There is no such thing as a short- term discipleship.

To some believers, the radical demands of Jesus may seem difficult and unreasonable, the result is that after they have traveled a short distance the path grows steep and rugged, they are like the disciples mentioned in John 6:66, "From that time many of His disciples turned back and no longer followed Him."

The evidences of discipleship are the following:

Total commitment or total surrender to His Lordship - Jesus said, "If you continue in My Word you are truly My disciple, and you will know the truth and the truth will make you free." (John 8: 31-32) The discipline to continue in reading and studying God's Word is the evidence of reality. We need to meditate and apply His Words into practice. A disciple of Christ not only studies His teachings but obeys His commands as well. Jesus said, "If you remain in me and My Words remain in you, ask whatever you wish and it will be given you. This is to My father's glory, that you bear much fruit, showing yourself to be My disciples." (John 15: 7-8)

"The fruit of the Spirit is, love, joy, peace, patience, kindness, goodness, faithfulness, gentleness and self-control." (Galatians 5:22-23) If there is no real fruit in our lives, we cannot claim to be a true disciple. The fruit of the Spirit is an authentic mark of discipleship. This is not automatic but conditional. Jesus made it clear when He said, "I tell you the truth, unless a kernel of wheat falls into the ground and dies, it remains only a single seed. But if it dies, it produces many seeds." (John 12:24) Jesus links the fruit bearing with His suffering and death in the cross. It is as we apply the cross to our lives and die to our self-dominated life that the spirit can make our lives fruitful.

Jesus said about love, "A new command I give you: Love one another. As I have loved you, so you must love one another. By this all men will know that you are my disciples, if you love one another. (John 13:34-35) Disciples' love must not be selective, not because we like them or because of family or social ties or because they are our neighbors geographically, but simply because we are obligated to share the love of God to others.

The Bible uses several different Greek words for "love." Philia describes the affection and admiration we have for a friend, while Eros is used for romantic love. A third term, agape, refers to sacrificial love, the greatest demonstration of which was Jesus Christ paying our deserved sin penalty with His own precious, sinless life. To help the Pharisees understand the heavenly Father's love, Jesus told parables about the lost sheep, a lost coin, and finally, a lost child. (Luke 15) From the story of the prodigal son we learn principles about how to express divine love to others who desperately need it, and how its awesome power can impact the people around us. While the word love has many definitions, love is really a commitment to another person's satisfaction, security, and development. In other words, we want someone else to feel safe, to have a sense of well being, and to learn and become all that God has in mind for his or her life.

Agape love is manifested in several ways:

First, by its ability to respond patiently in trying circumstances. When the son in the parable prematurely asked for his share of his inheritance, his father could have reprimanded him for such an unreasonable request, denied it, or warned him about dangers he might encounter. Instead, the father gave what the boy desired and then patiently watched him walk away. (Luke 15:12) When we are open to God's leading, He will help us express divine love, even in challenging or heartbreaking situations. Godly love also makes it possible to sacrifice without complaining. The boy's father was able to give a large portion of his estate without argument or complaint because he recognized where his son's heart was: the boy in some ways had already left.

Next, love facilitates calm waiting. In Luke 15's earlier parables of loss, the shepherd and the woman actively pursued the missing sheep and coin. However the prodigal's father did not rush out to convince the boy to return. Instead, the father stayed home, hopeful and watchful for his son's return. Eros and Philia love often times refuse to wait, that is why people step out of God's will. But Godly love can exhibit patience even when that is not our preference. When the son returned, notice what kind of reception awaited him. "While he was still a long way off, his father saw him and felt compassion for him, and ran and embraced him and kissed him" (Luke 15:20) As soon as he spotted the boy, he ran to him with arms outstretched in forgiveness, compassion and love. Jesus portrays selfless love, forgiving love and sacrificial love.

Selfless love – Even the noblest human love there is usually contains some element of self-interest. We love in part because of what we receive from it and the happiness it brings. Jesus loved us while we were still sinners (Romans 5:8) He loved and died for our sins. Our Lord's love was unselfish and unconditional.

Forgiving love - Although Jesus was doubted, denied, betrayed and forsaken, the Lord's love was not quenched. Jesus told Peter to forgive seventy times seven.

Sacrificial love – There was no limit to the sacrifices Jesus made to save us because of His love. His death on the cross was His ultimate sacrificial love. The supreme evidence of discipleship is genuine love for one another. "And though I have the gift of prophecy, and understand all the mysteries and all knowledge, and though I all faith, so that I could remove mountains, but have not love, I am nothing. And though I bestow all my goods to feed the poor, and though I give my body to be burned, but have not love, it profits me nothing. (1 Corinthians 13:2-3) We can preach, pray, give and even sacrifice, but without this love we gain nothing. One testimony from a previous unbeliever states, "It is surprising, you Christians seemed to solve all of the problems in this world through this love of Jesus."

This love should be developed at first between Jesus and His disciple, but it must soon become public evidence of true discipleship. Mother Theresa said, "We are called to plant seeds in God's kingdom. Not great things but small things but with great love. Love is the seed and the power is in the seed." One day I was praying, "Dear God, my heavenly Father, give me this kind of love just like Mother Theresa." The following day, my meditation reading in <u>My Utmost for His Highest</u> stated, "The only One who truly loves the Lord Jesus is the Holy Spirit, and it is He who has poured out in our hearts the very love of God. To be a disciple is to be devoted, bondservant, motivated only by love for the Lord Jesus. No one on earth has the passionate love for the Lord Jesus unless the Holy Spirit has given it to him. Whenever the Holy Spirit sees an opportunity to glorify Jesus through you, He will take your entire being and set you ablaze with glowing devotion to Jesus Christ. 1

Since that time I have been praying to the Holy Spirit to give me this kind of love, and everyday I include this prayer of St. Frances:

Prayer for the Holy Spirit

"Breathe in me, O Holy Spirit that my thoughts may all be holy

Act in me, O Holy Spirit that my work too will be holy

Draw my heart, O Holy Spirit that I may love only what is holy

Strengthen me, O Holy Spirit that I may defend all that is holy

Guard me, O Holy Spirit that I myself will be holy

St. Francis

"The characteristic of a disciple is not only that he does good things, but also he is good in his motives, having been made good by the supernatural grace of God. Jesus Christ came to place within anyone who would let Him a new heredity that would have a righteousness exceeding that of a scribe and Pharisee. Jesus is saying, 'If you are My disciple, you must be right not only in your actions, but also in your motives, your aspirations, and in the deep recesses of the thoughts of your mind.' Who can stand in the eternal light of God and have nothing for Him to rebuke? Only the Son of God, and Jesus Christ claims that through His redemption He can place within anyone His own nature and make that person as pure and as simple as a child. The purity that God demands is impossible unless we can be remade within, and that is exactly what Jesus has undertaken to do through His redemption." 2

If you read your Bible everyday and spend time with God in prayer and meditation, it is impossible to stay angry and bitter. If I am angry, I am unable to pray. I seriously have to repent first in order to have fellowship with God. Or when I am angry or have some misgivings in my heart and am still able to do my prayer, it will disappear after reading God's word. To be able to walk with God and have fellowship with Him, I have to forgive and must have God's love. I had to forgive Tony in spite of the hurt and the pain that he caused me. My father in law told me to be nice and stay friendly with him for our son's sake. I told him I would. I was thinking, as a Christian I have no other choice but to stay friendly with him.

After our divorce Tony got married. Within a few years after he got married I heard that he was having problems with his second marriage. He told my son that he had a series of bad luck and was unable to even get a decent job. Because of these problems and probably to make amends of his guilt of leaving me, he told our son Devin and our friends in Canada that he was going to return to me.

Then, my friend from Canada came for a visit. She called and asked if we could see each other. Our mutual friend Sonia and I decided to meet her in a Filipino restaurant. In the restaurant my friend asked me if I would take Tony back even if he had a child. I was shocked with her question. I did not even know that he was married. I only knew he was living with someone. I felt warmth and at the same time weakness all over my body, I couldn't wait to get home so I could ask Devin if all this was true. I confronted Devin and asked him why he was hiding the fact that he had a half brother, he told me that he promised his Dad that he would not tell me. Tony told Devin that he would tell me himself later. The hurt and the pain became alive once again. Exactly like the saying, "The old healed wound was opened." It was like reliving and rehearsing the pain of divorce. Thank God the pain was not as severe, but still uncomfortable.

I asked my older Christian friend for advice and she told me to fast and pray and to ask God for His guidance. I said to myself, I gave my life to God and His will be done.

As previously planned, we (Tony and I) attended Devin's graduation in New York. Before Devin's graduation Devin had already told me that his Dad was coming home to us just like the prodigal son in the Bible. He also said that we should forgive him and take him and his young child back.

After Devin's graduation in New York, we came back to LA. Tony stayed in our first floor bedroom.

Then a few days later Devin told me that his Dad had asked him for money to buy a plane ticket to Florida. He wanted to go back with his wife for the sake of his child who had been crying and missing Tony. Devin said, "Mom! I really hate Dad for doing this. But, anyway, this is the last time I'm giving him money, and if he will come back to us we will not accept or receive him!" Tony was crying when he said his farewell to me and said he was sorry. He was doing it mainly for his young child. I said, "It is fine with me. This child needs his father more than anything at his age."

Two days later Tony was back, he told me his wife left for Florida leaving their son and said she was filing for divorce proceedings. Tony and his child were devastated and both of them were crying. I agreed to take Tony and his child back out of pity for his child who was four and a half years old. I was hoping that someday when Tony would be financially stable he could be on his own. I also told him that I had one condition; he had to respect my vow to God. My vow was to stay single, not to marry again. He agreed and it was convenient to all of us because his child couldn't sleep without Tony beside him. Tony became the mother and the father of his child, Faustin.

My brothers and sisters were upset because I took Tony and his child back. They could not understand why I had to support them financially as well. My one brother was so upset that he stopped talking to me. My friends and co-workers were also surprised and could not understand my decision. One of my friends told me that like their neighbor, with a similar situation as mine, I would definitely encounter a lot of problems. She was begging me to change my mind for my sanity's sake. My Christian friend and my supervisor, (she was the one I told first that

Tony left me, the one who told me, "Why won't you kneel down and beg him to come back?") When she learned that Tony came back with his child she told me, "Are you out of your mind? He has a child now, send him away!"

My co-worker where I worked part time made this comment, "My God Elma! You will become a live-in baby sitter!" and added, "and as a maid without pay!" My brother Gilbert told me that when he told my story to his female friend she made this comment, "My, Gilbert! What is she thinking! Does she think she is Mother Theresa? I thought there is only one Mother Theresa!"

As everyone had predicted, it was not easy. What bothered me most was the guilt of living together with Tony and not being married. As a Christian, I am supposed to avoid the appearance of evil. I confessed and repented this sin. I gave this problem at the foot of the cross of Jesus and because of this sin I asked Jesus to do anything He wanted to do with my life, even death.

One year after Tony was back, Tony had his first heart attack. I was sure that it was due to stress. To support himself and his child, he was forced to take a low paying job and had to drive two hours to his work every day. He had this heart attack right after his shower. He was knowledgeable enough to call 911 just before he became unconscious. My neighbor called me at work telling me to come over to their house to pick up Tony's child because Tony was in the hospital. When I came to pick up Faustin, he looked very nervous and was throwing up every now and then. Everyone was in the hospital including Tony's family. I was at home baby-sitting with Faustin. Inside the Intensive Care Unit he called me to send Faustin to his mother in Florida, if something was to happen to him.

Evidences of Discipleship

The following day at around three in the afternoon I received a call from Monica, Tony's niece, telling me to come over as soon as possible because Tony's doctor told her to call everyone to come. Apparently Tony had a bad reaction to the medicine that was supposed to dissolve the blood clots and his doctor thought that Tony might not make it through the night. When I came to see him he was very pale and weak. When I looked up to his heart monitor His heart rate was between 48 to 52 beats per minute and his blood pressure was 54/40 to 58/44. I told him to get better for Faustin's sake and not to worry about anything because I would help him in anyway I could, including taking care of Faustin. Right after saying this, an amazing thing happened, his face lightened or brightened up and suddenly His heart rate and blood pressure went up. He made it through the critical period and in a few days he was able to tolerate the balloon procedure to dilate his arteries.

Five years later Tony had another heart attack. Because of his health I finally resigned to the idea of Tony not being able to work and have his own place to live. I was thankful that at least he was making a little money to help for his daily expenses. Day by day I was trying to live according to God's will. I tried to endure whatever trials and sufferings came my way, with the help of the Holy Spirit of course. The Holy Spirit gave me strength and helped me persevere as I yielded to Christ's presence and power moment by moment, every single day.

To be a disciple of Jesus, we have to follow His ways and obey His commandments; to love God and to love our neighbors. This love in particular is the agape kind of love, which means a sacrificial commitment dedicated to the well being of another person.

As Jesus' disciple I made a decision to take Tony and his son back in spite of what my family and friends said. As His disciple I had to pour my life to help Tony financially and to support him in raising Faustin. I made this decision because deep in my heart I knew that I was doing God's will. I knew it was going to be hard, but I also knew that God would help me because I was doing His will.

As Jesus' disciple I deliberately identify myself with God's interests in other people.

It was a great sacrifice in my part but I give all the glory to God and His supernatural grace. Because of His redemption, Jesus remade me within. He places His own nature in me. He gave me the power and strength, and enabled me to do the things that I could not do otherwise.

Chapter 14

MY SERVICE

"Behold My servant whom I uphold,
My Elect One in whom My soul delights!
I have put My Spirit upon Him;
He will bring forth justice to the Gentiles.
He will not cry out, nor raise His voice
Nor cause His voice to be heard in the street.
A bruised reed He will not break,
And smoking flax He will not quenched;
He will bring forth justice for truth.
He will not fail nor be discouraged,
Till He has established justice in the earth;
And the coastland shall wait for His law

(Isaiah 42:1-4)

Prophet Isaiah called the nation of Israel as the servant of Jehovah. Also, the Lord Jesus Christ is the servant of Jehovah and is so called in the Gospel of Mark. He made it very clear, "For even the Son of man came not to be ministered unto, but to minister, and to give His life a ransom for many." (Mark 10:45) In Matthew 12:17-21 there is an application of this prophesy to the Lord Jesus. "You call me Teacher and Lord, and you say well, for so I am. If I then, your Lord and Teacher, have washed your feet, you also ought to wash another's feet." "For I have given you an example, that you should do as I have done to you. Most assuredly, I say to you, a servant is not greater than his master; nor is he who sent him." (John 13:13-16)

Jesus' attitude is the pattern for the disciple. He acted out the master principle of service that the highest honor lies in the lowliest of service. He revealed to us that the life of God is spent in the service of humanity. There is no one so perpetually available as He. Jesus rules because He serves all.

"Learn a lesson that, if you are to do the work of a prophet, what you need is not a scepter but a hoe."

Bernard of Clairvaux

Richard J. Foster, in his book <u>Celebration of Discipline</u>, distinguished Self-righteous Service vs. True Service. He writes:

"If true service is to be understood and practiced it must be distinguished from self- righteous service.

Self-righteous service comes through human effort. It expends immense amounts of energy calculating and scheming how to render the service. Sociological charts and surveys may be devised so we can 'help those people.' True service comes from a relationship with the divine Other deep inside. We serve out of whispered promptings,

My Service

divine urgings. Energy is expended but it is not the frantic energy of the flesh. Thomas Kelly writes, 'I find He never guides us into an intolerable scramble of panting feverishness.'"

Self- righteous service is impressed with the "big deal." It is concerned to make impressive gains on ecclesiastical scoreboards. It enjoys serving, especially when the service is titanic. True service finds it almost impossible to distinguish the small and the large service. Where the difference is noted the true servant seems to be often drawn to the small service, not out of false modesty but because he genuinely sees it as the important service. He indiscriminately welcomes all opportunities to serve.

Self-righteous service requires external rewards. It needs to know that people see and appreciate the effort. It seeks human applause – with proper religious modesty of course. True service rests contented in hiding. It does not fear the lights and blare of attention, but it does not seek them either. Since it is living out of a new Center of Reference the divine nod of approval is completely sufficient.

Self- righteous service is highly concerned about results. It eagerly waits to see if the person served will reciprocate in kind. It becomes bitter when the results fall below expectations. True service is free of the need to calculate results. It delights only in the service. It can serve enemies as well as friends.

Self-righteous service picks and chooses whom to serve. Sometimes the high and powerful are served because that will ensure a certain advantage. Sometimes the low and defenseless are served because that will ensure humble image. True service is indiscriminate in its ministry. It has heard command of Jesus to be the "servant of all." (Mk. 9:35) Brother Francis of Assisi wrote in a letter, "Being the servant of all, I am bound to serve all and administer the balm-bearing words of my Lord."

Self-righteous service is affected by moods and whims. It can serve only when there is "feeling" to serve ("moved by the spirit" as we say.) Ill health or inadequate sleep will control the desire to serve. True service ministers simply and faithfully because there is a need. It knows that the "feeling to serve" can often be a hindrance to true service. It refuses to allow the feeling to control the service, but rather the service disciplines the feelings.

Self-righteous service is temporary. It functions only while the specific acts of service are being performed. Having served, it can rest easy. True service is a life-style. It acts from ingrained patterns of living. It springs spontaneously to meet human need.

Self-righteous service is without sensitivity. It insists on meeting the need even when to do so would be destructive. It demands the opportunity to help. True service can withhold the service as freely as perform it. It can listen with tenderness and patience before acting. It can serve by waiting in silence. "They also serve those who stand and wait.

Self-righteous service fractures community. In the final analysis (once all the religious trappings are removed) it centers in the glorification of the individual. Therefore it puts others into our debt and becomes one of the most subtle and destructive forms of manipulation known. The result is the rupture of the community.

My Service

True service on the other hand, builds community. It quietly and unpretentiously goes about caring for the needs of others. It puts no one under obligation to return the service. It draws, binds, heals, and builds. The result is the unity of the community."[1]

Mr. Foster continues to explain that there is humility in service.

"The grace of humility is worked into our lives through the discipline of service. Humility, as we all know, is one of those virtues that is never gained by seeking it. The more we pursue it the more distant it becomes. To think we have it is sure evidence that we don't. Therefore most of us assume there is nothing we can do to gain this prized Christian virtue and so we do nothing.

But there is something we can do. We do not need to go through life faintly hoping that someday humility may fall upon our heads. Of all the classical Spiritual Disciplines, service is the most conducive to the growth of humility. When we set out on a consciously chosen course of action that accents the good of others and is for the most part a hidden work, a deep change occurs in our spirit.

Nothing disciplines the inordinate desires of the flesh like service, and nothing transforms the desires of the flesh like serving in hiding. The flesh whines against service but screams against hidden service. It strains and pulls for honor and recognition. It will device subtle, religiously acceptable means to call attention to the service rendered. Every time we crucify the flesh we crucify our pride and arrogance." [2]

The apostle John wrote, "For all that is in world, the lust of the flesh and the lust of the eyes and the pride of life, is not of the Father but of the world." (1 John 2:16) We fail to understand the force of this passage because of our tendency to relegate it to sexual sin. "The 'lust of the flesh' refers to the failure to put under control – to discipline – the natural human passions. C.H. Dodd has said that the 'lust of the eyes' refers to the tendency to be captivated by the outward show. The 'pride of life' he defines as 'pretentious egoism.' In each case the same thing is seen: infatuation with natural human powers and abilities without any dependence upon God. That is the flesh in operation, and the flesh is the deadly of humility.3

The strictest daily discipline is necessary to hold this passion in check. The flesh must learn the painful lesson that it has no rights of its own. It is the work of hidden service that will accomplish this self-abasement. William Law made a lasting impact upon eighteenth-century England with his book, <u>A Serious Call to a Devout and Holy Life</u>. In it, Law urged that every day should be viewed as a day of humility. How do we go about making each day humble? by learning to serve others. Law understood that it was the discipline of service that brings humility into the life. If we want humility he counsels us to:

".... condescend to all the weaknesses and infirmities of your fellow-creatures, cover their frailties, love their excellencies, encourage their virtues, relive their wants, rejoice in their prosperities, compassionate their distress, receive their friendship, overlook their unkindness, forgive their malice, be a servant of servants, condescend to do the lowest offices to the lowest of mankind.

The result then of this daily discipline of the flesh will be the rise of the grace of humility. It will slip in upon us unaware. Even more than the transformation that is occurring within us, we are aware of a deeper love and joy

My Service

in God. Our days are punctuated with spontaneous breathings of praise and adoration. 4

For every kind of service rendered, we can't help to experience the fear of something like this: "If I do that, people will take advantage of me," "They will walk all over me," or "They will only use me or abuse me." Right here we must see the difference between choosing to serve and choosing to be a servant. When we choose to serve, we are still in charge. We decide whom we will serve and when we will serve, and if we are in charge we will worry a great deal about anyone's stepping on us i.e.: taking charge over us.

But when we choose to be a servant, we give up the right to be in charge. There is great freedom in this. If we voluntarily choose to be taken advantage of then we cannot be manipulated. When we choose to be a servant, we surrender the right to decide who and when we will serve. Therefore the fear that we will be taken advantage of and stepped on is justified. That is exactly what may happen. But who can hurt someone who has freely chosen to be stepped on?

A delightful story is told in, "The Little Flowers of St. Francis," about how Francis taught Brother Leo the meaning of perfect joy. As the two walked together in the rain and bitter cold, Francis reminded Leo of all the things that the world –including the religious world– believed would bring joy, adding each time, "Perfect joy is not in that." Finally in exasperation Brother Leo asked, "I beg you in God's name to tell me where perfect joy is." Whereupon Francis began enumerating the most humiliating self-abasing things he could imagine, adding each time, "Oh Brother Leo, write that perfect joy is there." To explain and conclude the matter he told him, "Above all the graces and gifts of the Holy Spirit which Christ gives to his friends is that of conquering oneself and willingly enduring sufferings, insults, humiliations and hardships for the love of Christ." 5

THE SERVICE OF SMALL THINGS

In Acts, there was a certain disciple called Tabitha, which is translated Dorcas. This woman was full of good works and charitable deeds. She used to make tunics and garments for widows. (Acts 9:39) She is a good example of doing service of small things.

Dietrich Bonhoeffer's, <u>Life Together,</u> talks about service: "The second service that one should perform for another in a Christian community is that of active helpfulness. This means initially simple assistance in trifling, external matters. There is a multitude of these things wherever people live together. Nobody is too good for the meanest service. One who worries about the loss of time that such petty, outward acts of helpfulness entail, is usually taking the importance of his own career too solemnly."

Francis de Sales says that the great virtues and the small fidelities are like sugar and salt. Sugar may have a more exquisite taste but its use is less frequent. Salt is found everywhere. The great virtues are a rare occurrence; the ministry of small things is a daily service. Large tasks require great sacrifice for a moment; small things require constant sacrifice.

Guarding the reputation of others is a service of a small thing. As Bernard of Clairvaux put it, the service of

My Service

"Charity." How necessary this is if we are to be saved from backbiting and gossip. The apostle Paul taught us to "speak evil to no one" (Titus 3:2.) We may clothe our backbiting in all the religious respectability we want, but it will remain a deadly poison. Nor should we be a party of slanderous talk of others. Bernard warns us that the spiteful tongue "strikes a deadly blow at charity in all who hear him speak and, so far as it can, destroys root and branch, not only in the immediate hearers but also in others to whom the slander, flying from lip to lip, is afterwards repeated. Guarding the reputation of others is a deep and lasting service. Gossiping is so common among men and women. Among church members sometimes they called gossip as sharing. Everyone should try hard not to gossip and avoid those who gossip. Remember, those who gossips to you are most likely will gossip of you.

I will include the following scriptures to help us avoid to gossip:

The Lord continued, "Never spread false rumors. Don't join forces with wicked people by giving false testimony."

Exodus 23:1

"Whoever gossips gives away secrets,
but whoever is trustworthy in spirit can keep a secret."
Proverbs 11:13

"A devious person spreads quarrels.
A gossip separates the closest friends."

Proverbs 16:28

"The words of a gossip are swallowed greedily
and they go down into a person's innermost being."
Proverbs 18:8

"Whoever goes around as a gossip tells secrets.
Do not associate with a person whose mouth is always open."
Proverbs 20:19

"Without wood a fire goes out,
and without gossip a quarrel dies down."
Proverbs 26:20

    Every disciple has the burning desire to serve and to please their master mainly because of their love for Him. A few months after I accepted Jesus as my Lord and Savior I volunteered to help one of the church members from our parish that was dying of cancer. She had no family and she needed someone to help her eat; she was very weak to even feed herself. The most convenient time for me was to help her during lunch. Since my work place was so close to the nursing home where she was, during my lunch hour I went to help her with her lunch. Sometimes because she did not like the food in the place where she was, I made her homemade soup and took it with me in a thermos bottle. Four months later she died.

My Service

I continued to work in this nursing home once a week for two hours because of my conviction that I was not tithing enough. I thought, "I would give my service instead." When I asked the director of this nursing home for permission to volunteer, she told me that I was the only Filipino that was doing this. Most Filipinos work extra hours for money.

I also attended a prayer group meeting once a week. It was held in Dominic Savio Church Elementary School during the evening. Most of the people attending this prayer meeting were Charismatic Catholic. We prayed like most evangelical Christians do, including prayer in tongue. A part of our prayer session was a quiet time. Then each member said encouraging scripture words, whatever the Holy Spirit was leading us to say. I was amazed at the power of God's word. When I mentioned God's Word at our prayer meeting, the same scripture that impressed me during my morning meditation, it helped one or two people in the group. One person was literally with tears in his eyes thanking me for sharing that scripture. He said that God had spoken to him through that Word. As St. Paul said in his letter to the Hebrews, "For the Word of God is living and powerful, sharper than any two edge sword, piercing even to the division of soul and spirit, and of joints and marrow, and is a discerner of the thoughts and intents of the heart,"

Because of my desire to learn more about the Bible, I arranged with Pastor Ed to have a Bible study in our house. In the clinic where I used to work I met patients that were on drug rehabilitation. I asked them if they were interested in attending a bible study and told them I would pick them up and drop them off. We had 6 to 8 people in our group. Some times patients from head trauma rehab program came as well. I made sure we had snacks after the bible study. Sometimes I got very discouraged because when I went to pick them up they wouldn't want to come. I talked to the Lord and said, "Lord I am really getting tired, I wonder if this is worthwhile doing all this." That evening our bible study was the most interesting and exiting and I learned a lot. We also had church service in our house every Sunday. Pastor Ed (who has a Theology Degree) preached in our service and sometimes we had guest Pastors do the preaching of God's Word. We had about 7 to 10 families attending and after our service we had our potluck lunch. Our fellowship was great being that our group was small. If we had questions about the sermon or if we wanted clarification about God's word we asked and discussed it during our lunch.

When I got divorced, because I was afraid to stay alone in our house, I rented one of my rooms. My tenant was a retired single lady and a Methodist Christian. We decided to have a bible study in our house. We decided that she would give the Bible study since she used to teach bible study before. I gave the bible study for the children that came with their parents. The children were from 5 to 9 years old. I remember being so frustrated because it seemed that they were not learning anything. Most of the time, they seemed to be not listening. I complained one time to my tenant and to their parents. I tried everything. I even promised to give them delicious snacks. I knew that their concentration and their attention span was short so every 5 minutes we stopped and sang hymns that required them to be standing and with hand actions. A few times, just to make sure they got something out of the bible study, I gave them a dollar for every homework they brought back. It is a good thing there were just few of them or I would have been broke.

My Service

In 2005, to my surprise, my friend and previous co-worker, Kilcha Chang, called me and told me she met the mother of one of the children that attended my bible study. This particular mother did not participate in adult Bible study but she would bring her two daughters for children's Bible study, especially when she had to go somewhere. This mother told her that she and her daughters were remembering me and wanted to talk to me. Kilcha gave me her telephone number. When I spoke to her she told me that, that short time of a bible study I gave to the children had some influence on her daughters' lives. They turned out to be good children and good students. One of her children was a college student in Long Beach Cal State. God's promise stating, "My words shall not return to Me void but it shall accomplish what I please" is very true. (Isaiah 55:11)

My hope of serving the Lord in a much bigger way was to start a foundation. I formed this foundation in 2002 mainly in following Jesus' command to spread the Gospel all over the world and to help the poor. The name of my foundation is New Life Family Outreach. This vision of mine came about because a few weeks after I became "Born Again", I dreamed that I was helping the poor, sick people, adult and children, in a small bamboo and nipa hut in a small village. I presumed the location would be in the Philippines.

My friends asked me why I chose the Philippines to do ministry. Why not Africa or Mexico? I chose Philippines, the hometown where I came from, because I want them to experience what I experienced as a "Born Again" Catholic. My purpose is to share God's word, the Bible, and to work on the ministry of reconciliation. I hope to help them to have a transformed life starting with my family and neighbors.

I dreamed to change my country as well. I am ashamed to admit that my country, Philippines, in the current survey is one as the most corrupt country in the world. I also heard from a foreigner who married a Filipino, after his first visit to the Philippines made this comment, "They are just a bunch of vultures out there!" I felt like hiding when I heard this. I wonder what he experienced in the Philippines to make such a statement. This is very hard to understand by the people, especially the Americans, knowing that the majority of the Filipinos are Catholics. My own explanation to this is because many Filipinos professed as believers of Jesus Christ but there is no genuine transformation of their lives. Another explanation is their lack of understanding of Jesus' teaching. They pick and choose what they want to believe. They only want to hear that God is love and full of mercy and grace. They forget that this same loving God we worship is also the God of judgment. Holy as He is, He will not overlook and ignore sin. He expects holiness from His children.

I love America, but I love my native homeland Philippines also, and I hope it will change back to his old name. Many years ago this country was called the "Pearl of the Orient" I strongly believe that God will change and bless this country by changing the people one person at a time, and nothing is impossible with God. The problem of every nation are the moral issues. They can be corrected if every person sincerely trusted our Lord Jesus and really got to know Him as their risen Savior. They must also know the power of Jesus' indwelling Spirit and trust that what Jesus said and taught was the truth that must be followed. The only way to know God is to read the Holy Bible. As the Psalmist said;" Taste and see that the Lord is good." If

My Service

you read the Bible cover to cover there is a sure guarantee that you will taste God's goodness. I am encouraged of what St. Paul said in his letter to Titus: "For the grace of God that brings salvation has appeared to all men. It teaches us to say "No" to ungodliness and worldly passions and to live self-controlled, upright and godly lives in this present age, while we wait for the blessed hope; the glorious appearing of our great God and Savior, Jesus Christ, who gave Himself for us, to redeem us from all wickedness and to purify for Himself a people that are His very own, eager to do what is good." (Titus 2: 11-15, NIV)

I formed this foundation mainly to change people's lives by giving or teaching them God's Words. I thought if God would use me to change a few people the way that He changed me, it would be of great help to the people in this village and hopefully this country. I started small, since I am doing it as a part time venture. Hopefully, God willing I will be devoting all my time as soon as I retire from my work as a school nurse. Presently I am supporting financially some local churches both Catholic and Baptist. I am also training my brother and my sister in-law with the help of the local pastor so that they could help me with the growth of my ministry. Our ministry is also helping and supporting two orphans to complete their college education. The ministry with the help of the local pastors is forming various bible study group. The last time I was there, fourteen people had decided to receive Jesus as their personal savior and I am hoping they will become disciples of Jesus with further training.

Jesus, the promised messiah, rendered the perfect devotion and service. He met the highest ideals of both His Father and of man. Jesus as "servant of the Lord" should be the pattern for all of us, His disciples.

Chapter 15

Raising Faustin

I need to tell you a brief history of how the four-year-old Faustin came into my life at the age of fifty-two. Tony planned to leave his second wife when he attended our son Devin's graduation in New York. Devin told me about his Dad's plan two months before his graduation. He added, "Mom, he is just like the prodigal son in the Bible. He is coming home to us and we have to forgive and accept him." Three weeks before Devin's graduation, our friend from Canada came to L.A. to visit her sister. We agreed to meet in a Filipino restaurant because our mutual friend would be there as well. Just before I left for home, she told me that she met Tony in Montreal. She added, "Tony was telling everyone that you are getting back together. What will happen to his son, I believe he is only four, is he going to stay with you? It is going to be hard!"

I said, "What! I did not even know he got married. When I heard the news I was shocked of course, but I did not show my emotions in front of the group. I drank my soda to help me gain my composure then said my goodbye and left.

I was still shaky when I got home. I called Devin immediately without considering the time difference of LA and New York. I confronted him of their awful secret and how he could do this to me, him of all people. Devin said, "Dad made me promise not to tell you. Besides, I was afraid you would get hurt and be depressed all over again." I told Devin to tell his Dad that I was very upset and not to bother me anymore. He still tried to call me, but I did not speak to him.

Devin's graduation event finally came and we both attended the ceremony as planned. Devin arranged the hotel for us. It was my first time seeing Tony and the first time talking to him after knowing he was married and had a child. Our time together in New York was hell on earth. I was so angry because of his deception and lies. I remember asking him when he came to see Devin if he got married. He lied to me through his teeth without blinking an eye. I wanted to hit him or throw something at him to release my anger.

The second day in New York Tony called his second wife in Florida to check on Faustin their son. I could see that Tony was crying because his eyes were red and swollen. He was sad and distraught. I did not bother to ask; I knew he was suffering. I was not in position to comfort him because I was still angry with him. I gave him a very cold and nasty treatment. I only talked civilly when we were around other people.

We arrived in Los Angeles and Tony decided to stay in our guest room in the first floor of our house. I could tell in his behavior and in his face that he was suffering because of his dilemma. He broke down crying after talking to Faustin on the phone. One time during his meal he was unable to eat because he had just started crying. I was still upset with him but at the same time I felt sorry for him because he reminded me of the suffering and pain I had felt a few days after he had left me. Seeing his condition I remembered my prayer when I said, "Lord, please let Tony feel what I am feeling! Let him feel the same misery and pain I am feeling!" I was just wondering if Tony really knew what I was feeling. I realized it then that it was a very mean prayer and seeing Tony suffering I wished that I had not prayed that. This was an example of a reckless and selfish prayer without thinking of the consequences. I heard of a saying, "Be careful of what you pray or wish for because you might get it." I was in pain and I just wanted Tony to know how I felt and what I was experiencing emotionally.

Two days later Tony told Devin that he would try to patch up his relationship with his second wife. He planned to leave for Florida as soon as possible. He asked Devin for money for his plane ticket and expenses. Devin told me about his Dad's plan. Devin was upset and said, "O.K. mom we will let him go, but that's it. If he comes back again we will not take him back. I told Dad just that." When I reached home from work Tony met me at the door and said he wanted to talk to me. He started to cry and said that he was sorry but he had to go back to his second wife for the sake of Faustin. Then he said, "I don't think I can live without my son!" I had mixed emotion and reaction. I was annoyed with his indecisiveness. He reminded me of what James said. "....a double-minded man, unstable in all his ways." (James 1:8)

On the other hand I felt sorry for him and his son. Then I thought of Abraham in the Bible. I remember Abraham loved Isaac so much because not only was he the promised son from God, but because Isaac was the child of his old age. Abraham loved his son, Isaac, both like his grandchild and as his son. People say that there is a different kind of love and affection towards grandchildren. Tony was forty-seven when he had Faustin, it is not old age of course, but what I mean here is that Faustin is not a child of Tony's youth, Devin was. That evening Tony left to stay in his friend's house. From there he planned to leave for Florida.

The following morning I went to work. I was early as usual. Instead of going to my workplace I stayed in my car to pray. I prayed like this, "Lord, I don't know your plan for my life but your will be done. If only I had known that he had gotten married and had a child I would not have prayed for him to come back to my life. Tony is better off with his small child. His child is better off to be with his father." Then I made a vow to God, "I will dedicate my whole life to Him and serve Him as a single person for the rest of my life."

A few days later while I was cleaning my garage, Tony showed up. To my astonishment I asked, "I thought you went back to Florida?" Tony's story was that when he told his wife that he was coming back and would be leaving for Florida soon, she told Tony to wait for her because she was coming to Los Angeles to visit her sister and she would be coming with Faustin. They had a pleasant reunion and were planning to leave for Florida together, but the following day his wife left for Florida without Faustin and without Tony's knowledge. Tony said he was still trying to talk to his wife and hoping that they would be together soon. He told me that Devin agreed to keep Faustin for the weekend while he was trying to get a place of his own.

THE FIRST TIME I SAW FAUSTIN

Devin and Faustin came back from Disneyland at around 11:00 p.m. that night. Faustin was sound asleep. Devin told me, "Mom I think we have to help Dad raise him." The first thing I noticed was his feet. Faustin's feet are a carbon copy of Devin's feet. I used to call Devin's feet banana feet because they looked like a not fully developed early stage of banana bunch. Nothing deformed but to me it seemed like the toes were just too close to each other. Faustin was cute and good-looking, very fair and had lots of hair.

I can't recall how I really felt this time, but I remember only feeling sorry for him, to be growing up without his mother if Tony and his wife did not get back together. I can't help remembering the kindergarten student we had from the school where I worked. The teacher told me that this boy did not participate in class and refused to respond, and later he went under his desk and refused to come out. They called the school psychologist and they found out his parents got divorced. His father went back to Mexico.

Saturday morning I made pancakes and eggs for breakfast, I heard him talking to Devin, "You are lucky Devin you have a nice mom. She made us nice breakfast."

In the afternoon I took Faustin to the park close to our house because he was looking kind of sad. I thought the swing and the slides would entertain him a little. He only played in the slide once and he refused to play in the swing. Instead, he was sitting in one of the picnic tables a little further than where I was; I was sitting on the grass under a shade. I allowed him to sit there for a while. Then he lay down on the bench of the picnic table. After a few minutes I approached him and asked, "What is wrong Faustin?" Then he started crying and said, "I miss my mom!" I tried to reassure him and said, "You will see your mom soon! You and your Dad are going back to Florida in a few days." He felt a little better and started to play. He wanted to lie down on the grass, so I got my blanket from my car and we both stayed there for one hour. Then we decided to walk for a while. We passed the area where the bars were. I asked him if he wanted to climb the bars and he said yes. I helped him to get up to the bars and the next thing I knew he was on the ground. I heard a big thug and I was so afraid that he was injured badly and could have had a head trauma. I could only pray and say, "O Jesus, Jesus! Thank God he was all right." Can you imagine if he was really hurt? This episode was the beginning of my bonding with Faustin.

Devin and Faustin were very close. I could tell that Devin loved Faustin so much. As an only child Faustin is the missing sibling that Devin never had. With their age difference Faustin could easily be mistaken as Devin's child. One day Devin needed a haircut; he took Faustin with him because he needed one also. The lady in the hair salon made this comment, "How nice! the father and son having a haircut together." Devin quickly responded, "He is not my son, he is my brother."

Tony and Faustin stayed in a studio apartment. His cousin helped to support him and Faustin. His brother Paul also helped him and gave him his credit card. This time Tony said his wife wanted a divorce and to save her from trouble he would be the one to file for divorce. Tony was not good in the housekeeping or something, because Faustin was frequently sick of colds and upper respiratory problems. I felt sorry for the way they were living.

Also, Tony's sister-in-law spoke to me indirectly that she thought they couldn't help Tony anymore. Since I was moving to a town house and Devin bought a house I asked Tony to move and stay with Devin, and he agreed. I was hoping Devin would help his Dad and Faustin, and they would all move to Devin's house when the deal would close in six months, but Devin had a plan of his own. He wanted his two friends to move in with him so they could help him pay his mortgage. Devin wanted his Dad to move in with me. Devin explained that his Dad needed help with Faustin. Besides, it was not good for me to live by myself considering the area where I moved in. He added, "Don't worry Mom! Dad will help you too. He promised to hire a regular housekeeper when he finds a job." I made sure Tony knew about my vow to God and he said not to worry because as soon as he gets settled and able to afford his own place they would leave.

Faustin was never separated from his Dad except that short time when Tony attended Devin's graduation. Since his birth he slept in a sofa bed next to Tony. I noticed later that Faustin did not sleep if Tony was not at his side. They were very close. One of the reasons why I took Tony back was because of Faustin. The other reason was because I was committed to helping Tony as a Christian. I was motivated to take them back because of my love for Jesus. Don't forget that because of my trials and because of living as a divorcee for five years, my relationship with Jesus became more intimate as I matured as a Christian. As a Christian who loves Jesus, I thought we should be our brother's keeper, helping and supporting each other no matter what. I knew this is what the Lord wanted. Tony was in great need for sure, financially and he needed support in raising Faustin. Besides, Devin was not in a position to be able to help him because he was not making much as a Resident. Hospital residency program's salary as everyone knows, is not much.

Tony and Faustin stayed in our guest room in the first floor of our house. I kept my busy schedule working full time as a school nurse, cleaning and cooking. I also worked every Saturday in my part time job. I was also taking courses in the evening weekdays towards my school nurse credentials. I did not have much time to spend with them. Tony did all the work taking care of Faustin. Devin and I only supported him.

Tony found a temporary job with his cousin's help. He thinks he was overqualified for this job but he took it anyway because he needed a job so badly. This job took him two hours every day traveling to and from work. He told us after a few days that the traffic was costing him his nerves. Faustin was placed in a nursery and Tony dropped by and picked him up everyday. When he was stuck in traffic he would call me to pick up Faustin from the nursery. I noticed that Faustin was dismayed every time I picked him up from his school. He only wanted Tony to pick him up.

One time when he saw me, he went to another area and continued to play just ignoring me. The nursery teacher had to prod him to pick up his things so we could leave. On our way to our car all of a sudden he hit me with his jacket for no other reason except that I was the one who picked him up from his pre-school instead of his father. The zipper of his jacket hit the bone of my hand and it was really painful. I was about to scold him right there when he hit me but there were some people close to us so I waited. When I asked him why did he hit me he did not give me an answer but kept quiet. After I calmed down I told him that I was not taking his mother's place or taking his Dad away from him. I also told him that I had no plan of marrying his Dad. I was only trying to help his Dad by taking care of him and that was all.

After this talk his attitude towards me was a little better. Tony told him to call me "mom." He had a hard time calling me mom in the beginning and I told him that I considered him as my godchild and therefore I was his godmother, so it was all right to call me "mom."

When Devin was a child I was not a "Born Again" person and I had been wishing that I had been so I could teach him early in his age about God. I decided to teach Faustin about the Bible every time I had the chance. Every time he was in playing mood he would come to me. I taught him Bible stories that I used to teach when I was giving Bible studies to the children six years prior in my home when I was living by myself. Faustin was very sharp, bright and full of spirit. He remembered the stories in detail even after many months. One time I was telling him the importance of staying close to God by praying and talking to Him. I said, "If you take one step towards God, He will take two steps towards you." Many weeks later in our kitchen, while talking to someone I think to his Dad, he said, "If you take one step to God, God will take two steps to you." And he was showing the number of steps. I taught him all the Christian songs that I knew and he loved to sing. His aunts, uncles, and his brother and sisters were wondering why he only knew Christian songs, the simple answer- that was the only songs that he heard. Since he was late to enter kindergarten, I taught him the Alphabets and Numbers. I taught him how to whistle and I taught him a few dance steps. At five , I used to put him on the coffee table to be my partner in dancing disco, swing and the "boogie" dance. Now that he is in high school he is not shy but loves to dance and is very good at it. I bought him a picture Bible and I used to read it to him until he knew how to read on his own.

Another incident was not a big miracle but I treasured it in my heart. While watching the Christian Broadcasting Network (CBN), I heard Terry Meewsen telling in the program about their new video for children. I only heard the title "Spunky," I thought that any Christian cartoon must be good for Faustin and it would keep him busy as well so I ordered the video. This cartoon was about a puppy called Spunky and his first Christmas with his new family. Faustin, as little as he was, must have identified himself to this puppy; being new to our family. I cannot count the number of times he watched this video, I know that I have watched it with him about eight times.

At the end of the movie there was a salvation prayer and every time this prayer came, Faustin bowed his head and prayed with Terry. One day, coming from work I was wondering where Faustin was, he was awfully quiet in the room by himself. When I entered the room I found him at the foot of the bed praying the salvation prayer with the video "Spunky" that he was watching. I thanked God for the video and for using me for Faustin's salvation. You might call this a coincidence but I will say it was the divine hand of God that made me get this particular video in a timely manner. I believe Faustin needed this video at this particular moment in time.

There are a few incidents that I need to tell. This happened when Faustin was five years old. I was wrapping the Christmas gifts, (Christmas bags were not us popular at that time.) Faustin insisted that he would wrap some of the gifts. I let him wrap one, but later I re-did it because it was messy. When he saw me re-do the wrapping that he did he was angry and said, "You! You!" (a pause) and added, "You old woman!" With a straight face, I told him, "That was not nice to say Faustin," but inside I was laughing.

One time, our friend from Canada came for a visit. After a few greetings Tex said to me in front of Faustin, "My, Elma! You still look good!" Faustin responded quickly and said, "O Uncle she has artificial teeth." He knows my teeth problem because I had a tooth implant and needed a frequent visit to my Periodontist. He was behaving typical to his age and funny but true.

Another funny incident was when Tony and Faustin went to the grocery store to buy his diapers. Faustin was very late to be toilet trained. He was a little over six years old during this time. According to Tony, when the cashier in the counter looked at the diaper and then to Faustin she seemed to wonder because of Faustin's age. Faustin quickly said, "That is not for me, (pointing to the bag of large diapers) it is for my Dad!"

At the age of five and maybe 2 months old, I took Faustin with me to Costco to pick up something for our dinner. I had become a member to this store recently. When we got there, after frantically searching for my card I remember that I did not put my membership card back in my purse but in my other jacket. I was kind of upset at myself and started to head back home to get my card. Then Faustin said, "Mom, why not go there and tell them you left your card?" I told him that we could not get into the store, not unless we showed our membership card. He insisted to try and tell the man that we left our card. I finally agreed with him. There was no problem at all. We were told to ask for a temporary card and we were able to shop. This was the first time I realized that this kid was sharp.

When he was seven or eight years old I was concerned that he still rode his bike with the training wheels. He got his bike from Devin during his first Christmas with us, when he was six years old. Everyone was busy and no one had the time to teach him how to ride his bike without the training wheels. One Saturday during my vacation I thought it was about time for Faustin to ride a bike without training wheels. So I planned for a picnic in Legg Lake Park so we could train Faustin to ride his bike without training wheels. Before leaving for the park we removed his bike's training wheels. Tony tried to teach him while holding his bike in the back but gave up after ten to fifteen minutes. Devin spent time with Faustin but gave up as well. It was late and we would be going home soon and Faustin still didn't know how to ride his bike. I thought, "If Faustin won't learn it this time he will be like me, does not know how to ride a bike. What a pity!" So I decided to train him myself. We kept at it until finally he went off without me holding the bike. What an excitement. I can't help remembering the same excitement when I taught Devin to ride his bike many, many years ago. Faustin was very excited and happy that he could balance without me holding his bike. He kept riding and I saw that he was heading towards a group of people who were sitting in the grass eating their picnic food. I saw Faustin with no sign of slowing down and he was getting close to running into these people. So I ran and dove to stop the bike. We both fell. At least I saved him from running into a group of people. Devin made this statement, "Mom! I am surprised you can still do that at your age. You were like a football player doing a tackle." I told Devin, "It is the Adrenalin working!"

Raising Faustin

A few months after Tony and Faustin moved in with us Tony had a heart attack. His first and second divorce, taking care of Faustin, the stress of his job, and the drive back and forth in the freeway traffic must have taken its toll off his health. I mentioned it in the previous chapter, the emotional trauma of Tony's family, especially on Faustin. It was during this time that the doctor thought Tony was not going to make it and called all of Tony's family to come to the hospital. During this time I made a promise to Tony in his sick bed, that I would help him raise Faustin and would help him in anyway. As I was talking, all of a sudden a remarkable miracle happened. Right in front of my eyes Tony's eyes began to sparkle and the reading in his bedside monitor changed from very low blood pressure and low heart rate into a better and stable reading.

The next day, Faustin and I went to visit Tony in the hospital. We were told to wait in the lobby and to wait for our turn as only two visitors were allowed each time. Faustin was not allowed in the Intensive Care Unit so we took turns to stay with him in the lobby. He was doing something with the hospital furniture so I stopped him. He answered, "So what, you are just my step mom!"

I said, "No, I am your god-mom and you still need to listen to me." This remark coming from Faustin made me think and made a decision that when it came to discipline, Tony would be in charge. Later, when I discussed this incident with Tony he said, "I don't know about that, I think I had the heart attack because he made me so angry and I had to spank him the night before I had my heart attack." However, if he misbehaved I reminded Faustin that as any elder person, I needed to be respected by him and he needed to listen to me. I learned my lesson; not to be so temperamental. Maybe because I am a changed person I have more patience now than when I was raising Devin. Devin told me a few times that I let Faustin get away with many things than when he was growing up. I tried not to raise my voice when I was reprimanding. It is because when I asked Devin what he hated most when he was growing up he told me that it was when I shouted at him.

The last time Billy Graham did a crusade it was in San Diego, I planned to take the whole family, including Devin and his wife Mala to attend this awesome event. My main reason was to have all of us, including Faustin, recommit our lives to the Lord. Also, it was for Mala to receive Jesus for the first time. When the altar call came, (for my Catholic brothers and sisters, altar call means calling to those who want to receive Jesus as their savior to come forward to the altar, but in crusades, to come forward near the platform.) Devin and Tony both agreed that since we were too far up, it would take us a long time to go down. They decided not to go down but jut to stay in our seats to receive Jesus. "We will just do it here! It won't make a difference." Tony said. I really wanted for all of us would go down, but before I could say anything Faustin said, "We came here for this reason and we are all here anyway, let's all go down!" and we did. I was so thankful for Faustin. I told him that I would never forget this and I really appreciated what he did because going down was important and meant so much to me. If we did not go down Mala would have missed knowing and meeting the nice lady that gave her the pamphlet and her explanation about salvation.

With lots of prayer, thanks God, Faustin turned out to be a good boy. My neighbor told me we did a good job raising him. I told her, "I cannot receive all the credit because he goes to his mother every other weekend and in his vacations. They must have some influence in his life as well. I am just happy that he turned out to be a smart and decent boy in spite of what he had been through – a product of dysfunctional family." Faustin's life proved that even with a single parent raising a child, when there is enough love and nurturing and enough support from relatives, they will turn out all right. I told this repeatedly to so many parents and students with the same problem. There was one particular grade-five student who came many times to our Health Office crying because his father left them. He refused to come to school and his grade suffered because of poor attendance. With much love, empathy and understanding, and sharing Faustin's experience to him and his mother, he finally accepted his situation and was back to his normal life. With my hands on experience with Faustin, my advice was more effective to these people with similar problems of divorce.

Faustin, as a teenager, is experiencing difficulties at times like most teenagers do. This age is also hard for parents to handle. However, with effective and loving discipline, I believe we will get through this confusing and difficult age. Faustin seemed to be in dilemma of his situation. He needs a lot of understanding, support and guidance. At this time he is not reading his Bible regularly. However, I told him and he understands that we can only take him to the water but we cannot force him to drink. He has to have the initiative to come to Jesus himself. At present, Faustin is attending the first year of the two years program in preparation for his confirmation in St. Mary's Assumption Church.

Many well meaning Catholics and Christians hurt their children spiritually. They hurt their children by being inconsistent in their own walk as a believer and in the way they are disciplining them. But mostly they hurt them by taking lightly the salvation of their children. Most of the parents say;" they are too young" and some say, "they will decide themselves by the time they grow up."

This is the primary context of Mathew 18 when Jesus was talking about relationships in God's kingdom.

"At that time the disciples came to Jesus saying, 'Who then is greatest in the kingdom of heaven?' And Jesus called a little child to Him, set him in the midst of them, and said, 'Assuredly, I say to you, unless you are converted and become as little children, you will by no means enter the kingdom of heaven. Therefore whoever humbles himself as this little child is the greatest in the kingdom of heaven. And whoever receives one little child like this in My name receives Me. But whoever causes one of these little ones who believe in Me to sin, it would be better for him if a millstone were hung around his neck, and he were drowned in the depth of sea.'" (Matthew 18: 1-6)

Faustin was blessed to receive Jesus at the age of five aside from his infant baptism. He re-committed his salvation at the age of ten during Billy Graham's crusade in San Diego. The daughter of Billy and Ruth Graham, Gigi Graham Tchividian, received the Lord at the age of three. She wrote about her children coming to Christ,

"When our oldest son was three, he was sitting beside his daddy on the balcony of our home in Switzerland enjoying the view. Suddenly he asked, "Daddy, how can I ask Jesus into my heart?" That day our eldest became a child of God and has never wavered. Years later, as a teenager, he was putting his youngest sister to bed. As he tucked her in, he quoted the verse, "Behold, I stand at the door and knock; if anyone hears My voice and opens the door, I will come in to him, and will dine with him, and he with Me." (Rev. 3:20) He explained that this was Jesus knocking at the door of her life. Would she like Him to come in and live with her? She said "yes" and prayed to receive Christ.

Gigi went on to say, 'The great theologian Karl Barth was once asked what he thought was the greatest theological truth. He answered, 'Jesus loves me this I know, for the Bible tells me so.'" [1]

The best people in the entire world to lead children to Christ are the parents. I heard from a Christian Pastor that it is good to bless our children too. I blessed Devin and Faustin.

A parent who is never at home or who never has time to be with the children possibly will not be available when the Holy Spirit pricks a tiny heart.

Anne Graham Lotz, another daughter of Billy and Ruth Graham, was telling about her mother,

"What my mother has taught me and that which I seek to pass on to her grandchildren, is that God is enough – period. Growing up, I had a bedroom directly over hers. No matter what time I went to bed at night, I could see the light from her room reflected on the trees outside. Were I to slip downstairs, I would find her on her knees beside her bed. There was no use waiting for her rise – she would be there, in prayer, for hours, at a time. No matter what time I arose in the morning, I would see the light from her room. When I arrived downstairs, she'd be at her desk reading one of 14 different Bible translations. She knows God well." What a tribute! She knows God well. How many people can you say that about? Could your children say that about you? " [2]

I firmly believe that if at all possible, Mom should be home when children are there.

Charles Stanley, world famous author and preacher, explained how he was raised by a single Mom who had to work to support them. He said he knew the financial issues, but it does not lessen the trauma or the loneliness because both parents worked out of necessity.

Dr. Stanley was a latchkey kid, long before the term was thought of. He said, "I remember what it sounded like. I remember the sickening feeling in my stomach when I inserted the key into the keyhole and knew no other human being was on the other side of the door. I felt totally alone."

My son Devin (Faustin's half- brother,) was a latchkey kid. I am ashamed to mention it here, but I want to share this important experience as a parent so that others may learn from it. Devin was six years old. He was in grade one. He came home at 2:30 PM and I arrived home from work at 3:30 PM. He was alone at home for one hour until I got home. I told him to have a snack when he got home and then to watch television. It was all right until winter came. One cold and snowy day in windy Toronto, Canada, Devin was not able to open our door for some reason. Maybe his hand was frozen or something. When I got there he was in our front door crying and shivering almost frozen. I can't believe that not one of our neighbors was home either. Thank God kidnapping was not common during this time (1976) Right after this incident, I found a baby sitter close to Devin's school.

Dr. Stanley went on to say, "I don't say this to inflict guilt to anyone. God knows your circumstances. You may be saying, 'Well, Dr. Stanley was a latchkey kid raised by a single working mother for many years, and he turned out okay.' But you have not seen all the years of working through the feelings of isolation and loneliness that accompanied my early childhood. It is a sheer grace of God and I give Him all the praise and glory for what he has done in my life. If you must work and your children must be cared by others, bathe them, and the caregivers, in prayer. Pray. Pray. Pray. God knows your circumstances. He loves your children more than you do." 3

The Bible tells us to; " train up a child in the way he should go, and when he is old he will not depart from it." (Proverbs 22:6) We are to train up a child concerning the way he should go, and parents are to find out that way. They are not to bring up a child in the way they think he should go, but in the way God wants him to go. In Deuteronomy Chapter 4, Moses gave his final instruction to the people:

"Hear now O Israel, the decrees and laws I am about to teach you. Follow them so that you may live and may go in and take possession of the land that the Lord, the God of your fathers, is giving you. Do not add to what I command you and do not subtract from it, but keep the commands of the Lord your God that I give you.

You saw with your own eyes what the Lord did at Baal Peor. The Lord your God destroyed from among you everyone who followed the Baal of Peor, but all of you who held fast to the Lord your God are still alive today.

See, I have taught you decrees and laws as the Lord my God commanded me, so that you may follow them in the land you are entering to take possession of it. Observe them carefully, for this will show your wisdom and understanding to the nations, who will hear about all these decrees and say, 'Surely this great nation is wise and understanding people.' What other nation is so great as to have their gods near them the way the Lord our God is near us whenever we pray to Him? And what other nation so great as to have such righteous decrees and laws I am setting before you today?

Only be careful, and watch yourselves closely so that you do not forget the things your eyes have seen or let them slip from your heart as long as you live. Teach them to your children and to their children after them. Remember the day you stood before the Lord your God at Horeb, when He said to me, 'Assemble the people before me to hear My words so that they may learn to revere me as long as they live in the land and may teach them to their children. You came near and stood at the foot of the mountain while it blazed with fire to the very heavens, with black clouds and deep darkness. Then the Lord spoke to you out of the fire. You heard the sound of words but saw no form; there was only a voice. He declared to you his covenant, the Ten Commandments, which He commanded you to follow and then wrote them on two stone tablets. And the Lord directed me at that time to teach you the decrees and laws you are to follow in the land that you are crossing the Jordan to possess.

You saw no form of any kind the day the Lord spoke to you at Horeb out of fire. Therefore watch yourselves very carefully, so that you do not become corrupt and make for yourselves an idol, an image of any shape, whether formed like a man or woman, or like any animal on earth or any bird that flies in the air, or like any creature that moves along the ground or any fish in the waters below.

And when you look up to the sky and see the sun, the moon and the stars—all the heavenly array –do not be enticed into bowing down to them and worshipping things the Lord your God has apportioned to all the nations under heaven. But as for you, the Lord took you and brought you out of the iron-smelting furnace, out of Egypt, to be the people of His inheritance as you now are. The Lord was angry with me because of you, and He solemnly swore that I would not cross the Jordan and enter the good land the Lord your God is giving you as your inheritance. I will die in this land; I will not cross the Jordan; but you are about to cross over and take possession of that good land. Be careful not to forget the covenant of the Lord your God that He made with you; Do not make for yourselves an idol in the form of anything the Lord your God has forbidden. For the Lord your God is a jealous God.

After you have had children and grandchildren and have lived in the land a long time—if you then become corrupt and make any kind of idol, doing evil in the eyes of the Lord your God and provoking Him to anger, I call heaven and earth as witnesses against you this day that you will quickly perish from the land that you are crossing the Jordan to possess. You will not live there long but will certainly be destroyed. The Lord will scatter you among the peoples, and only few of you will survive among the nations to which the Lord will drive you. There you will worship man-made gods of wood and stone, which cannot see or eat or smell. But if from there you seek the Lord your God, you will find Him if you look for Him with all your heart and with all your soul. When you are in distress and all these things have happened to you, then in later days you will return to the Lord your God and obey Him. For the Lord your God is a merciful God; He will not abandon or destroy you or forget the covenant with your forefathers, which He confirmed to them by oath.

Ask now about the former days, long before your time, from the day God created man on the earth; ask from one end of the heavens to the other. Has anything so great as this ever happened, or has anything like it ever heard of?

Has any other people heard the voice of God speaking out of fire, as you have, and lived? Has any god ever tried to take for himself one nation out of another nation, by testing, by miraculous signs and wonders, by war, by a mighty hand and an outstretched arm, or by great and awesome deeds, like all the things the Lord your God did for you in Egypt before your very eyes?

You were shown these things so that you might know that the Lord is God; besides Him there is no other. From heaven He made you hear His voice to discipline you. On earth He showed you His great fire, and you heard His words from out of fire. Because He loved your forefathers and chose their descendants after them, He brought you out of Egypt by His Presence and His great strength, to drive out before you nations greater and stronger than you and to bring you out into their land to give it to you for your inheritance, as it is today.

Acknowledge and take to heart this day that the Lord is God in heaven and on the earth below. There is no other. Keep His decrees and commands, which I am giving you today, so that it may go well with you and your children after you and that you may live long in the land the Lord your God gives you for all time."[4] (Deuteronomy 4:1-40, TNKJB)

One of Moses' instructions was to teach the laws or commandments to their children and to their children after them. (Deut. 4:9) Our actions are the best way to teach our children. Actions speak louder than words as the saying goes, and it is true. To be able to teach God's commandments to our children, we parents must follow and obey it ourselves. We fail to train our children the way God told us to, and then we wonder why they grow up the way they do. We cannot just let the church or the school teach and train them. We should remember that before our children listen to our priests, pastors, or teachers, they are watching their parents to see whether they follow it themselves. We need godly parents to stay strong enough to teach their children to paddle against the current of worldly things that stray us away from God and His teachings.

Some parents, because of their past experiences and the way they were raised, fail to discipline their children. Recently I saw a mother on TV say that she was unable to discipline her daughter because she wanted her daughter to feel that she was her best friend. You cannot discipline a child if they look at you as a friend and not as a mother that deserves honor and respect. Another mother in the show said that she couldn't discipline her three kids because she felt sorry for them because they didn't have a father (she was a divorcee.) Another single mother in the show said, that she gave in to her children's whims and demands because she was afraid that if she refused they might not love her anymore; one of her daughters was over twenty years old and already married.

One counselor made a comment that in our present society most people are not receiving any love from others except the love from their children and that is why they cannot discipline them. They are afraid of losing that only love that they receive from their children. The counselor suggested for all the parents to follow this golden rule, "Say no and mean it," and I will add to it, if you make a promise keep it. Broken promises or promises not kept are very frustrating to a child. All parents should not make a promise that they cannot keep. Sometimes we make a promise to get out of a difficult situation, or to get them out of our way. One child was asked why she had such bad temper tantrums, she said it was because her parents made promises to her many times and they failed to keep them. She gave the example that they promised to play with her or to watch TV with her. She was told, "Later we will watch with you!" But her parents continued to watch a program that the child could not watch. The parents did not keep their promise until it was her bedtime and she could not watch TV or play anymore.

Children are treasures in our world. We have to tell them that they are important and that they are loved a lot. However, balance is needed because children's rights are getting out of hand sometimes. The Bible says the following verses:

"Foolishness is bound up in the heart of a child; the rod of correction will drive it far from him." (Proverbs 22:15)

"A child left to himself brings shame to his mother." (Proverbs 29:15)

"Correct your son, and he will give you rest; yes, he will give delight to your soul." (Proverbs 29:17) These proverbs remind us parents of the need to bring consistent discipline.

Balance includes a large amount of love. That is what our heavenly Father does, He disciplines. The Bible says that if He did not discipline us, we would not be treated like His children. (Hebrews 12:8) On the other hand, our Father loves us a lot. He loves us so much that He gave His only begotten Son to die for us. He constantly affirms it in His word. We are precious in His sight. As His children, and knowing we are chosen by Him, we preserve our self-esteem.

I am grateful to God for the opportunity that I had to receive and raise Faustin, because Jesus said, "Whoever receives one of these little children in My name receives

Me; and whoever receives Me, receives not Me but Him who sent me." (Mark 10: 37)

A few weeks prior to Faustin's confirmation I had been praying for the Holy Spirit's anointing over him. I prayed about this frequently, every time I could remember; in my daily meditation and in Church, especially during the Mass celebration. Faustin's confirmation day was Wednesday May 13th. This particular morning, when I was having my prayer and meditation time, the scripture reading was taken from 2nd Peter Chapter 1 and it says: "But for this very reason, add to your faith virtue, to virtue, knowledge, to knowledge self control, to self control perseverance, to perseverance godliness and to godliness, love. (2 peter 1: 5-6) Then I thought of God's love for me. God loves me not because I am lovable, but because it is God's nature to do so. In knowing how God loved me beyond all limits, it should compel me to love Him back and do service for his glory. Then I remembered last Sunday's Gospel reading. "Whoever remains in Me and I in him will bear much fruit. (John 15:5) The priest added that one of these fruits is doing service in God's vineyard (kingdom). I realized that I was not really doing enough service for God's kingdom. I started to cry and talking to God I said, "Lord! I am not fruitful and I am not doing any service to you. Is my life acceptable and pleasing to You? Is my life a service to You? The only thing I do for You is give Tony and Faustin a home. But then I am not doing a good job in this service at all because I complain about my situation every now and then, especially during difficult times." Then I thought, "I have to start volunteering in the hospital soon." (Since I retired, I have been thinking of doing volunteer work in the nearby hospital but I kept putting it off.) I finally had my volunteer orientation and will be starting next month.

The following day, (Wednesday,) was Faustin's confirmation. After the confirmation we went to Smith Hall to pick up Faustin's confirmation certificate. There, Faustin introduced me to his confirmation class teacher. She then told me, "I have been telling Faustin I wanted to meet you! I wanted to know the person who raised him." She added, "You raised him well, he is so godly and holy!" Her comment was a surprise to me. Faustin is godly and holy? It takes a lot of effort from me to wake him up so we would not be late for Church every Sunday morning.

When I asked Faustin about his teacher's comments He told me, "Mom remember I told you I always participate in our class discussion and we always talk after our class about spiritual things? My teacher used to ask me why I know all these things and I told her, 'My mom taught me these things.'" I can't remember in particular what I shared with him except a few times that I shared and read my meditation book with him. A few times I read the book of Proverbs and Psalms to him if it pertained to what we were experiencing that day. I am glad I made a bit of a difference in Faustin's spiritual life. God answered my question when I asked Him if my life was a service to Him. He is so faithful. He always answers us if we are serious, sincere, and honest with Him.

Oswald Chambers said this: "The people who influence us the most are not those who detain us with their continued talk, but those who live their lives like the star in the sky and 'the lilies of the field' – simply and unaffectedly. Those are the lives that mold and shape us." [5]

I would like to end this topic with a story because this story is a dream of every parent including myself. O how I wish that I have a child like Peter in this story.

PETER'S WISH LIST

"You're going Christmas shopping today, aren't you?" Peter asked his mother as she dropped him off at Junior High.

"Maybe," she teased, "And maybe not."

"Well I know you are," Peter said. "You have your sneakers and you only wear those when you're headed for the mall. So here's my list!" Peter smiled and pressed an envelope into his mother's hand. He kissed her goodbye and bolted from the car before she could respond. "Love ya, Mom!" he called out to her.

Margaret sat in the car holding the envelope that read "Peter's Holiday Wish List." It felt thick, like there were several sheets of paper folded inside of it. She was disappointed.

Margaret and her husband Paul, had done their best to teach Peter about sharing with others and understanding the value of money, and that peer pressure was having more of an influence over her boy than the good examples she and her husband tried to give him.

Once inside the mall, Margaret bought herself a cup of coffee and sat at a small table. She pulled out the list she'd prepared over the last few months of gifts she wanted to buy for her family and friends. In Peter's column she'd written the name of a series of books she knew he wanted. Now she wondered if Peter's "mega list" had any books on it at all. What was he asking for, anyway? Video games/a drum set, maybe? A dirt bike?

She pulled his envelope from her purse, thinking about the conversation she would have to have with her son that evening. As she removed the folded papers from the envelope, ten $10 bills floated onto the table.

Margaret quickly unfolded the pages. Peter's wish list included items like Plant a tree, cook for Meals on Wheels, sponsor an exchange student, work at a soup kitchen, and read to the kids at the children's hospital. There was also a note:

Dear Mom and Dad,

I know how lucky I am to have you for parents. And how fortunate I am to be related to the grandparents and cousins and other loving relatives that make up our family tree.

But I've only just realized how many people don't have compassion in their lives, and how much isn't getting done in our world only because nobody's stepping up to it. This is my way of stepping up.

I'll need your help because it could only take a couple of years for me to accomplish everything on my list and keep up with school, too. So you can "nudge" me any time you want.

All my love,

Peter

P.S. The money is for you, Mom! After you wear yourself out shopping for everybody else, have a pedicure on me!

Margaret wiped the tears from her eyes. She was overwhelmed by Peter's thoughtfulness. And like any parent, Margaret hoped she could make her son's wishes come true.

(Taken from St, Frances de Salle Church Bulletin, Riverside California)

Chapter 16

Basics of Catholic Faith

In order for Catholics to explain about their beliefs, they need to know the basics of their beliefs. In knowing our basic faith, all of us Catholics will realize that we have more things in common with what evangelical Christians believed. In my opinion, basing with my own experience, most of us Catholics do not fully understand our faith. For Catholics that did not go through catechism, and if they have not read the Bible cover to cover, they do not know the basics of the Catholic faith. Most of the Catholics that do not know much about their faith were unable to answer the questions or clarify the misconceptions that our evangelical Christian brothers have. Some of them instead of seeking for the answer, out of confusion moved out of the Catholic Church and joined the other denomination.

I will mention a few of the basics of our Catholic faith for the sake of both Catholics and Evangelical Christians. Hopefully, it will clear some of the misconceptions and equip the Catholics that did not go through catechism or like me, forgot what we learned as a children.

What is faith? Our Lord Jesus' first command was "...repent, and believe in the gospel" (Mark 1:15) and the New Testament clearly states that salvation is received by faith in God through Jesus Christ. Catholics firmly believe in the importance of faith in accepting God's gift of salvation. "Truly, truly I say to you," Jesus said, "he who hears my word and believes Him that sent me, has eternal life; he does not come into judgment, but has passed from death to life." (John 5:24) Many other New Testament texts affirm that faith in Jesus Christ leads to salvation.

The New Testament shows faith to be much more than an intellectual assent to the proposition that God exists or that Jesus Christ is Lord and Savior. This assent may be a first step, but it is not sufficient for salvation. Even evil spirits recognize and acknowledge Jesus' true identity. An unclean spirit cried out: "I know who you are, the Holy one of God." (Mark 1:24) James declared, "Even the demons believe and shudder." (James 2:19)

The faith that leads to salvation is an act of acknowledging our utter dependence on God and committing our lives totally to Him. When Jesus spoke about faith proclaiming, "...believe in God, believe also in me," (John 14:1) He meant "give your whole life to Me: follow Me; obey Me; become my disciple." True Christian faith means entrusting your whole life to God. It is a commitment to put God first and to do whatever he commands or asks. As the Second Vatican Council he explained:

"By faith, man freely commits his entire self to God, making the full submission of his intellect and will to God....

The Catholic Church today emphasizes the preeminence of faith in its official teaching. The 'Decree on the Apostolate of the Laity' sums up this teaching as well:

'The Church's mission is concerned with the salvation of men; and men win salvation through the grace of Christ and faith in Him.'"

"Many Christians today equate "faith," with a decision for Christ—a conscious, personal acceptance of Jesus Christ as the Lord and Savior of your life. This terminology is used mostly by Evangelical Protestants, but Catholics agree that all mature Christians must make a conscious choice to accept Jesus Christ as their Lord and Savior and commit themselves to follow Him. Catholics make such a public recommitment every year when they renew their baptismal promises during the Easter liturgy. The practice of regular, even daily, personal "acts of faith" in Jesus Christ is a part of Catholic tradition." [1]

Unfortunately, some Catholics including myself, before accepting Jesus as their Lord and Savior, have neglected the importance of this conscious, personal commitment to Jesus Christ. Catholics sometimes assume that persons who are baptized, attend Mass, and receive the sacraments regularly, have obviously accepted Jesus Christ as the Lord and Savior of their lives. A few years after I accepted Jesus as my Lord and Savior, when I shared my new life with enthusiasm to a few of my Catholic friends, I was really hurt because some of them told me that I was becoming a Protestant. This incident shows that not so many Catholics know that Catholic faith and the Catholic Church believe in a personal relationship in Jesus or as what Alan Schreck said, " a conscious choice to accept Jesus as their Lord and Savior." Many Catholics have not yet made a deliberate, adult decision to believe in Jesus Christ and give their lives fully to Him. In response to this, the Catholic Church has placed a strong emphasis in recent years on evangelization (even of the baptized,) on continual conversion to Christ, and on spiritual renewal. The goal of all these is to lead all Catholics and eventually all people to a full personal faith in Jesus Christ.

In my own experience, this spiritual renewal will not be adequate because it is easily taken for granted like the sacrament of Eucharist, and it won't create a change of life or as what we Catholics say a devout Catholic life or a genuine conversion. We need to be educated of what salvation means, how to get salvation, and what Jesus meant when He said, "Most assuredly, I say to you, unless one is born again, he cannot see the kingdom of God." (John 3:3) Also, extensive study of God's Word, the Bible (both The Old Testament and The New Testament,) and regular or daily self-study and meditation is needed. In my case, by studying and daily reading and meditating God's word, I begin to know God's will and purpose for my life. I learned that I was not created for myself, but for Him, therefore the reason God created me is to bring Him honor and glory. "For by Him all things were created that are in heaven and that are on earth, visible and invisible, whether thrones or dominions or principalities or powers. All things are created through Him and for Him. And He is before all things, and in Him all things consist." (Colossians 1:16-17) By studying His Word I learned and understood that His important agenda for my life is my salvation for His kingdom. In knowing this, it is much easier for me to follow and obey Him.

"It is also a part of Catholic teaching to consider 'faith' as a way of life rather than a major decision that happens once, twice, or a few times in one's life. Catholics realize the importance of the initial conversion and commitment to Christ, but they also emphasize the challenge of living out faith in Jesus Christ every day, by God's grace and with the guidance of the Holy Spirit. God provides the power or grace to live out our faith through many channels: through daily prayer, the sacraments, and our life and fellowship with other Christians. Thus, these means of God's grace are also significant for our salvation, since they enable us to stay persevered in our faith and live it out day by day.

Even though many things play a part in receiving God's gift of salvation, faith is primary for two reasons. First, a Christian's good works flow from a firm belief and trust in God. Second, receiving the sacraments, observing Church teaching, and using the other means of grace are meaningless without a living faith in God." [2]

Sacrament and Salvation –Catholics believe that the sacraments are channels by which the grace of Jesus Christ comes to us. They too are part of God's plan of salvation. The Bible attests that baptism is the way a person becomes a part of the body of Christ, the Church. St. Peter, at the end of his sermon during Pentecost, told the people what they had to do in order to be saved: "Repent and be baptized every one of you in the name of Jesus Christ for the forgiveness of your sins; and you shall receive the gifts of the Holy Spirit." (Acts 2:28) Through baptism, converts to Jesus Christ first received forgiveness of their sins, the gift of the Holy Spirit, and became members of the community of Christians, the Church. But does baptism have anything to do with salvation? Jesus said, "He who believes and is baptized will be saved." (Mark 16:16) He told Nicodemus that, "unless one is born of water and the Spirit, he cannot enter the kingdom of God." (John 3:5) The Church of the New Testament times responded to this teaching by immediately baptizing the new converts. (See Acts 2:23,41; 18:8; 19:5; 22:16)

"Does the Eucharist, or Lord's Supper, have any significance for salvation? Jesus said, 'unless you eat the flesh of the Son of Man and drink His blood, you have no life in you: he who eats my flesh and drinks my blood has eternal life, and I will raise him up in the last day.' (John 6:53-54) The apostle Paul explained that eating the flesh of Christ and drinking His blood refers to partaking of the bread and cup of the Eucharist. [3]

Church and Salvation – the church is the community or body of persons committed to following Jesus Christ. Catholic Christians believe that the normal way to be saved is to become a follower of Jesus, and thus to become part of "the church," which is His, (Christ's) body." (Ephesians 1:22-23)

"For centuries, Christians accepted the teaching of St. Cyprian of Carthage, a great bishop-martyr of the third century, who said, 'Outside of the Church there is no salvation.' Cyprian's teaching was based on certain presuppositions that were shared by the authors of the New Testament. They presupposed that one was saved by becoming a follower of Jesus and those followers of Jesus were members of His body, the Church. They also presupposed that the Church's members would respect and obey their leaders because Jesus Christ had given them authority to guide God's people. All of this seemed self-evident to the early Christians. There was no salvation outside the Church because it was only within the Church that a person had access to the ways by which he could come into contact with Jesus and thus, be saved. (See Acts 3 and 4) Therefore, Catholics believe that the Church itself is an important means of salvation. Jesus Himself indicated this when He told Peter that 'the powers of death shall not prevail against it,' (the Church.) (Mathew 16:18) This does not mean that Catholics believe that a person must belong to the Catholic Church to be saved. In fact as recently as 1949, the Roman Catholic Church vigorously rejected an opinion, attributed to Fr. Leonard Feeney of Boston, that only Catholics could be saved." 4

St. Augustine, in The City of God, said that some persons would be saved if they were ones who truly loved God, even if they were not formally members of the Catholic Church. On the other hand, St. Augustine warned his fellow Catholics that some baptized members would not be saved if they did not love God and live in charity. Church membership may be a great help to an individual in attaining salvation, but it is never an automatic "ticket to heaven." The Catholic Church's official teaching is very similar to St. Augustine's. The Second Vatican Council, after spelling out what it means to be a "fully incorporated" member of the Church, insisted:

"He is not saved, however, who, though he is a part of the body of the Church, does not persevere in charity. He remains indeed in the bosom of the Church, but as it were, only in a 'bodily' manner, and not 'in his heart.' All the sons of the Church should remember that their exalted status is to be attributed not to their own merits but to the special grace of Christ. If they fail moreover to respond to that grace in thought word, and deed, not only will they not be saved, but they will be the more severely judged.

This is a stern warning to 'nominal Catholics.' They will not escape rigorous judgment by God on the last day simply because they are Catholics." 5

Are Catholics "Born Again" or "Spirit Filled?"

Many Christians today say that a person must be "Born Again," "Spirit –filled," or baptized in Holy Spirit," in order to be saved. Catholics and other Christians often ask what the Catholic Church teaches about this because these terms do not originate in Catholic teaching and Theology. The simple answer is that the Catholic Church basically affirms the reality and truth of what this phrase points to. The term "Born Again" came from Jesus's words in John Chapter 3. "Truly, truly, I say to you, unless one is "Born from above" or "Born Again," he cannot see the kingdom of God… Unless one is born of water and the Spirit, he cannot enter the Kingdom of God." (John 3:3, 5) Catholics believe that they are first born again of water and the Holy Spirit when they receive the sacrament of baptism. Therefore, a person who has been validly baptized has been "born of water and the Spirit," and can attain salvation. However, Catholics also believe that baptism only begins the work or mission of the Holy Spirit in the life of the believer. The Spirit also comes in new and deeper ways in the other sacraments of the Church, and through the fervent and expectant prayer of Christians.

Salvation, as we have seen, is a lifelong process that depends upon continually living in the power of the Holy Spirit and by the Spirit's guidance. Paul in his letter to the Romans said that it is those who live according to the Spirit of God who will attain salvation, "…for if you live according to the flesh you will die, but if by the Spirit you put to death the deeds of the body you will live. For all who are led by the Spirit of God are sons of God." (Romans 8:13-14)

Alan Schreck in his book, <u>Catholics and Christians</u> explained what Catholic Theologians said about baptism in the Spirit:

"Catholic theologians have reflected on the work of the Holy Spirit in our lives and have discussed some important questions about how 'baptism in the Spirit' is related to other forms of God's action among His people. The reason for these proposals is to acknowledge that 'baptized in the Spirit' is a biblical term that probably should not be used to describe one particular type of experience of the Holy Spirit. To speak of 'the baptism in the Spirit,' is even more misleading if it implies that there is only one event in a person's life that could properly be called by that name. God can pour out the Holy Spirit in a new and significant way many times in a person's life if God wishes. The first time that this happens to a person is often the most dramatic because it may be experienced by the person as a totally 'new thing.'"

Fr. Frances Sullivan, S.J. refers to St. Thomas Aquinas' teaching in this subject and he states:"I conclude from this teaching of St. Thomas that there is no reason why Catholics, who believe that they have received the Holy Spirit in their sacramental initiation, should not look forward to new 'sendings' of the Spirit to them, which would move them from the 'state of grace,' in which they already are into some 'new act' or 'new state of grace.' Now if we recall that in biblical language, 'sending the spirit,' 'pouring out the Spirit' and 'baptizing in the spirit' are simply different ways of saying the same thing, the conclusion follows that it is quite in accord with traditional Catholic theology for baptized and confirmed Christians to ask the Lord to 'baptize them in the Holy Spirit.' What they are asking for, in the language of St. Thomas, is a new 'sending' of the Holy Spirit, which would begin a decisively new work of grace in their lives. As we have seen from the examples which St. Thomas gives, (working miracles, prophecy, etc.) he would obviously not be surprised if such a new work of grace involved a charismatic gift."

"...and are seeking a fuller release or outpouring of the power of the Holy Spirit in their lives. Many of these Catholics like myself have been regularly receiving the sacraments and striving to live uprightly, but they experience 'something missing,' – the desire and need for more of God and His Holy Spirit. Hence, they are right to pray to God and seek the prayers of others to be 'baptized in the Holy Spirit.' Catholics do not believe, however, that any particular gift, such as 'speaking in tongues' always necessarily accompanies being 'baptized in the Spirit.' (See 1 Cor.12: 29-31; 14:5) 6

A. SACRAMENT

Sacrament, per definition, is one of the ceremonies of a Christian Church. The Sacraments are simply channels through which the grace of God, flowing from the cross of Jesus, comes to us. They are not the only channels of God's grace through Jesus, but they are reliable channels that never run dry. We believers, receive the benefits of the grace and salvation that Jesus won for us by simply coming to Him in faith. We must, "Come to Him, to that living stone, rejected by men but in God's sight chosen and precious." (1 Peter 2:4) One way of coming to that living stone is through the sacraments. Catholic Christians believe that the grace of Jesus Christ is present in the sacraments because the Bible, the activity of the apostles, and the tradition of the early Church all testify to this belief. The sacraments are a prime example of God's "inhuman" way of approaching and relating to humankind. This means that God doesn't only share His life in us in an invincible or "spiritual" way, but also through things, persons, and events that we can touch and experience with our senses.

The Catholic Church teaches that the first and primary sacrament is Jesus Himself. God chose to save humankind and communicate the fullness of His life and grace by taking our humanity, living and walking among us. The first letter of John begins:

"That which was from the beginning, which we have heard, which we have seen with our eyes, which we have looked upon and touched with our hands, concerning the word of life– the life was made manifest, and we saw it and testify to it, and proclaim to you the eternal life which was with the Father and was made manifest to us…(John 1: 1-2)

The Church, although is not explicitly called a "Sacrament" in the Bible, the Church functions as a sacrament because it is a visible body that carries on a mission of Jesus Christ in the world and draws people to God. It is a channel, a sign, and an instrument of God's grace to all humankind.

The Catholic Church has seven sacraments:

Baptism – the sacrament of spiritual rebirth through which we are made children of God and heirs of heaven. The Bible emphasizes the importance of baptism in receiving God's gift of salvation:

"Amen, Amen I say to thee, unless a man be born again of water and the Holy Ghost, he cannot enter into the kingdom of God."(John 3:5)

Infant Baptism – The first converts to Christianity were adults. The New Testament does not explicitly state whether infants or children were also baptized, but there is some indication that they were. In Acts Chapter 2 Peter states: "Repent, and let everyone of you be baptized in the name of Jesus Christ for the remission of sins: and you shall receive the gift of the Holy Spirit. For the promise is to you and to your children, and to all who are afar off, as many as the Lord our God will call." (Acts 2:38-39) "The Bible does not explicitly command that infants and children be baptized, but neither does it forbid the practice. There is no explicit testimony before the second century that infants were baptized in the early Church. After this however, there is considerable evidence that infants and children were baptized, and by the first century this was a universally accepted practice throughout the Church of Jesus Christ." [1]

Confirmation – is the official prayer of the Church for the full outpouring of the Holy Spirit. This sacrament confers the Holy Spirit to make us strong and perfect Christians and soldiers of Jesus Christ. Peter and John were sent to converts in Samaria "and prayed for them that they might receive the Holy Spirit; for it had not yet fallen on any of them, but they had only been baptized in the name of the Lord Jesus. Now when the apostles, who were in Jerusalem, had heard that Samaria had received the word of God, they sent unto them Peter and John. Who, when they were come, prayed for them, that they might receive the Holy Spirit... Then they laid hand on them, and they received the Holy Spirit." (Acts 8: 14-17)

Eucharist – The Eucharist, or the Lord's Supper, makes present the central mystery of the Christian faith – the passion, death, and the resurrection of the Lord Jesus. Catholics consider it the highest form of Christian prayer. It is not just the prayer of the individual, nor of the priest who presides it but it is truly the prayer of the whole Church, gathered to worship Jesus, our Savior and great high priest. (Heb. 7:26 27; 8:1)

"The second Vatican Council's "Constitution on the Sacred Liturgy" affirms this when it says that:

"...the liturgy (the Mass) is the summit toward which the activity of the Church directed; at the same time it is the fountain from which all her power flows. For the goal of apostolic works is that all who are made sons of God by faith and baptism should come together to praise God in the midst of His Church, to take part in her sacrifice and to eat the Lord's Supper." [2]

This sacrament, is also known as Holy Communion, which nourishes the soul with the true Flesh and Blood, Soul and Divinity of Jesus, under the appearance, or sacramental veil, of bread and wine: "And whilst they were eating, Jesus took bread; and blessing, broke, and gave to them, and said, Take ye. This is my body. And having taken the chalice, giving thanks, He gave it to them: This is my blood of the New Testament, which shall be shed for many." (Mark 14:22-24. See also Matt. 26:26-28, Luke 22:19-20)

Penance – the sacrament, also known as reconciliation, or confession, through which Christ forgives sins and restores the soul to God's grace. Jesus had the authority as the Son of God to forgive sins, and He gave this same authority to His apostles. To Peter He said, "And I will give you the Keys to heaven, and whatever you bind on earth will be bound in heaven, and whatever you loose on earth will be loosed in heaven." (Mathew 16:19) Later, He told the other apostles the same thing in Mathew 18:18. In John's gospel, Jesus appeared to the apostles on Easter and said, "Receive the Holy Spirit. If you forgive the sins of any, they are forgiven; if you retain the sins of any, they are retained." (John 20:22-23)

Extreme unction- the sacrament, sometimes called the last anointing, which strengthens the sick and sanctifies the dying. This sacrament has been practiced since the earliest days of the Church, but its focus has shifted at times. Until recently, the emphasis was on preparation for death, but the Second Vatican Council restored an emphasis on prayer for physical and spiritual healing for all seriously ill persons. This sacrament does not preclude the importance of individual Christians praying for the sick, or even anointing them with blessed oil. It simply acknowledges Jesus' command to His apostles to anoint and heal the sick and recognizes the power that has always been at work through their ministry and through that of the elders who succeeded them. "Is any man sick among you? Let him bring in the priests of the Church, and let them pray over him, anointing him with oil in the name of the Lord. And the prayer of faith will save the sick, and the Lord will raise him up. And if he has committed sins, he will be forgiven." (James 5:14-15)

Sacrament of Holy orders – the sacrament of ordination, which empowers priests to offer the Holy Sacrifice of the Mass, administer the sacraments, and officiate over all the other proper affairs of the Church. Jesus set apart certain men, especially the apostles to have a unique responsibility to carry on His mission and ministry.

"The original apostles insured the continuation of the Church's leadership by appointing elders to succeed them, and conferring upon these elders the same authority that Jesus had given to them. By the late century A.D. these elders were known as bishops, presbyters and deacons – was the norm for the entire Christian world. The Catholic Church has preserved this basic pattern of official leadership and succession from the first or second century to the present day." "For every high priest taken from among men is appointed for men in things pertaining to God, that he may offer both gifts and sacrifices for sins. He can have compassion on those who are ignorant and going astray, since he himself is also beset by weakness. Because of this he is required as for the people, so also for himself, to offer for sins. And no man takes this honor to himself, but he who is called by God, just as Aaron was." (Hebrews 5:1-4) "Therefore, take heed to yourselves and to all the flock, among which the Holy Spirit has made you overseers, to shepherd the Church of God which He purchased with His own blood." (Acts 20:28) [3]

Sacrament of Matrimony – the sacrament that unites a man and woman in a holy and indissoluble bond. Many Christians recognize marriage as an important part of Christian life, but Roman Catholics consider it a sacrament. The roots of a Christian marriage are found in the Old Testament and confirmed by Jesus: "Have you not read that He who made them from the beginning made them male and female and said, 'For this reason a man shall leave his father and mother and be joined to his wife, and the two shall become one flesh? So they are no longer two but one flesh. What therefore God has joined together, let not man put asunder.'" (Mathew 19:4-6) Why is marriage a sacrament? First, because it is an action of God: "what God has united, man must not divide." Jesus is adamant about this, and reestablished the indissolubility of marriage that existed before the fall of man; He said to them, "For your hardness of heart Moses allowed you to divorce your wives, but from the beginning it was not so. And I say to you: whoever divorces his wife, except for un-chastity, and marries another, commits adultery." (Mathew 19:8-9) Marriage is a sacrament because it is a visible, outward sign of Jesus' presence and love in the world. The love of a husband for his wife for example is a sign of Christ's love for His Church:

"Husbands, love your wives, as Christ loved the Church and gave Himself up for her... For no man hates his own flesh, but nourishes and cherish it, as Christ does the Church, because we are members of His body... This is a great mystery, and I mean in reference to Christ and the Church." (Ephesians 5:25, 29-30, 32)

Anointing of the Sick – The scriptural roots of the sacraments of anointing the sick are very clear: Jesus healed the sick and commanded and empowered his disciples to do the same. " And they cast out many demons, and anointed with oil many that were sick and healed them" [Mk 6:13].

This sacrament has been practiced since the earliest days of the Church, but its focus has shifted at times. Until recently, the emphasis was on preparation for death, but the Second Vatican Council restored an emphasis on prayer for physical and spiritual healing for all seriously ill persons. This sacrament does not preclude the importance of individual Christians praying for the sick, or even anointing them with oil. [4]

B. HIERARCHY OF TRUTHS

"One of the principles that guide the Catholic Church is the hierarchy of truths. Catholics believe that God reveals the fullness of truth to Christians through the Bible and through the ongoing guidance of the Holy Spirit. There is a wide range of truths that Catholics believe are revealed by God. Nearly all Christians, such as the divinity of Jesus, the Trinity, Jesus' intention to establish a church, and many others, accept some of these truths. Other truths are accepted by Catholics, but not by other Christians, such as the importance of Mary in God's plan of salvation, the intercessory role of the saints, the existence of purgatory, and so on. Catholics believe that both the former and the latter categories are part of the fullness of Christian truth. So, Catholics do not distinguish between "Christian truths" and "Catholic truths" as if Catholic beliefs are added on to "basic Christianity." Rather, Catholics understand the official teachings of the Catholic Church to be a faithful presentation of the fullness of divine truth that God has revealed through the Bible and the ongoing revelation of the Holy Spirit. However, having said this, an important qualification needs to be made in order to understand Catholic teaching correctly. Catholics do not believe that all revealed truths are equally central to the basic gospel message or are equally important for salvation.

This is what the Catholic Church means when it teaches that there is "hierarchy of truths." Practically speaking, this means that the beliefs that are most important for Catholics are truths such as the divinity of Jesus, the necessity of His death on the cross for our salvation, the reality and power of the Holy Spirit, and so on. Here, Catholics find a common ground of understanding and cooperation with other Christians, because Catholics and most other Christians usually agree on the most central and basic doctrine of Christianity. However, Catholics believe that there are other Christian truths such as those concerning Mary, the saints, the purgatory, and so on that are indeed true, but are not the central points of the gospel message.

It is important for both Catholics and other Christians to recognize this distinction. Sometimes, Catholics are guilty of viewing and talking about Mary, the saints, purgatory, and similar beliefs as if they were the most important truths. This often produces an unnecessary obstacle to unity with other Christians, and may actually be a distortion of authentic Christianity. On the other hand, sometimes other Christians focus unduly on Catholic beliefs about Mary, the saints, purgatory, indulgences, and the like (often rejecting them in a one-sided way, even when they have some basis in the Bible,) in order to portray Catholics as "un-Christian," or to accuse the Catholic Church of distorting the gospel of Jesus Christ. These extremes should be avoided and corrected where they exist." [1]

Catholic Christians want to be faithful to the full gospel and to the guidance of the Holy Spirit. If the Bible and the experience of Christians over the course of centuries testify to certain truths about Mary, the saints, the next life, certain ways of prayer and worship and so on, Catholics want to acknowledge and embrace these truths, even if they are less central in the "hierarchy" of Christian truths. Rather than rejecting these truths as non-essential, Catholic Christians try to retain them in the proper perspective, not exaggerating them or focusing on them unduly. Catholics admit that in practice they have not kept the proper balance in their beliefs. They have not always lived out the fullness of Christian truth that the Catholic

Church professes to preserve and proclaim in its official doctrine. This is why Catholics admit their need and desire for ongoing repentance and renewal. [2]

C. THE MASS CELEBRATION

"The Mass is the fellowship and the worship celebration of Catholic people in the Church. Jesus commanded His Apostles to 'Do this in remembrance of me.' (1 Cor. 11: 24, Luke 22:19,) the Eucharist soon became the primary act of Christian worship in the primitive Church. This reenactment of the Lord's Supper was accompanied by readings from the Old Testament, accounts of Jesus' life and teaching and prayers. This 'prayer service,' with the Eucharist at the center, came to be called 'the Mass' by Catholics. Although the mass has developed somewhat over the centuries, its parts are essentially the same as the worship services of the early Church. This weekly celebration of the Lord's Supper or the Eucharist was held on Sunday, the day of Jesus' resurrection. In the early Church, it was generally assumed that all Christians who were physically able would gather every Sunday to worship the Lord and partake of His body and blood. St. Paul in his letter to the Hebrews warns against '...neglecting to meet together, as in the habit of some...' (Heb. 10:25) The Catholic Church today follows this practice in requiring its members to worship together on Sunday as a community. This is something that a faithful follower of Jesus and member of His body, the Church, should do anyway." [1]

The Catholic Christian Church considers the second part of the Mass, the Liturgy of the Eucharist, as a representation or perpetuation of Jesus' one sacrifice of Himself on Calvary for the sins of all people. However, the term "sacrifice of the Mass" is confusing and even scandalous to many Christians. The letter to the Hebrews states clearly that Jesus Christ has been sacrificed once for our sins and now stands interceding for us in the presence of the Father. (Heb7:25, 9:24-28)

"The Catholic Church has never taught that in the Mass Jesus is "re-sacrificed" or offered up to suffer again. The Catholic Mass is called a sacrifice because it "re-presents" "reenacts," or presents once again before us, the one sacrifice of Christ on Calvary. Jesus Christ was sacrificed once, but God, in His mercy, makes present to us once again the sacrifice of Christ through the Mass so that we human beings can enter more deeply into the reality and significance of sacrifice. Catholics believe that this is possible because 'Jesus Christ is the same yesterday and today and forever.' (Heb. 13:8) What Jesus did in the past – His death on the cross – is present to God. God can make this sacrifice present to us when Christians gather to celebrate the Lord's Supper or Eucharist in His memory. Therefore, Catholic Christians believe that Jesus is not "re-sacrificed" in the Mass, but that His one sacrifice at Calvary is made real and present to us by God, so that we enter into this central mystery of our faith in a new way. The apostle Paul said, 'For as often as you eat this bread and drink this cup, you proclaim the Lord's death until He comes.' (1 Cor.11:26) Indeed, participation at Mass is not some magic rite in which the passive presence individual is adequate. In fact, the Roman Catholic Code of Canon Law sates that the Eucharistic celebration should be 'planned to bring about conscious, active, and full participation of the people, motivated by faith, hope and charity.'" 2

I think it is only fair to everyone if I share the order of the Mass and some of the prayers to give you more understanding of the Catholic Mass celebration.

I. Entrance Song –

II. Greetings – The priest greets the people with this prayer: "May the grace of our Lord Jesus Christ and the love of God and the fellowship of the Holy Spirit be with you all." And the people respond: And also with you."

III. Penitential Rite – Priest and the people recite: "I confess to almighty God, and to you, my brothers and sisters that I have sinned through my own faults, in my thoughts, in my words, and in what I have done, and in what I failed to do, and I ask the blessed Mary, all the angels and saints, and to you my brothers and sisters to pray for me to the Lord our God." Then the priest says, "May almighty God have mercy on us and forgive us our sins and bring us to everlasting life, Amen."

Then everyone will sing: "Lord have mercy"

IV. Gloria or praises – The choir and the people sing together:

"Glory to God in the highest,

And peace to His people on earth

Lord God, heavenly King,

Almighty God the Father,

We worship You, we give You thanks,

We worship You for Your glory.

Lord Jesus Christ, only Son of the Father,

Lord God Lamb of God,

You take away the sin of the world:

Have mercy on us;

You are seated at the right hand of the Father:

Receive our prayer.

For You alone are the Holy One,

You alone are the Lord,

You alone are the Most High,

Jesus Christ

With the Holy Spirit,

in the glory of God the Father. Amen"

V. First Reading of Scriptures (Scriptures are taken from Old or New Testament.)

VI. Responsorial Psalms – The cantor will sing 2-3 verses of Psalms and the people respond: For example, "The Lord is good and His mercy endures forever."

VII. Second Reading of Scriptures

VIII. Gospel reading – we all sing ALLELUIA before the priest reads the Gospel and we all stand up for the reading. This is followed by the priest' homily or sermon.

Basics of Catholic Faith

IX. Profession of Faith – we all recite the Nicene Creed (every Sunday and every holiday obligation observed by the Catholic Church.)

"We believe in one God,

The Father, the Almighty,

Maker of heaven and earth,

Of all that is seen and unseen.

We believe in one Lord, Jesus Christ,

The only Son of God,

Eternally begotten of the Father,

God from God,

Begotten, not made, one in Being with the Father.

Through Him all things were made.

For us men and for our salvation

He came down from heaven:

(Bow) By the power of the Holy Spirit

He was born of the Virgin Mary, and became man.

For our sake He was crucified under Pontius Pilate;

He suffered, died and was buried.

On the third day He rose again

In fulfillment of the scriptures;

He ascended into heaven

And is seated at the right hand of the Father.

He will come again in glory to judge the living and the dead,

And His kingdom will have no end.

We believe in the Holy Spirit, the Lord, the giver of life,

Who proceeds from the Father and the Son.

With the Father and the Son He is worshiped and glorified.

He has spoken through the prophets.

We believe in one Catholic and apostolic Church.

We acknowledge one baptism for the forgiveness of sins.

We look for the resurrection of the dead,

And the life of the world to come. Amen."

X. General Intercession – Prayer for the Faithful

The priest says: "As priestly people we unite with one another to pray for today's needs."

For every petition the people answer, "Lord hear our prayer."

XI. Preparation for Altar and Gifts –

The priest prays, "Blessed are You Lord,

God of all creation, through Your goodness we have this bread to offer,

Which earth has given and human hands have made.

It will become for us the bread of life."

All will respond: "Blessed be God forever."

"Blessed are You Lord

Through Your goodness we have this wine to offer,

Fruit of the vine and work of human hands.

It will become our spiritual drink."

All respond, "Blessed be God forever."

The priest continues to pray:

"Pray brethren, that our sacrifice may be acceptable to God, the Almighty Father."

The people respond:

"May the Lord receive the sacrifice at your hands.

For the praise and glory of His name,

For our good and the good of all His Church. (notice we Catholics pray for the good of all of God's Church every single Mass given throughout the whole world every single day. I myself usually add in this part a quick prayer; "Lord! Unite all Your Church.")

    XII.   Collection of Offerings – The choir and people sings.

    XIII.   Preface of the Eucharistic Prayer

Priest: "The Lord be with you"

Respond: "And also with you"

Priest: "Lift up your hearts!"

Respond: "We lift them up to the Lord"

Priest: "Let us give thanks to the Lord our God!"

Respond: "It is right to give Him thanks and praise."

Everyone Prays: "Holy! Holy! Lord,

God of power and might

Heaven and earth are full of your glory

Hosanna! Hosanna in the highest

Blessed is he who comes in the name of the Lord

Hosanna! Hosanna in the highest."

X1V. – Eucharistic Prayer (choice of prayer 1 to prayer 4)

Eucharistic Prayer 1

"We come to You Father,

With praise and thanksgiving,

Through Jesus Christ Your Son.

Through Him we ask You to accept

And bless

These gifts we offer You in sacrifice.

We offer them for Your Holy Catholic Church,

Watch over it, Lord, and guide it;

Grant it peace and unity throughout the world.

We offer them for –our Pope

For --our bishop,

And for all who hold and teach the Catholic faith

That comes to us from the apostles.

Remember Lord your people,

Especially those whom we now pray N. and N.

Remember all of us gathered here before You.

You know how firmly we believe in You

Basics of Catholic Faith

And dedicate ourselves to you.
We offer You this sacrifice of praise
For ourselves and those who are dear to us.
We pray to You, our living and true God,
For our well-being and redemption.
We honor Mary, the ever-virgin mother of Jesus Christ
Our Lord and God.
We honor Joseph, her husband,
The apostles and martyrs
Peter and Paul
James, John Thomas
James, Phillip,
Bartholomew, Mathew, Simon and Jude;
We honor Cletus, Clement, Sixtus,
Cornelius, Cyprian, Lawrence, Chrysogonus
John and Paul, Cosmas and Damian
And all the saints.
May their merits and prayers
gain as our constant help and protection
Through Christ our Lord. Amen.
Father accept this offering
From your whole family.
Grant us Your peace in this life,
Save us from final damnation,

And count us among those You have chosen

Through Christ our Lord. Amen.

Bless and approve our offering;

Make it acceptable for You'

An offering in spirit and in truth.

Let it become for us

The body and blood of Jesus Christ,

Your only Son, our Lord.

Through Christ our Lord. Amen.

The day before He suffered

He took bread in His sacred hands

And looking up to heaven, to You His Almighty Father,

He gave You thanks and praise.

He broke the bread,

Gave it to His disciples, and said:

'Take this all of you and eat it:

This is My body which will be given up for you.'

When supper was ended,

He took the cup.

Again He gave You thanks and praise,

Gave the cup to His disciples, and said:

'Take this all of you and drink from it:

This is the cup of My blood,

The blood of the new and everlasting covenant.

It will be shed for you and for all
So that sins may be forgiven.
Do this in memory of me.'
Let us proclaim the mystery of faith:
Christ has died,
Christ is resin,
Christ will come again. (or)
Dying You destroyed our death,
Rising You restored our life,
Lord Jesus, come in glory."

XVI.   Communion Rite

The priest invites all to join in the Lord's Prayer: (or sing)
"Our Father, who art in heaven
Hallowed be thy name;
Thy kingdom come,
Thy will be done on earth as it is in heaven.
Give us this day our daily bread;
And forgive us our trespasses,
As we forgive those who trespass against us;
And lead us not into temptation,
But deliver us from evil. Amen."
The priest pray:
"Deliver us Lord from every evil,

And grant us peace in our day.

In Your mercy keep us from sin

And protect us from all worthless anxiety,

As we wait in joyful hope

For the coming of our Savior, Jesus Christ."

All: "For the kingdom, the power, and the glory,

Are yours, now and forever more."

Sign of Peace: The priest will pray:

"Lord Jesus Christ, You said to Your apostles:

I leave you peace, My peace I gave to you.

Look not on our sins, but on the faith of Your Church,

And grant us peace and unity of Your kingdom

Where You live forever and ever."

All: "Amen."

Priest: "The peace of the Lord be with you always."

Response: "And also with you."

Priest: "Let us offer each other a sign of peace." (The people exchange a sign of peace, according to local custom.)

    XVII.   Breaking of the Bread

Prayer:

"Lamb of God, You take away the sins of the world:

Have mercy on us.

Lamb of God, You take away the sins of the world:

Grant us peace."

Communion:

The priest says:

"This is the Lamb of God

Who takes away the sins of the world.

Happy are those who are called to His supper."

Response:

"Lord I am not worthy to receive You,

But only say the word and I shall be healed."

XVIII.   Concluding Rite

Greeting: "The lord be with you"

Response: "And also with you."

Blessing:

"May almighty God Bless you,

The Father, the Son and the Holy Spirit"

Response: "Amen"

Dismissal: "Go in peace to love and serve the Lord"

Response: "Thanks be to God".

End of the Mass and the priest leaves the altar, and so with the congregation. [Taken from Catholic Today's Missal]

The following are the Eucharistic Worship of Pope John Paul 11:

"Lord Jesus,

Born Again Catholic

We are gathered here before you.

You are the Son of God made man,

Crucified by us and raised up by the Father.

You, the living One,

Actually present among us.

You the way, the truth, and the life:

You who alone have words of eternal life:

You the sole foundation of our salvation

And the sole name to invoke

If we are to have hope.

You, the image of the Father

And the giver of the Spirit;

You, Love: Love not loved!

Lord Jesus, we believe in you,

We worship you,

We love you with all our heart,

And we proclaim your name above every other name.

In this solemn moment

We pray to you for our city.

Watch over it. O Christ from your cross,

And save it

Watch over the poor, the sick.

The old people, the outcast,

The young men and girls
Who have embarked on desperate roads,
The many families in trouble and afflicted by misfortune
And society's ills.
Look and have pity!
Look at those who no longer know how to believe
In the Father who is in Heaven,
Who no longer perceive His tenderness,
Those who cannot
Read your face,
O crucified One,
Their pain, their poverty
And their sufferings.
See how many are lying in sin, far from you.
Who are the source of living water:
The only One who takes away thirst
And soothes the yearning and restless anxiety
Of the human heart.
Look at them and have pity!

Bless our city and our neighborhood.
Bless all the workers
Who by their daily toil
See to the needs of families and the progress of society.

Bless the young,

So that hope of the better world

Is not extinguished in their hearts,

Nor the wish to devote themselves generously to build it.

Bless those who govern us, that they may work for justice and peace.

Bless the priests who lead the communities,

The men and women willing to accept the call

To give themselves completely to the service of the Gospel

And their brothers and sisters.

O Lord Jesus, allow

Our parish community to be confirmed in the faith of baptism,

So that it may possess the joy of the truth,

The only road that leads to life!

Give it the grace of reconciliation

That spills from your pierced heart,

O crucified One:

So that, reconciled and united,

It may become a force

That transcends divisions,

And leavened by a new mentality

Of solidarity and sharing,

Is a living call to follow you

Who become the brother of us all.
Finally, let it be a community that is a
Messenger of hope
Spur them to commit themselves,
To work for a more united and peaceful world,
Conforming to the will of your Father,
Our Creator.
Lord Jesus
Give us peace, you are peace
And on your cross transcended every division.
And make us
True workers for peace and justice:
Men and women
Who are submitted to build
A world that is more just,
More united and more fraternal.

Lord Jesus,
Return among us
And make us vigilant
In expectation of your coming.
Amen." 3

June 16,1985 (Taken from The Private Prayers of Pope John Paul 11 Atria.)

Once I became "Born Again," I was more understanding of our Catholic faith. Now I love and enjoy my church, specially the mass celebration, a lot more. Before, I did not understand the meaning of some of our Catholic rituals, but by studying and learning, now I can follow our rituals with more meaning, more feeling and understanding. As I mentioned before, I used to attend Mass for brownie points or to get my blessing and if I was in need or wanted a favor from God. I went to mass because I was afraid that if I didn't attend God would punish me. So when I attended Mass, I used to keep watching for the time on my wristwatch wondering when the one-hour would be over. Now, I attend the Mass celebration because I want to. Because I love the Lord, I want to be in His presence and I want to fellowship, worship and praise Him. Many times in the mass I can actually feel His glory so much, that many times I get emotional and cry during worship, during the Eucharistic prayer and when we sing or pray the "Our Father." When my family asks me why I am crying, I smile and say, "I just feel God's presence and His love for me." Now I find that the Mass and the sermon are too short and I wish that our Mass were like the service of Evangelical Christians Church, that lasts longer

D. Common Questions other Denominations often asked about Catholic Faith

"Catholic Church Has the Answer" written by Paul Whitcomb is a booklet that the Catholic Church put out to explain some of the contradictory opinions of our Christian brothers and others. This was written to minimize or avoid incomplete and distorted information about the Catholic

Basics of Catholic Faith

faith. "The right place to go for information about Catholic belief – in fact the only place to go for complete and authoritative information – is the Catholic Church herself. As any detective will tell you, no investigation is quite so complete as an on-the-spot investigation. Hence, dear reader, if you are a Protestant, an unaffiliated Christian, or an agnostic, who wants to know the truths about the Catholic belief, take this friendly advice: Seek out a Catholic priest and put your questions to him. You will find him a very understanding and obliging person. Or read this booklet; this booklet was written by a Catholic who knows the questions that you are likely to ask, as well as the answers, because once, he too was outside of the Catholic Church looking in. The questions in this booklet are basically the same ones he put to a Catholic priest, and the answers are basically the same ones given him by that priest. Read this booklet; then forget all the fiction you have heard about the Catholic Church, for you will have the Gospel truth." [1]

The following questions and answers are the most common questions that most of my Christian friends asked and discussed. They are all taken from this same booklet that I mentioned, "The Catholic Church has the Answer," by Paul Whitcomb.

Why do Catholics believe that their Church is the true Church of Jesus Christ? Wouldn't it more reasonable to believe that Christ's true Church is a spiritual union of all Christian denominations?

Answer: Catholics believe that theirs is the one true Church of Jesus Christ, firstly, because theirs is the only Christian Church that goes back in history to the time of Christ, secondly, because theirs is the only Christian

Church which possesses the invincible unity, the intrinsic holiness, the continual universality and the indisputable apostolicity which Christ said would distinguish His true Church; thirdly, because the Apostles and primitive Church Fathers, who certainly were members of Christ's true Church, all professed membership in this same Catholic Church, (See Apostles Creed and the Primitive Christian letters.) Wrote Ignatius of Antioch, illustrious Church Father of the first century; "Where the Bishop is, there let the multitude of believers be; even as where Jesus is, there is the Catholic Church."

Our Lord said: "There shall be one fold and one shepherd," yet it is well known that the various Christian denominations cannot agree on what Christ actually taught. Since Christ roundly condemned inter-denominationalism ("And if a house be divided against itself, that house cannot stand." Mark 3:25) Catholics cannot believe that He would ever sanction it in His Church.

If the Catholic Church never fell into error, how explain the worldly Popes, the bloody Inquisitions, the selling of indulgences and the invention of new doctrines?

Answer: A careful, objective investigation of Catholic history will disclose these facts: The so-called worldly Popes of the Middle Ages – three in number – were certainly guilty of extravagant pomposity, nepotism and other indiscretions and sins which were not in keeping with the dignity of their high Church office – but they're certainly not guilty of licentious conduct while in office, nor were guilty of altering any part of the Church's Christ-given deposit of faith. The so –called bloody Inquisitions, which were initiated by the civil governments of France and Spain for the purpose of ferreting out Moslems and

Jews who were causing social havoc by posing as faithful Catholic citizens – even as priests and bishops – were indeed approved by the Church. (Non– Catholics who admitted that they were non – Catholics were left alone by the Inquisition.) And the vast majority of those questioned by the Inquisition, (including St. Theresa of Avila) were completely cleared. Nevertheless, the Popes roundly condemned the proceedings when they saw justice giving way to cruel abuses, and it was this insistent condemnation by the Popes that finally put an end to the Inquisitions.

The so – called selling of indulgences positively did not involve any "selling"- it involved the granting of spiritual favor of an indulgence (which is the remission of the debt of temporal punishment for already –forgiven sins) in return for the giving alms to the Church for the building of Christendom's greatest house of prayer – St. Peters Basilica of Rome. One must understand with regard to indulgences that there are always two acts to be fulfilled by the one gaining the indulgence: 1. Doing the deed (e.g. alms-giving) and 2. (Saying of some prescribed prayers with proper spiritual dispositions. In the case in point, the first act for gaining the indulgence was "giving alms." If the almsgiver thereafter failed to say the requisite prayers, he would not receive the indulgence because he failed to fulfill both required acts. The indulgences therefore were not "sold;" the very giving of money was itself the first two requisite acts for gaining indulgence in question.

The so-called invention of New doctrines, which refers to the Church's proclamation of new dogmas, is the most baseless and ridiculous charge of all – for those "new" dogmas of the Church were actually old doctrines, dating back to the beginning of Christianity. In proclaiming them to be dogmas, the Church merely emphasized their importance to the Faith and affirmed that they are, in truth, part and parcel of divine revelation. The Catholic Church followed the same procedure when, in the fourth century, she Proclaimed the New Testament to be divinely revealed. Hence, it is obvious that the Catholic Church did not fall into error during the Middle Ages as some people allege, for if she had, she could not have produced those hundreds of medieval saints – saints the caliber of St. Francis, St. Bernard, St. Bonaventure, St. Claire, St. Anthony, St. Jonn of the Cross, St. Thomas Aquinas, St. Elizabeth and St. Vincent Ferrer (who performed an estimated 40,000 miracles)

Why do Catholics pray to Mary and the other saints when Sacred Scriptures states that there is one Mediator between God and man – Christ Jesus? (1 Timothy 2:5)

Answer: When Catholics pray to Mary and the other saints in Heaven they are not bypassing Christ, whom they acknowledge as the sole Mediator between God and man. They are going to Christ through Mary and other saints to intercede for them before the throne of Christ in Heaven. "For the continual prayer of the just man availeth much." (James5:16) How much more availing is the unceasing prayer of the sinless Mother of Our Lord Jesus Christ! St. Paul asked his fellow Christians to intercede for him: "Brethren, pray for us." (2 Thess. 3:1) And again: "I beseech you therefore, brethren, through our Lord Jesus Christ, and by the charity of the Holy Ghost, that you help me in your prayers for me to God…(Romans 15:30) Christ must particularly approve of our going to Him through Mary, His Blessed Mother, because He chose to come to us through her. And at Cana, He performed His first miracle after a word from His Mother. (John 2:2-11)

It is clear in Sacred Scripture that the saints in Heaven will intercede for us before the throne of Christ if they are petitioned in prayer, (Rev. 8:3-4) and it is clearing the records of primitive Christianity that the first Christians eagerly sought their intercession. Wrote St. John Chrysostom in the fourth century: "When thou perceivest that God is chastening thee, fly not to His enemies, but to His friends, the martyrs, the saints, and those who were pleasing to Him, and who have great power." If the saints have power with God, how much more His own mother.

Why do Catholics worship Mary as though she were a goddess, when it is clear in Scripture that she was not a supernatural being?

Answer: Catholics DO NOT worship Mary, the Mother of Christ—as though she were deity. Of all the misconceptions about Catholic belief and practice, this one is the most absurd. Catholics are just aware as Protestants that Mary was a human creature, and therefore not entitled to the honors which are reserved to God alone. What many non-Catholics mistake for adoration is a very profound love and veneration, nothing more. Mary is not adored, first because God forbids it, and secondly because the Canon Law of the Catholic Church, which is based on Divine Law, forbids it. Canon Law 1255 and the 1918 Codex strictly forbids adoration of anyone other than the Holy Trinity. However, Catholics do feel that Mary is entitled to a great measure of exaltation because, in choosing her as her Mother of Redemption, God Himself exalted her—exalted her more than any other person before or since. Catholics heap tribute and honor on Mary because they earnestly desire to be "followers of God, as most dear children." (Ephesians 5:1) Mary herself prophesied: "For behold henceforth all generation shall call me blessed.

Because he that is mighty, hath done great things to me; and holy is His name." (Luke 1:48-49) Catholics know that every bit of the glory they give to Mary redounds to the glory of her divine Son, just as Mary magnified God, not herself, when Elizabeth blessed her. (Luke 1:41-55) They know that the closer they draw to her, the closer they draw to Him who was born of her. In the year 434 St. Vincent of Lerins defended Christian devotion to Mary this way: "Therefore, may God forbid that anyone should attempt to defraud Holy Mary of her privilege of divine grace and her special glory. For by a unique favor of our Lord and God, she is confessed to be the most true and the most blessed Mother of God." Today 75% of all Christians still hold to this view.

Why do Catholics refuse to concede that their Church became doctrinally corrupt in the Middle Age, necessitating the Protestant Reformation?

Answer: Catholics refuse to concede such a thing out of faith in Jesus Christ. Christ solemnly pledged that the gates of Hell would never prevail against His Church (Mathew 16:18,) and He solemnly promised that after His Ascension into Heaven He would send His Church "another Paraclete…. the Spirit of truth," to dwell with it forever (John 14:16-17,) and He inspired the Apostle Paul to describe His Church as "the pillar ground of the truth." (1 Timothy 3:15) If the Catholic Church, (which Protestants admit was the true Church of Jesus Christ before Luther's revolt,) became doctrinally corrupt as alleged, it would mean that the gates of Hell had prevailed it – it would mean that Christ had deceived His followers. Believing Christ to be the very essence of truth and integrity, Catholics cannot in conscience believe that He could be guilty of such deception. Another thing: Catholics cannot see how the division of Christianity into hundreds of rival camps and doctrinal variations can be called a "reformation" of the Christian Church. In the Catholic mind, hundreds of conflicting interpretations of Christ's teachings do not add up to a true interpretation of Christ's teachings.

Why do Catholics believe that Peter the Apostle was the first Pope, when the word "Pope" doesn't even appear in Catholic Bibles? Just where does the Pope get his authority to rule over the Catholic Church?

Answer: True, the word "Pope" doesn't appear in the Bible – but then neither do the words "Trinity," "Incarnation," "Ascension," and "Bible" appear in the Bible. However, they are referred to by other names. The Bible for example is referred to as "Scripture." The Pope, which means head bishop of the Church, is referred to as the "rock" of the Church, or as the "shepherd" of the Church. Christ used that terminology when He appointed the Apostle Peter the first head bishop of His Church, saying: "Blessed art thou, Simon Bar-Jona...Thou art Peter, and upon this rock I will build my Church." (Mathew 16:17-19) "There shall be one fold and one shepherd." (John 10:16) "Feed my lamb...feed my sheep." (John 21:15-17) The words "rock" and "shepherd" must apply to Peter, and they must distinguish him as the head Apostle, otherwise Christ's statements are so ambiguous as to be meaningless. Certainly the other Apostles understood that Peter had authority from Christ to lead the Church, for they gave him the presiding place every time they assembled in council (Acts 1:15,5:1-10,) and they placed his name first every time they listed the names of the Apostles. (Mathew 10:2, Mark 3:16, Luke 6:13-14, Acts 1:13) In addition, there is the testimony of the Church Fathers. In the second century, St. Hegessipus compiled a list of Popes to the time of Anicetus (eleventh Pope,) which contained the name of St. Peter as first. Early in the third century, the historian Caius wrote that Pope Victor was the "thirteenth Bishop of Rome from Peter." In the middle of the third, St. Cyprian related that Cornelius, (twenty –first Pope) "mounted the lofty summit of the priesthood …the place of Peter." Even Protestant historians have attested to Peter's role as first bishop of Rome, first Pope of Catholic Church. Wrote the eminent Protestant historian Cave in his Historia Literaria: "That Peter was at Rome, and held the See there for some time, we fearlessly affirm with the whole multitude of the ancients." Hence the source of the Pope 's authority to rule over the Catholic Church is quite obvious: It was given him by none other than Jesus Christ –by God Himself.

Why does the Catholic Church base some of her doctrines on tradition instead of basing all of them on the Bible? Did Christ not tell the Pharisees that in holding to tradition they were transgressing the commandment of God?

Answer: Observe that in the Bible there are two kinds of religious tradition – human and divine. Observe that when Christ accused the Pharisees He was referring to "precepts of men," (Mark 7:7) to their human traditions. Christ wanted divine tradition preserved and honored because He made it part and parcel of the Christian deposit of faith – as the Apostle Paul affirmed: "Stand fast; and hold the traditions which you have learned, whether by word or by our epistle." (2 Thess. 2:14. Also see 2 Thess. 3:6) This divine tradition to which Paul refers – this revealed truth which was handed down by word rather than by letter – is the tradition upon which, along with sacred scripture, the Catholic Church bases her tenets of faith – as the primitive Christian Fathers affirmed. Wrote St. Augustine: "These traditions of the Christian name, therefore, so numerous, so powerful, and most dear, justly keep a believing man in the Catholic Church." The New Testament itself is a product of Christian tradition. Nowhere in the New Testament is there any mention of New Testament.

Why do Catholics repeat the same prayer over and over again when they pray the Rosary? Is this not vain repetition condemned by Christ in Mathew 6:7?

Answer: Catholics do not just repeat the same prayer over and over again when they pray the Rosary. The Rosary is a progression of many prayers – The Apostles Creed, the Lord's Prayer, the Gloria, the Hail Mary and the Salve Regina – and these prayers are accompanied by many holy meditations. As the Rosary progresses, Catholics meditate on the joyful, the sorrowful, and the glorious mysteries of the life of Christ and His Mother. True, the Hail Mary is repeated many times during the course of the Rosary, and some of the other prayers are repeated several times, but this is not "vain" repetition, certainly not the vain repetition condemned by Our Lord. The vain repetition He condemned is that of people who pray standing "in the corner of the streets, that they may be seen by men." No prayer is vain, no matter how often repeated, if it is sincere, for Christ Himself engaged in repetitious prayer in the Garden of Gethsemane (" ...he went again: and he prayed the third time, saying the selfsame word" – Mathew 26:39, 42,44) And we are informed in the Apocalypse (Revelation 4:8) that the angels in Heaven never cease repeating, night and day, the canticle: "Holy, Holy, Holy, Lord Almighty, who was, and who is to come." The publican humbly repeated the prayer: "O God, be merciful to me, a sinner," and he went away justified, whereas the Pharisee went home unjustified after his long-winded, extemporaneous prayer. (Luke 18:9-14) God was likewise pleased with the repetitious prayer of the three young men in the fiery furnace, whom He preserved miraculously untouched by the flames. (Dan. 3:52-90) Protestants also engage in repetitious prayer: the same prayers at mealtime grace, the same prayers at Benediction, etc. The time lapse is no factor; it is still repetitious.

Why do Catholics believe in a place between Heaven and Hell called Purgatory? Where is purgatory mentioned in the Bible?

Answer: The main body of Christians has always believed in the existence of a place between Heaven and Hell where souls go to be punished for lesser sins and to repay the debt of temporal punishment for sins which have been forgiven. Even after God forgave Moses, he was still punished for his sin. (2 Kings or 2 Samuel 12:13-14) The primitive Church Fathers regarded the doctrine of Purgatory as one of the basic tenets of the Christian faith. St. Augustine, one of the greatest doctors of the Church, said the doctrine of Purgatory "has been received from the Fathers and it is observed by the Universal Church." True, the word Purgatory does not appear in the Bible, but a place where lesser sins are purged away and the soul is saved "yet so as by fire," is mentioned. (1 Cor. 3:15) Also, the Bible distinguishes between those who enter Heaven straightaway, calling them "the church of the firstborn" (Heb. 12:23,) and those who enter after having undergone a purgation, calling them "the spirit of the just made perfect." (Heb.12:23) Christ Himself stated: "Amen I say to thee, thou shalt not go out from thence till thou repay the last farthing." (Mathew.5:26) And: "Every idle word that men shall speak, they shall render an account for in the day of judgment." (Mathew 12:36) These are obviously references to Purgatory. Further, the Second Book of Machabees, (which was dropped from the Scriptures by the Protestant Reformers,) says: "It is therefore a holy and wholesome thought to pray for the dead, that they may be loosed from sins."(2 Machabee 12:46) Ancient Christian tomb inscriptions from the second and third centuries frequently contain an appeal for prayers for the dead – which is meaningless if there is no Purgatory – was universal among Christians for the fifteen centuries preceding the Protestant Reformation. Furthermore, ordinary justice calls for a place of purgation between Heaven and Hell.

Take our own courts of justice for example. For major crimes a person is executed or sentenced to the life imprisonment (hell,) for minor crimes a person is sentenced to temporary imprisonment for punishment and rehabilitation, (Purgatory,) for no crime at all a person is rewarded with the blessing of free citizenship, (Heaven.) If a thief steals some money, then regrets his deed and asks the victim to forgive him, still insists on restitution. God, who is infinitely just, insists on holy restitution. This is made either in this life, by doing penance (Matt.3:2, Luke 3:8,13:3, Apoc.3:2-3, 19,) or in Purgatory.

Also what Christian is there who, despite his faith in Christ and his sincere attempts to be Christ-like, does not find sin and worldliness still in his heart? "For in many things we all offend." (James 3:2) "Yet there shall not enter into it (the new Jerusalem, Heaven) anything defiled." (Apoc. or Rev.21:27) In Purgatory, the soul is mercifully purified of all stain, there, God carries out the work of spiritual purification which most Christians neglected and resisted on earth. It is important to remember that Catholics do not believe that Christ simply covers over their sinful souls, like covering a manure heap with a blanket of snow (Martin Luther's description of God's forgiveness.) Rather,

Christ insists that we be truly holy and sinless to the core of our souls. "Be you therefore perfect, as also your heavenly Father is perfect." (Mathew 5:48) This growth in without sin – in Christian virtue and holiness – is of course the work of an entire lifetime, (and is possible only through the grace of God.) With many, this cleansing is completed only in purgatory. If there is no Purgatory, but only Heaven for the perfect and Hell for the imperfect, then the vast majority of us are hoping in vain for life eternal in Heaven.

Why do Catholics confess their sins to priests? What makes them think that priests can absolve them the guilt of their sins? Why don't they confess their sins directly to God as Protestants do?

Answer: Catholics confess their sins to priests because it is clearly stated in Sacred Scripture – God in the Person of Jesus Christ authorized the priests of His Church to hear confessions and empowered them to forgive sin in His Name. To the Apostles, the first priests of His Church, Christ said: "Peace be to y\ou. As the Father hath sent me, I also send you... Receive ye the Holy Ghost. Whose sins you shall forgive, they are forgiven them; and whose sin you shall retain, they are retained." (John 20:21-23.) Then again: "Amen I say to you, whatsoever you shall bind upon earth, shall be bound also in heaven; and whatsoever you shall loose upon earth, shall be loosed also in heaven." (Matt.18:18) In other words, Catholics confess their sins to priests because priests are God's duly authorized agents in the world, representing Him in all matters pertaining to the ways and means of attaining eternal salvation. When Catholics confess their sins to a priest they are in reality, confessing their sins to God, for God hears their confessions and it is He who, in final analysis, does the forgiving. If their confessions are not sincere, their sins are not forgiven. Furthermore, Catholics do confess their sins directly to God as Protestants do; Catholics are taught to make an act of contrition at least every night before retiring, to ask God to forgive them their sins of that day. Catholics are also taught to say this same prayer of contrition if they should have the misfortune to commit a serious sin (called a "mortal sin" by Catholics.)

Why do Catholics believe that Christ is sacrificed in each and every Mass, when scripture plainly states that He was sacrificed on Calvary once and for all?

Answer: Most non-Catholics do not realize it, but Christ Himself offered the first Mass at the Last Supper. At the last supper He offered (sacrificed) Himself to His Father in an un-bloody manner, that is, under the form of bread and wine, in anticipation of His bloody sacrifice on the cross to be offered on the following day, Good Friday. In the Mass, not now by anticipation, but rather in retrospect, Christ continues to make that offering of Himself to His Father – by the hands of the priest. "And whilst they were at supper, Jesus took bread, and blessed, and broke: and gave to His disciples, and said: 'Take ye, and eat. This is my body.' And taking the chalice, He gave thanks, and gave to them, saying: 'Drink ye all of this. For this is my blood of the New Testament, which shall be shed for many unto remissions of sins.'" (Mathew 26:26-28) Christ ordered His Church to perpetuate that sacrificial rite for the continued sanctification of His followers, saying, "Do this for a commemoration of me"(Luke 22:19) – so the Catholic Church complies with His order in the Mass. In other words, every Mass is re-enactment of Our Lord's one sacrifice of Calvary. The Mass derives all its value from the Sacrifice of the Cross; the Mass is that same sacrifice, not another. It is not essentially a sacrifice offered by men (although men also join in,) but rather it is the sacrifice of Jesus Christ.

Christ's bloody sacrifice on Calvary was accomplished "once," (Heb.10:10) just as Scripture says. The Catholic Church likewise teaches that the sacrifice of the Cross was a complete and perfect sacrifice – offered "once." But the Apostle Paul – the same Apostle who wrote this text in the book of Hebrews – also bears witness that the sacrificial rite which Christ instituted at the Last Supper is to be perpetuated – and that it is not only important for man's sanctification, but is the principal factor in man's final redemption. In 1 Corinthians 11:23-26, St. Paul tells how, at the Last Supper, our Lord said: "This do ye, as often as you shall drink, for the commemoration of me. For as often as you shall eat this bread, and drink the chalice, you shall show the death of the Lord, until he come." Thus at every Mass, the Christian has a new opportunity to worship God with this one perfect sacrifice and to "absorb" more of Christ's saving and sanctifying grace of Calvary. This grace is infinite, and the Christian should continuously grow in this grace until death. The reason the Mass is offered again and again is not from any imperfection in Christ, but from imperfect capacity to receive.

Finally, the holy sacrifice of the Mass fulfills the Old Testament prophecy: "For from the rising of the sun even to the going down, my name is great among the gentiles, and in every place there is sacrifice, and there is offered to my name a clean oblation: for my name is great among the gentiles, saith the Lord of hosts. (Mal. 1:11) The sacrifice of the Mass is offered every day throughout the world, and in every Mass the only truly "clean oblation" is offered, that is, Christ Himself, thus, the Mass is the perfect fulfillment of this prophesy.

Why do Catholics believe that good works are necessary for salvation? Does not Paul say in Romans 3:28 that faith alone justifies?

Answer: Catholics believe that faith and good works are both necessary for salvation, because such is the teaching of Jesus Christ. What Our Lord demands is "faith that worketh by charity." (Gal.5:6) Read Matthew 25:31-46, which describes the Last Judgment as being based on works of charity. The first and greatest commandment, as given by Our Lord Himself, is to love the Lord God with all one's heart, mind, soul and strength, and the second commandment is to love your neighbor as oneself. (Mark 12:30-31) When the rich young man asked Our Lord what he must do to gain eternal life, Our Lord answered: "keep he commandments." (Matt. 19:17) Thus, although faith is the beginning, it is not the complete fulfillment of the will of God. Nowhere in the Bible is it written that faith alone justifies. When St. Paul wrote, "For we account a man to be justified by faith, without the works of the law," he was referring to works peculiar to the old Jewish Law, and he cited circumcision as an example.

The Catholic Church does not teach that purely human good works are meritorious for salvation: such works are not meritorious for salvation, according to her teaching. Only those good works performed when a person is in the state of grace - that is, a branch drawing its spiritual life from the Vine which is Christ. (John 15:4-6) – only these good deeds work toward our salvation, and they do so only by the grace of God and the merit of Jesus Christ. These good works, offered to God by a soul in the state of grace (i.e…free of mortal sin, with the Blessed Trinity dwelling in the soul,) are thereby supernaturally meritorious because they share in the work and in the merits of Christ. Such supernatural good works will not only be rewarded by God, but are necessary for salvation.

St. Paul shows how the neglect of certain good works will send even a Christian believer to damnation: "But if any man have not care of his own, and especially of those of his house, he has denied the faith, and is worse than an infidel." (1 Tim.5:8) Our Lord tells us that if the Master (God) returns and finds His servant sinning, rather than performing works of obedience, He shall "shall separate him, and shall appoint him his portion with unbelievers." (Luke 12:46)

Furthermore, Catholics know they will be rewarded in Heaven for their good works. For the Lord Himself said: "For the Son of Man ...will render to every man according to his works." (Matt. 16:27) "And whosoever shall give to drink to one of this little ones a cup of cold water in the name of a disciple, amen I say to you, he shall not lose his reward. (Matt. 10:42) Catholics believe, following the Apostle Paul, "every man shall receive his own reward, according to his own labor." (1 Cor. 3:8). "For God is not unjust, that He should forget your work, and the love which you have shown in His name, you who have ministered, and do minister to the saints." (Heb.6:10) "I have fought a fight, I have finished my course, I have kept the faith. As to the rest, there is laid up for me a crown of justice, which the Lord the just judge will render to me in that day, and not only to me, but to them also that love His coming." (2 Tim. 4:7-8)

Still, Catholics know that, strictly speaking, God never owes us anything. Even after obeying all God's commandments, we must still say: "We are unprofitable servants; we have done that which we ought to do." (Luke 17:10) As St. Augustine stated: "All our good merits are wrought through grace, so that God, in crowning our merits, is crowning nothing but His gifts."

Had St. Paul meant that faith ruled out the necessity of good works for salvation, he would not have written: "...and if I should have all faith, so that I could remove mountains, and have not charity, I am nothing." (1 Cor. 13:2) If faith ruled the necessity of good works for salvation, the Apostle James would have not written: "Do you see that by works a man is justified and not by faith only? "...For even as the body without the spirit is dead; so also faith without works is dead." (James 2:24-26) Or: "What shall it profit my brethren, if a man say he hath faith, but hath not works? Shall faith be able to save him? (James 2:13) If faith ruled out the necessity of good works for salvation, the Apostle Peter would have not written: "Wherefore, brethren, labor the more, that by good works you may make sure your calling and election. For doing these things, you shall not sin at any time. For so an entrance shall be ministered to you abundantly into the everlasting kingdom of our Lord and Savior Jesus Christ." (2 Peter 1:10-11) If faith ruled out the necessity of good works for salvation, the primitive Christian Fathers would not have advocated good works in such powerful words. Wrote St. Irenaeus, one of the most illustrious of the primitive Fathers: "For what is the use of knowing the truth in word, while defiling the body and accomplishing the works of evil? Or what real good at all can bodily holiness do, if truth be not in soul? For these two, faith and good works, rejoice in each other's company, and agree together and fight side by side to set man in the presence of God." (Proof of the Apostolic Preaching) Justification by faith alone is a new doctrine; it was unheard of in the Christian community before the sixteenth century.

Why do Catholics believe their Holy Communion is the actual Flesh and Blood of Jesus Christ? Why don't they believe as Protestants do that Christ is only present symbolically, or spiritually, in the consecrated bread and wine?

Answer: Catholics believe that their Holy Communion, the Blessed Eucharist, is the actual Flesh and Blood of Jesus Christ because that is what Christ said It was: "This is My body...This is My blood" (Matt. 26:26-28, see also Luke 22:19-20 and Mark 14:22-24) because that is what Christ said they must receive in order to have eternal life: "...Except you eat the flesh of the Son of man, and drink His Blood, you shall not have life in you..." (John 6:48-52, 54-56,) and because that is what the Apostles believed: "The chalice of benediction, which we bless, is it not the communion of the blood of Christ? And the bread, which we break, is it not the partaking of the body of the Lord?" (1 Cor. 10:16) Therefore whosoever shall eat this bread, or drink the chalice of the Lord unworthily, shall be guilty of the body and of the blood of the Lord. But let a man prove himself: and so let him eat of that bread and drink of the chalice. For he that eateth and drinketh unworthily, eateth and drinketh judgment to himself, not discerning the body of the Lord." (1 Cor.11:27-29) Also, Catholics believe that Holy Communion is the actual Flesh and Blood of Jesus Christ because that is what all Christians believed until the advent of Protestantism in the 16th century.

Wrote Justin Martyr, illustrious Church Father of the second century: "This food is known among us as Eucharist...We do not receive those things as common bread and common drink; but as Jesus Christ our savior, being made flesh by the Word of God." Wrote St. Cyril of Jerusalem, venerable Church Father of the fourth century: "Since then Christ has declared and said, 'This is my body,' who after that will venture to doubt? And seeing that He has affirmed and said, 'This is my Blood,' who will raise a question and say it is not His Blood?" In addition to the witness of the Sacred Scripture and Christian tradition, Catholics have the witness of the Eucharist itself: On numerous occasions, great and awesome miracles have attended its display, and seldom has its reception by the Catholic faithful failed to produce in them a feeling of joyful union with their Lord and Savior. In the face of all this evidence, Catholics could hardly be expected to adopt the Protestant position.

If the Church really honors the Bible as the holy Word of God—if she really wants her members to become familiar with its truths-Why in times past did she confiscate and burn so many Bibles?

Answer: The Bibles which were collected and burned by the Catholic Church in times past—notably the Wycliff and the Tyndale Bibles—were faulty translations, and therefore, were not the holy Word of God. In other words, the Catholic Church collected and burned those "Bibles" precisely because she does honor the Bible, the true Bible, as the holy Word of God and wants her member to become familiar with its truths. Proof of this is seen in the fact that after those Bibles were collected and burned, they were replaced by accurate editions. There can be no doubt that the Wycliff and Tyndale translations were corrupt and therefore deserving of extinction, for no church has ever attempted to resurrect them. Nor can there be any doubt that the Bibles which replaced them were correct translation, because they have been long honored by both Protestants and Catholics. 2

E. COMMON CATHOLIC PRAYERS AND PRACTICE:

ANGELUS

The Angel of the Lord declared unto Mary…..

And she conceived by the Holy Spirit

Hail Mary….

Behold the Handmaid of the Lord….

Be it done unto me according to your Word.

Hail Mary…

The Word was made flesh…

And dwelt among us.

Hail Mary

Pray for us, O Holy Mary, Mother of God,

That we may be made worthy of the promise of Christ.

Let us pray: Pour forth, we beseech You, O Lord,

Your grace into our hearts that we to home the

Incarnation of Christ, Your Son, was made known by the message of an

Angel, by His Passion and Cross, be brought to the glory of

His resurrection through the same Christ our Lord, Amen.

Queen of Angels

Queen of Heaven , rejoice, alleluia:

For He whom you merited to bear,

Alleluia,

Has risen, as He said, alleluia.

Pray for us to God ,

Alleluia.

Rejoice and be glad, O virgin

Mary, alleluia.

For the Lord is truly risen, alleluia.

Let us pray:

O God, Who by the Resurrection of Your Son, our Lord Jesus Christ, granted joy to the whole world, grant we beg You, that through the intercession of the Virgin Mary, His mother, we may lay hold of the joys of Eternal Life, through the same Christ our Lord. Amen. (Prayed from Easter Vigil to Pentecost in place of Angelus)

The above prayers recall the Mystery of the INCARNATION, when God became man. Its name is Latin from the first word "the angel." Traditionally the Church bells toll for the Angelus to be prayed at 6:00 AM, 12 NOON and 6:00 PM

DIVINE PRAISES

Blessed be God.

Blessed be His Holy Name.

Blessed be Jesus Christ, True God and True man.

Blessed be the Name of Jesus.

Blessed be His Most Sacred Heart.

Blessed be His Most Precious Blood.

Blessed be Jesus in the Most Holy Sacrament of the Altar.

Blessed be the Holy Spirit, the Paraclete.

Blessed be the great Mother of God, Mary most Holy.

Blessed be her Holy and Immaculate Conception.

Blessed be her Glorious Assumption.

Blessed be the name of Mary, Virgin and Mother.

Blessed be St. Joseph, her most chaste spouse.

Blessed be God in His Angels and in His Saints.

The Divine Praises prayer, traditionally recited after BENEDICTION of the Blessed Sacrament, was composed in 1800 to atone for sins of disrespect and abuse of God's Name.

PRAYER FOR THE ROSARY

APOSTLES CREED

I believe in God, the Father Almighty,

Creator of Heaven and earth, and in Jesus,

Christ, His Only Son, our Lord, who was conceived by the

Holy Spirit, born of the Virgin Mary, suffered under

Pontius Pilate; was crucified, died, and was buried.

He descended to the dead. On the third day

He rose again. He ascended into

Heaven, is seated at the right hand of the

Father. He will come to judge the living and the dead.

I believe in the Holy Spirit. The

Holy Catholic Church, the

Communion of Saints, the forgiveness of sins

The resurrection of the body, and

Life Everlasting. Amen.

LORDS PRAYER

Our Father, who art in

Heaven, hallowed be thy Name.

Thy Kingdom come;

Thy will be done on earth as it is in Heaven.

Give us this day our daily bread,

And forgive us our trespasses as we forgive

Those who trespass against us.

And led us not into temptation but deliver from evil.

Amen.

HAIL MARY

Hail Mary, full of grace.

The Lord is with you.

Blessed are you among women, and blessed is the

Fruit of your womb, Jesus.

Holy Mary, Mother of God,

Pray for us sinners, now and at the hour of our death.

Amen.

GLORY BE

Glory be to the

Father and to the Son and to the

Holy Spirit.

As it was from the beginning,

Is now, ever shall be, world without end.

Amen.

O MY JESUS

O my Jesus, forgive us our sins, save us from the fires of

Hell, and lead all souls in Heaven, especially those in most need of

Your mercy. Amen.

HAIL HOLY QUEEN

Hail, Holy Queen, Mother of Mercy, our life, our sweetness, and our hope!

To you do we cry, poor banished children of Eve.

To you do we send up our sighs, mourning and weeping in this valley of

Tears,

Turn then, O most gracious Advocate, your eyes of mercy toward us.

And after this our exiles, show unto us the

Blessed Fruit of your womb, Jesus.

O clement, O loving, O sweet Virgin Mary.

Pray for us, O Holy Mother of God:

That we may be made worthy of the promises of Christ.

Let us pray:

O God, Whose Only- Begotten Son, by His life Death and

Resurrection has purchased for us the rewards of Eternal Life.

Grant, we beseech You, that by meditating upon these mysteries of the most

Holy Rosary of the Blessed Virgin Mary, we may both imitate what they

contain and obtain what they promise, through the same

Christ our Lord. Amen.

ROSARY MEDITATIONS

There have been traditionally 15 mysteries of the Rosary to meditate on the Life of Jesus: 5 Joyful, 5 Sorrowful, and 5 Glorious. Pope John Paul 11 recommended on October 16, 2002, five new mysteries, known as the Mysteries of Light or the Luminous Mysteries.

Basics of Catholic Faith

JOYFUL MYSTERIES:
- Annunciation — Luke 1: 26-38
- Visitation — Luke 1: 39-45
- Nativity — Luke 2: 1-20
- Presentation — Luke 2: 22-38
- Finding in the Temple — Luke 2: 41-51

LUMINOUS MYSTERIES:
- Baptism of Jesus in the Jordan — Mathew 3: 13-17
- His Self- manifestation at the Wedding of Cana — John 2:1-11
- His proclamation of the Kingdom of God, with His call to conversion — Mathew 4:12, 7:29
- His Transfiguration — Mathew 17:1-8
- Jesus institution of the Eucharist, as the Sacramental expression of the Paschal Mystery — Mathew 26:26-29

SORROWFUL MYSTERIES:
- Agony in the Garden — Mark 14:32-42
- Scourging at the Pillar — Mark 15:1-15
- Crowning with Thorns — Mark15: 16-20
- Carrying of the Cross — Luke 23:26-32

- Crucifixion   Mark 15:22-41

GLORIOUS MYSTERIES:

- Resurrection   Mark 16:1-8
- Ascension   Acts 1:6-12
- Descent of the Holy Spirit   Acts 2:1-13
- Assumption of Mary   Genesis 3:15
- Coronation of Mary   Revelation 12:1

CATHOLIC THEOLOGICAL VIRTUES

Faith – Personal Belief and Commitment to God

We believe in God and all that He has said and revealed to us, and that Holy

Church proposes for our belief, because God is truth itself.

Hope – Trust in God

We desire the Kingdom of Heaven and Eternal Life as our happiness, placing our

Trust in Christ's promises, relying not on our strength, but on the help of the

Grace of the Holy Spirit.

Charity – Self-giving Love of God and Others

We love God above all things for His own sake, and our neighbor as ourselves

for the love of God.

MORAL CARDINAL (Principal) VIRTUES

Prudence – Right Judgment

Practical reason to true good in every circumstance and choose right means of
achieving it.

Justice – Fair Trust to God and Others

Constant and firm will to give their due to God and neighbor

Fortitude – Courage

Firmness in difficulties and constancy in the pursuit of the good.

Temperance – Moderation

Moderates attraction of pleasures and provides balance in the use of created goods.

(Catechism of the Catholic Church, # 1812- 1828, 1806-1809)

GIFTS OF THE HOLY SPIRIT

Wisdom – Judgment using Divine Norms that flows from a loving union with God

Understanding – Deeper insights into Divine Truths

Knowledge – Grasp Truths of Faith

Counsel – Receptive to God to make right decisions

Piety – Worship of God and relate to all as children of God

Fortitude – Strength and power infused by God

Fear of the Lord – Reverence and love of God

1(Spiritual Theology, Aumann, p. 97.)

FRUITS OF THE HOLY SPIRIT:
CHARITY, JOY, PEACE, PATIENCE, KINDNESS, GOODNESS, GENEROSITY, GENTLENESS, FAITHFULNESS, MODESTY, SELF-CONTROL, CHASTITY
(Galatians 5: 22-23)

Charisms of Holy Spirit:

- Administration
- Encouragement
- Giving
- Mercy
- Teaching
- Discernment
- Voluntary Poverty
- Evangelism
- Missionary
- Hospitality
- Pastoring
- Celibacy
- Healing
- Prophecy

- Wisdom
-

Intercessory Prayer

- Craftsmanship
- Faith
- Music
- Helps
- Leadership
- Service
- Witnessing

(Taken from St. Mary's Of Assumption Church Bulletin May 2009)

F. ECUMENISM

I will begin this topic with the prayer of Pope John Paul 11:

"Let us pray for the unity of all Christians! This great gift that only God can grant can transform hearts, divisions, and the wounds of centuries, and expand the prayer that Jesus addressed to the Father for the unity of His Disciples: 'That they may all be one; even as thou art in me, and I in thee.' With this prayer we begin the ecumenical week, turning to our Christian brothers who are not yet fully united with us, and we invoke this unity as a gift from on high. Amen.

Pope John Paul 11 January 19, 1992

Richard J. Mouw, President of Fuller Theological Seminary in Pasadena, California, in his foreword of the book <u>Catholics and Evangelicals</u> wrote:

"In 1875 the great American evangelist Dwight L Moody received a letter from a Catholic monk in Wales. 'I must send one word of affectionate greetings in our Precious Redeemer's name,' the monk wrote, 'to say how rejoiced I am to hear and read of your powerful gifts from 'The Father of Lights,' good and perfect gifts indeed.' The monk went on to assure Moody that while his community engaged in 'the perpetual adoration of the Holy Sacrament' – a practice that he knew would make the evangelist nervous – he and his fellow monks also preached 'Jesus only as perfect, finished, and present salvation to all who are willing to receive Him. And the only work of evangelist is to give knowledge of salvation to His people.'

Moody was pleased to receive this letter, he seemed to have no doubt that the prayers of these monks were offered up by fellow Christians who had a deep commitment to the cause of the Gospel. In a recent biography of Moody, Lyle Dorsett provides several other examples of how Moody refused to conform to the typical evangelical anti-Catholicism of his day. While living in New England, the evangelist even made a personal contribution to the building fund in a local Catholic parish!

Moody's name was highly revered in the evangelical environs in which I was raised, but no one told me any stories about his friendly relations with Roman Catholics. The evangelicalism of my youth was rigidly anti-Catholic. I regularly heard preachers proclaim with considerable self-confidence that the Pope was the Anti-Christ. I also had first-hand experience with evangelicals who believed that Catholicism was uniformly a religion of 'pagan darkness,' and that the only hope that that the Catholics had was that they might get to heaven 'in spite of what their church teaches.'

All of this was forever changed for many of us in evangelical world by the Second Vatican Council. Indeed, it could be argued that the obvious signs of post –Vatican 11 rapprochement between evangelicals and Catholics is one of most important ecumenical developments of the past half-century. Not that these developments have ever taken a very 'official' shape. The 'Evangelicals and Catholics Together' documents, for example, received the endorsement of no ecclesial bodies. The new patterns of cooperation between Catholics and evangelicals have been largely local and ad hoc. This is the kind of arrangement, of course, that suits evangelicals nicely. We have not been much attracted to 'conciliar' ecumenism or ambitious denominational mergers. The Billy Graham crusade - where Christians of various denominations work together in a specific evangelistic effort – has been a more natural style of task –oriented ecumenism for us. Our new- found friendships with Roman Catholics, then has taken the form of what Timothy George has labeled 'an ecumenism of the trenches,' where evangelicals and Roman Catholics have found common cause on a number of issues that are a concern in the public arena, especially right-to life matters and other causes associated with a recent 'culture wars.' But these efforts have also inspired many grass roots evangelicals and Catholics to begin praying and studying the Bible together.

It would be irresponsible, however, simply to ignore theological discussion in all of this. Doctrinal concerns are too important to both of our communities. This is why this book of essays is an important gift to both Catholics and evangelical Protestants. The authors have been intensely involved in Catholic-evangelical dialogue, and they take on the 'big' topics on which the two communities have significant agreements: salvation, ecclesiology, authority, the sacraments, and evangelism. There are no attempts here at an easy consensus. But there are serious - and I think quite successful - the efforts to get past long-standing pattern of talking past each other. Important issues are engaged with deep respect and an obvious desire to find real commonalities.

In his book, <u>Christianity and Liberalism</u>, one of the classics of American evangelical thought, J. Gresham Machen – who was in the midst of intense debates with Protestant liberals of his day – observed that a wide 'gulf' existed between evangelical and Catholic thought. 'But profound as it is,' Machen continued, 'it seems almost trifling compared to the abyss which stands between us and many ministers of our own Church.' Catholics and evangelicals, said Machen, share a common commitment to the authority of Scripture and the affirmations of the classical creeds.

Machen was wise to highlight the differences between gulfs and abysses. In our post- Christian era, the abyss that separates historic Christianity and the culture of unbelief is indeed great. By comparison, while the space that separates evangelicals and Catholics may still be a gulf, it is not nearly as wide as it appeared to be in Machen's day. And the theological bridging efforts represented by these essays are clear evidence that the gap continues to narrow. 1

"Today, Catholic Christians are engaged in seeking to restore unity among Christians. This movement, 'fostered by the grace of the Holy Spirit, for the restoration of unity among all Christians,' is called ecumenical movement. It includes all who invoke the triune God and confess Jesus as Lord and Savior. Ecumenism is not an option for Catholic Christians today. The second Vatican Council called all Catholics to work and pray for the restoration of the unity of the Church. Pope John Paul 11 reaffirmed and deepened this teaching in his encyclical letter Ut Unum Sint ("That They May Be One..." issued on May 25, 1995.) The 'Decree on Ecumenism' spelled out The Catholic Church's approach to other Christians. This document takes pains to reassure Christians who might fear that Catholic ecumenism is only a disguised way to lure other Christians back to the Catholic Church. The second Vatican Council does not make a distinction between a true Church (the Catholic Church) and other 'false Churches,' but the bishops of the council preferred to speak of a fullness of the means of grace and salvation present in Catholic Church, with other Christian Churches or ecclesial communities having some share in that fullness. This means that Catholics can honestly approach other Christians as brothers and sisters in Christ without necessarily having in mind 'bringing them back to the fold' of the Catholic Church. The 'Decree on Ecumenism' shows the Catholic Church's respect for other Christians: 'All those justified by faith through baptism are incorporated into Christ. They therefore have a right to be honored by the title of Christian, and are properly regarded as brothers in the Lord by the sons of the Catholic Church."[2]

The Second Vatican Council also states that many elements and endowments of the Church of Christ and even the grace of Salvation may be found outside of the Catholic Church, especially in other churches and ecclesial communities. "The Dogmatic Constitution on the Church" states that "many elements of sanctification and truth can be found outside of her (the Catholic Church's) visible structure." The "Decree on Ecumenism" states that the worship and liturgical actions of other Christian bodies "can truly engender a life of grace and can be rightly described as capable of providing access to the community of Salvation.

A protestant leader, Samuel Mcera Cavert, examined the "Decree on Ecumenism" and came to this conclusion: The promise of a new era is especially evident in the new way in which the Decree speaks of non-Catholic Christians. No one can read it without being impressed by the respect shown for those outside of the Roman obedience and by the care which is taken to understand their position and to state it fairly. Moreover, instead of dogmatically insisting on their return to Rome as the only possible movement toward unity, the Decree is concerned with a movement toward Christ. From a protestant angle, this fresh orientation is of the highest consequence and is pregnant with creative possibilities." 3

The "Decree on Ecumenism" directs Catholics to work for Christian unity, but to leave the accomplishment of unity to God: "This most sacred synod desires that the initiatives of the sons of the Catholic Church, joined with those separated brethren, go forward without obstructing the way of divine Providence and without prejudging the future inspiration of the Holy Spirit. Further, this synod declares its realization that the holy task of reconciling all Christians in the unity of the one and only church of Christ transcends human energies and abilities. It therefore places its hope entirely in the prayer of Christ for the Church, in the love of the Father for us, and the power of the Holy Spirit. 'And hope does not disappoint because the love pf God is poured forth on our hearts by the Holy Spirit who has been given to us.' (Romans 5:5)

Basics of Catholic Faith

"Catholics are encouraged to share their faith, but this sharing is not just a one-way street. Catholics can also be strengthened in their faith and live the gospel by the witness of Evangelical Christians. This actually happened to me because I grew in the knowledge of our Lord and Savior through our Christian brothers. The "Decree of Ecumenism" also reminds us: "Nor should we forget that whatever is wrought by the grace of the Holy Spirit in the hearts of our separated brethren can contribute to our own edification. Whatever is truly Christian never conflicts with genuine interests of the faith; indeed, it can always result in a more ample realization of the very mystery of Christ and the Church." 4

Another new relationship of evangelicals and Catholics is represented by "Evangelicals and Catholics Together" (ECT,) a loose knit group of scholars organized by Richard John Newhaus, a convert to the Catholic Church and editor of the journal "First Things," and Charles Colson, former White House Counsel, now deeply involved in prison ministry. ECT's first effort was the unofficial statement, "Evangelicals and Catholics Together: The Christian Mission in the Third Millennium," signed by twenty Catholics and twenty Evangelical scholars after an eighteen- month consultation. Though theologically sophisticated, it tends to focus on those moral and social concerns shared by Catholic neo-conservatives and the religious right, among them opposition to abortion, euthanasia, pornography, and the ideas of marriage, parenthood, and family, tolerance "requires the promotion of moral equivalence between the normative and deviant." The statement supports the transmission of "our cultural heritage" and parental choice in public education, "a vibrant market economy," as part of a free society, and a renewed appreciation of western culture. 5

Thomas P. Rausch, S.J. Professor of Catholic Theology and chair of the Department of Theological Studies at Loyola Marymount University in Los Angeles writes:

"Catholics could learn a great deal about what Pope John Paul 11 has called the 'new evangelization,' calling those no longer involved with the church to a living sense of faith, from Evangelical Christians. Some Catholics are beginning to take them seriously, calling for new cooperation and learning from them about the needs of Hispanic Catholics. Evangelicals are showing a new interest in ecumenism. Some are learning to work with Catholics rather than presuming that joining a Protestant community is the only way to live a renewed life of faith. When Pope John Paul 11 visited New York in October 1995, there were several Evangelicals among the Christian leaders who met with him. At the gathering, Pat Robertson, Founder of CBN, pledged to work for unity between Catholics and Evangelicals.

He added: "At a recent meeting of our local dialogue, I listened to an Evangelical pastor – a very charismatic Hispanic, educated at Harvard University and Fuller Seminary – talking about members of his congregation who were former Catholics, as were his own parents. One was a grandmother, very catholic; her home full of shrines to the saints, but who never went to church. Another had been a member of the very large local Catholic parish, 'but not a Christian; she was doing drugs.' After her conversion, she wanted to be baptized, but the pastor did not allow her to until later, when her own parents also asked to become members of the church. A third remained active at the same

Catholic parish, but came each Wednesday night for Bible study, finding that his own life in Christ was beginning to deepen. A forth also remained in her parish, but finding its liturgy cold, came to the Evangelical church for its warmth and fellowship.

What if the pastors of the two churches were to begin their own local dialogue about the needs of their people? What if Catholic parishes or dioceses were to consider forming some of their lay ministers and evangelists in programs like Campus Crusade and Young Life? What if the growing interchange between Hispanic seminarians were to lead a new interest, by Evangelical pastors of tomorrow, in liturgical prayer and a sense for the catholicity and universality of the church? What if Catholics and Evangelicals were to admit how much they could learn from each other? 6

David E Bjork, who has been doing missionary work in France to work with Roman Catholic communities in the area of evangelism and discipleship training, wrote this essay, "When Obedience Leads into the Unknown," he writes part report and part personal testimony: "I am sad to have admit that it took three and a half years for God to overcome my religious prejudices. The first hurdle was recognizing Father Norbert as my brother in Christ. That hurdle was overcome rather quickly. As I got to know Father Norbert, as I witnessed the vitality of his faith and the consistency of his obedient submission to the spirit and the Scriptures, I was not only convinced of his relationship with the Savior, but challenged in my own walk with Christ. The second hurdle was more difficult to overcome. I was still plagued by the question: How can Father Norbert be an obedient disciple of Jesus Christ and remain a practicing Roman Catholic priest? The words of

Paul Billheimer, a former Radio pastor and Bible College president, helped me to understand that this is a question between Father Norbert and God, and not a question between Father Norbert and me;"

"If you are scripturally born again you are a member of the Body of Christ and a son of my very own Father. As a member of the same family, you are my own brother, whether you realize it or acknowledge it or not. As far as I am concerned, this is true whether you are a Charismatic or an anti-Charismatic; whether you believe that everyone should speak in tongues or whether you believe that speaking in tongues is of the devil; whether you believe that the gifts of the Spirit are in operation in the Church today or whether you believe they ceased at the close of the Apostolic age; whether you are an Armenian and believe in eternal security or in falling from grace: whether you accept only the "King James" or prefer a modern version; whether you believe in baptismal regeneration or no ordinances at all; whether you believe on immersion or sprinkling, infant or adult baptism; whether you wash feet or you don't; whether you are Methodist, Baptist, Presbyterian, Disciples of Christ, Church of Christ, Mennonite, Anish, Seventh Day Adventist, Episcopalian, Catholic or no denomination at all; whether you believe in female or only male ordination; whether you think that Saturday is the true Sabbath and should be kept holy or whether you think that the day is indifferent; whether you eat meat or vegetarian; whether you drink coffee, tea and soft drinks or only water, fruit juices or milk; whether you wear a toupee or sport a bald head; whether you color your hair or not; whether you are a pre- , a post -, or an amillennialist; whether you are a Republican, a Democrat or a Socialist; whether your skin is white, black, red, brown or yellow; and if there be any other doubtful matters...over which we differ…if you are born again, we are still members of the same family and organic parts of the same spiritual Body. I may think some of your beliefs are as crazy as a loon, but if I have sufficient love for God, agape love, I will not reject you as a person." (Paul Billheimer)

"As I got to know Father Norbert I began to realize that God's family extends beyond the limits of my own church denomination and reaches even into unexpected places. Perhaps Jesus was alluding to this reality when He said: 'I have other sheep that are not of this sheep pen. I must bring them also. They too will listen to my voice and there shall be one flock and one shepherd.' (John 10:16) I learned through a slow, painful, and drawn-out process, that my ability to fellowship with Father Norbert could not be based on shared theological understandings, liturgical practices, or on concepts and opinions concerning 'non-essentials.' If we were to come together it would be on agreement over Evangelical truths which are basic to salvation and on our common life in Christ." 7

I am so glad that I found this material in my research. I could not have agreed more to David Bjork's last comment. I experienced it first hand, his question about Father Norbert; how can I be obedient to Jesus Christ and remain a practicing Roman Catholic. The same exact question my Christian acquaintance asked me. The fact that Catholics bow or believe of the saints, there is no way that I am saved or that I am a Christian, so they told me, and they wanted me to leave Catholic Church at once. It has also been said that the Pope is the anti-Christ. I just know that this essay and the words of Paul Billheimer will help a lot of people and will stop the criticism and animosities between different denominations, particularly between Catholics and Evangelical Christians.

Cecil M. Robeck, Jr.; Associate Professor of Church History and Ecumenics at Fuller Seminary, Pasadena, is an Assemblies of God minister, in his essay, "Evangelicals and Catholics Together," he wrote seven guidelines for consideration for the future Ecumenism of Catholics and Evangelicals:

1. We must know our own traditions and be able to look at them with an objective eye, willing to acknowledge both strengths and weaknesses. This is frequently difficult for any of us to do, since all of our training within our respective traditions is spent in helping us see what is right about us and wrong about the other. We need to be honest and admit that all of us are flawed, and that all of us are something of the genius of God.

2. We must be willing to try to understand one another from the other's perspective, rather than merely our own perspective. But I suggest that this act, as much as anything, will help us to break down preconceived notions and long-nourished stereotypes. There is nothing like spending time together and listening to one another in a genuine attempt to get into each other's shoes that will ultimately help us gain greater understanding for one another.

3. We must be willing to compare strength for strength and weakness for weakness, and to admit it when we have violated this standard. Once again, this is a very difficult task. We are not used to doing this. But it seems to me to be only fair. It is very easy for us to proclaim our strengths and curse the weaknesses of others

but, without parity in the process, we run the risk of slandering one another or contributing to the bearing of false witness about one another instead of recognizing that we are both strong and flawed, and that we are attempting to serve the same Lord Jesus Christ.

4. Together we can approach the scriptures and ask what they say to our situation, if anything. I believe that this can be done without violating our confessional patterns; that is, Catholics need not deviate from magisterial teachings, and Evangelicals need not deviate from a position which allows both personal and communal attempts at exegesis. Whatever way it happens, it must be done openly and honestly, with all presuppositions on the table.

5. We need to be careful not to make premature or inappropriate judgments about one another, especially about the motives which we think the other might have for wanting the discussion in the first place. I recognize that this is a place where we risk some things, but within the Pentecostal community, as well as the remainder of the Evangelical community, there are many who fail at this point. They ascribe motives to Roman Catholics who look forward to dialogue with Evangelicals who are reminiscent of the pronouncement of Pope Pius X1 that any such conversation is a devious attempt to get Evangelicals back into the arms of Rome. But frequently they fail to assess that their own motives for attempting to persuade

Catholics to leave their own churches and join Evangelical ones.

It seems to me that sooner or later we must recognize that like all things which we do in our Christian walk, the pursuit of genuine understanding, to say nothing of unity, requires both honesty and risk taking. Not to ascribe preconceived motives is an act of trust, an act of faith in the One who called us as sisters and brothers to share at the one table. It would be a shame to miss the opportunity to do so, simply because we presume that the other partner cannot be trusted.

6. We need to avoid any willingness to compromise for the sake of some presumed level of unity. Genuine unity often comes even when we disagree profoundly over an issue, but we agree to disagree. This search for greater unity between us, for visible manifestations of unity between us, is like marriage. We will not agree on everything. We are entitled to our own opinions. Any attempt not to recognize this, or to smooth over differences as though they do not exist, is not helpful. We need to know where the rocks are. We need to be honest about our differences. People in dialogue with one another must know who they are and what they believe. They cannot be people who are prone to "spiritual insecurity" for that is what ultimately breeds to compromise, and compromise results in a false sense of unity.

7. Finally, we need to be open to the surprises which God might have in store for us, even up to and including what we might now be willing to call a new reality. I have already mentioned the dreams of Father O.C. Edwards and the National Council of Churches. I have mentioned, too, the dreams of Professor Mark Heim for the World Council of Churches. I have noted the proposal of Father Avery Dulles for an "ecumenism of mutual enrichment." To be quite honest, we do not know what form our life together as Christians will take in the future. But we must be willing to enter the future together with faith in the One who has called to us to oneness, even as He and the Father are One.

Robeck added in his conclusion: "If I could emphasize just one point, it would be the need for Evangelicals and Catholics to get to know one another. It is in the day-to-day life, in table talk, in dialogue, in personal sharing where the stereotypes will be dealt with, the fears will begin to dissipate, and real differences can be settled. If we are not there yet we can at least pause and pray together. There is something that is particularly humbling about kneeling at the foot of the cross before our common Lord and Savior, Jesus Christ. I find the words of Pope John Paul 11, in his encyclical "Ut Unum Sint," to be an especially good reminder of what love is all about. He writes:

"Love is the great undercurrent which gives life and adds vigor to the movement towards unity. This love finds its most complete expression in common prayer. When brothers and sisters who are not in perfect communion with one another come together to pray, the Second Vatican Council defines their prayer as the soul of the whole ecumenical movement. The prayer is 'a very means of petitioning for the grace of unity, a genuine expression of the ties which even now bind Catholics to their separated brethren.' Even when prayer is not specifically offered for Christian unity, but for other intentions such as peace, it actually becomes an expression and a confirmation of unity. The common prayer of Christians is an invitation to Christ Himself to visit the community of those who call upon Him: 'Where two or three are gathered in my Name, there I am in the midst of them.' (Mt.18:20) 8

Chapter 17

MY TESTIMONY

"Modern man listens more willingly to witnesses than to teachers

and if he listens to teachers he does so because they are witnesses."

Pope Paul VI

Testimony is defined: a witness; a statement made to establish fact.

Our personal testimony is a powerful tool. It is the expression of what God has done and is doing in our lives.

According to George Barna, fifty-two per cent of Americans reject the idea that sharing religious beliefs with others is a personal responsibility. Sixty-eight per cent of "Born Again" believers embrace this:

When you share what Jesus had done in your life, Jesus is the center of attention, then your testimony will sow the seed that the Holy Spirit will nourish into life. In sharing your testimony, you are doing evangelism. Evangelism involves presenting to God the person you are and the gifts He has given you and asking Him to show you how he wants to use you in people's journey toward Jesus. Your witness – your testimony—

Can mean the difference between heaven and hell for others. Most people want to hear first hand about what God has done in your life.

A few months after I became "Born Again" with the encouragement of our friend, Pastor Ed Lacaba, I wrote the following brief testimony that I shared with my family and friends. (1978)

My Testimony

I belong to a Catholic denomination which I acquired from birth. Since childhood, I prayed regularly (the memorized prayer that I learned from catechism,) and I went to Church every Sunday and holidays of obligation. My friends considered me a very religious person.

After a few years I got married and became less serious about my religion. My husband, who was a Hindu, didn't go to church and I hated to go alone. I was also preoccupied with my child and my schoolwork, (I went back to school to get my nursing degree.)

Somehow I started to doubt God's presence, especially when I took up "Introductory Philosophy," where we covered the Philosophy of Religion. The book's author was very convincing in saying that man created God. My doubts were even enhanced when I took up Biology where we covered the evolution theory, which stated that man evolves within his environment.

My Testimony

Six years after I finished my degree, I felt that something in my life was missing. I was busy being busy. I was promoted to a head nurse position, we bought a house in a nice area, but there was still a void in my life. I started to question, "What is my real purpose in this world?" During this time I realized that I was beginning to search for the truth. I started to read any religious book, and became interested with other religions. One of the religious books I read was the book by a certain religious sect in India called, "The way to Sainthood." In its introductory cover it was written that after reading the book, one was guaranteed to become a better person regardless of whatever religion he or she belonged to.

The Holy Spirit must have enlightened me a great deal because I started to see some truth. I became a better Catholic and went to church every Sunday and holiday obligation. I went to confession and received communion. However, at the back of my mind I still had doubts that Jesus is really the Son of God and if He really resurrected from death.

By then we moved to California, I met a friend at work who was a "Born Again" Christian. I did not know at first that she was also a Baptist missionary and a wife of a Pastor. I noticed that whenever we had a talk, we always ended up talking about God because whatever topic we discussed always had some connection with God. I admired her relaxed and composed personality, but most of all, the peace within her being was written all over her.

Later, her husband Ed came to know my husband Tony. Ed took my husband to Bible Studies and gave him a Bible. To make a long story short, my husband was baptized. I saw the change in Tony, he started reading the

Bible and started going with me to attend mass in Catholic Church. However, He still practiced his Hindu beliefs.

Tony decided to have a Bible study at home. Being a die-hard Catholic, I refused. After many arguments and disagreements I finally consented to have the Bible study at home, but I refused to attend. Sometimes, Ed would bring someone with him, but most of the time only Tony and Ed were having the Bible study. I am sure that they were praying for me because after a few weeks I started to attend the Bible study and started to show some interest in reading the Bible myself even if I did not understand most of it. I attended the Bible study and at the same time I was worried about what my Catholic friends and my family would say because I was having Bible study with a Baptist Pastor. During this time I still had doubts. In fact, I was so worried about this that I had to confess this embarrassing thing to our attendant who was a Christian at work. Then, in our Bible study, we discussed that Faith was a gift from God. I therefore prayed to God for Him to give me this gift.

Ed and his wife Nellie invited us for a Christian retreat in the mountains. In one of the services I went forward to accept Jesus as my Savior but I did not feel any change in me. I still had doubts and I even asked myself why I had made such a fool of myself by going forward during the altar call.

The following Saturday after I went forward to respond to that altar call I decided to read the Bible. After reading the Bible for two solid hours, I decided to stop and closed the Bible. While I was in deep thoughts thinking about my acceptance of Jesus during the retreat, I was unconsciously flipping the pages of the Bible, and my eyes were fixed to that part that said, "I am the Alpha and the Omega, the Beginning and the End. I will give of the fountain of the water of life freely to him who thirsts. (Rev.21:6)

I knew that Jesus was talking to me, saying that He is the Son of God, the part of the Triune God, and therefore He is God the Son. It had touched me so deeply, and for the first time I saw some light of the truth that I had been searching for; I started to cry. Since that time I have believed completely in Jesus Christ. I was given the gift of faith that I had prayed for, "Praise the Lord," I just had to open my heart and there He was, and the Holy Spirit came in. I believe the Holy Spirit guided me to read that part and enlightened me to its meaning. I have read this particular portion several times in the Scripture reading in Church, and I have heard it also through sermons and preaching, but it had not touched me at all.

After that experience I considered myself being reborn because I could feel the change in me. Religion still bothered me though. I still thought that Catholicism was the best and had the authority because Jesus appointed Peter to be the first leader of the Church and Peter was the first Pope. It bothered me because we Christians have so many different denominations. Why couldn't we Christians have one church since we all believed in the Father, His Son Jesus Christ and the Holy Spirit?

These questions were answered through my prayers. One Sunday, while we were attending the Catholic Church Mass, the priest said in His sermon that everyone should pray for the unity among Christians. He mentioned that we should respect and understand the other denominations and love them. He also said that Christian Churches are like pipelines and there is more than one pipeline that reaches God.

I'm very thankful to God that I came to know Him. I wish I knew Him earlier because my life would have been peaceful and more meaningful. I have more patience at work and in my home now. If I am upset or get angry, I repent and get over it very quickly. My worrying about something used to last for a long time, but it's different now.

I came to realize that religion did not help me get to know Jesus or get closer to Him. Instead, I find it a hindrance. To me, the most important thing is my true personal relationship with God through His Son Jesus.

I hope that this testimony of mine will bring my family and friends closer to God and allow them to experience what I have experienced. It's too bad I cannot express nor explain what I feel as a "Born Again" Christian. I can only say that there is inner change in me. I feel God's presence in me and I am more aware of His guidance. Also, now that I know Him, I can see and feel His many blessings which I failed to see and realize before.

Now I have the peace of God, and because I have peace I am more joyful, and most of all, my life is more meaningful.

Your sister in Christ,

Elma M. Chopra

1978

God uses us by commanding us to share his gospel with others. He can use us in different ways with our specific gifts and interests. I feel God wanted me to share my faith with others by inspiring me to write this book.

My Testimony

Pope John Paul II encouraged all of us Catholics and Christians to be a witness to others.

He writes:

Be Witnesses

"I would like to urge you today: Be witnesses. Witnesses of the hope that is rooted in faith. Witnesses of the invisible in a secularized society, which too often ignores every transcendent dimension.

Yes, consecrated souls: among the people of this generation, who are so immersed in the relative, you must be voices that speak of the absolute. Perhaps you have, so to speak, thrown all your resources into the scales of the world, gladly tipping them toward God and the goods promised by Him? You have made a decisive choice about your life: you have opted for generosity and giving in the face of greed and self-interest; you have chosen to count on love and grace, challenging those who consider you ingenuous and ineffectual; you have placed every hope in the kingdom of Heaven, when many around you are striving only to assure for themselves a comfortable stay on earth.

It is up to you now, to be integrated, in spite of every difficulty.

The spiritual destiny of many souls is linked to your faith and your integration.

You must be a constant reminder of that destiny which unfolds in time but has eternity as its goal, bearing witness with our words, and even more with our lives, that we must of necessity direct ourselves toward the one who is the inescapable end point of the parabola of our existence.

Your vocation
makes you the advance guard
of mankind on the march:
in your prayers
and in your work,
in your joy
and in your suffering,
in your successes
and in your trials,
mankind must be able to find
the model and the future
of what it too,
is called to be,
in spite of its own burdens
and its own compromises." [1]

Pope John Paul 11
Bologna, April 18, 1982

Taking An Interest In The World In Order To Transform It

My Testimony

"Christians, and especially you members of the laity, are called by God to become interested in the world in order to transform it according to the Gospel. Your personal commitment to truth and honesty occupies an important position in fulfillment of that task, because a sense of responsibility to truth constitutes one of the fundamental meeting points between the Church and society, between the Church and each man or woman. The Christian faith does not provide ready-made solutions to the complex problems of contemporary society, but it does provide a deep understanding of human nature and its needs, calling you to tell the truth in charity, to take up your responsibilities as good citizens, and to work along your neighbor, to construct a society in which genuine human values are fostered and intensified through a shared Christian vision of life." 2

Pope John Paul 11; Nairobi, May 7, 1980

The World Needs Your Testimony

"The world today needs to see your love for Christ, it needs public testimony of the religious life as Paul V1 once said: 'Modern man listens more willingly to witnesses than to teachers, and if he listen to teachers he does so because they are witnesses.' If the nonbelievers of this world are to believe in Christ, they need your faithful testimony---testimony that springs from your complete in the generous mercy of the Father and in your enduring faith in the power of the cross and the resurrection. Thus the ideals, the values, the convictions that are the basis of your dedication to Christ must be translated into the language of daily life.

Among the people of God, in the local ecclesial community, your public testimony is part of your contribution to the mission of the Church. As St. Paul says: 'You are a letter from Christ...written not with ink but with the spirit of the living God, not on tablets of stone but on tablets of human hearts." 3

The best way to end this chapter is to pray for the lost souls. Jill Briscoe in her book <u>Prayer That Works</u> wrote this prayer:

A Prayer About Lostness

"Oh God of love
Who would not that 'any' should perish
But that all would come to Christ and be forgiven:
Hear us now in this quiet moment.
Convince us that your word is true
And that choices are for now,
That there is a heaven where you live
And a hell where you do not.
Jesus said so.

Thank You Savior,
That we can have You in our hearts

My Testimony

And lives forever.

We pray for missionaries, pastors and teachers,
That would be bold to tell the bad news---
The reality of our lostness---
And then the good news that we can be found,
Saved from our sins,
Our emptiness, and our wishful wishes.

We pray, too, for our children,
That they believe while young,
Grow quickly into Christian maturity,
And serve You till they see You face to face!
In Christ's name,
Amen.

Chapter 18

CATHOLIC SAINTS

Catholics usually use the word "saint" to refer to people of outstanding holiness, especially those they believe to be with the Lord in heaven. Sometimes we hear an exceptionally holy person on earth called a "saint," like Mother Theresa of Calcutta often was during her life. In the New Testament however, the word has a broader meaning. Paul called all his fellow believers "saints," not just the notably holy ones (see Rom.12:13, 16:15,1 Cor. 16:1, Eph 1:1, Phil1:1, 4:21-22, Phlm 5.) Some Bibles translate "saints," as "holy ones," which has the same meaning. This is also what the Apostles Creed, one of the earliest statements of Christian faith, means when it proclaims: "I believe in the communion of saints."

The phrase "the communion of saints," refers to the bond of unity among all those, living and dead, who are or have been committed followers of Jesus Christ. St. Paul's favorite image for this unity or communion is the "body of Christ." He says of believers that, "so we, though many, we are one body in Christ, and individually members of one another." (Rom 12:5) The members of Christ's body are so united that "If one suffers, all suffer together…" (1 Cor

12:26) Jesus prayed that His followers would be united to each other just as closely as he was united to the Father (see Jn 17:20-23)

"This close, living unity among all who belong to God through Jesus is what the Creed calls 'communion.' When Catholics profess that they believe in the communion of saints, they are professing their unity with all the faithful followers of Jesus Christ.[1]

For Catholics, the communion of saints includes all of God's people—those in heaven, those on earth, and even those in a state of purification, (purgatory.) All of these people are in a communion because they are all in a real relationship with God through Jesus Christ, and hence are "one body in Christ, and individually members of one another."

Traditional Catholic Theology has called those saints still on earth the "church militant" (still fighting the good fight of faith,) those in purgatory the "church suffering" and those in heaven the "church triumphant." But these are not three distinct "churches," but together make up the one church of Jesus Christ: "All partake in the same love of God and neighbor, and all sing the same hymn of glory to our God." [2]

Canonization of Saints:

Canonization is an act by which a Christian Church declares a deceased person to be a saint, inscribing that person in the canon, or list, of recognized saints.

"In the Roman Catholic Church, the act of canonization is now reserved to the Holy See and occurs at the conclusion of a long process requiring extensive proof that the person proposed for canonization lived, and died, in such a way that he or she is worthy to be recognized as a saint. Originally, however, individuals were recognized as saints without any formal process, as happened, for instance, in the case of Saint Peter and the Blessed Virgin Mary.

Protestant practices, like the Lutherans, have a calendar of saints, but most protestant theologians and denominations, in an attempt to avoid veneration of certain believers above others, reject the notion of an official or recognized list of 'saints.' Protestants often appeal to the Bible's apparent recognition of all Christian believers as saints, in Acts and in Paul's letters. Also, since most Protestants reject prayer requests of the dead as impossible, much of other churches' motivation for canonization is removed in Protestant practice." [3]

"The process of canonization involves a careful investigation of the life of a person who has died to determine whether God has attested to their holiness through miracles, conversions, examples of exceptional holiness, and many other indicators. Those who are canonized, or officially recognized as saints by the Catholic Church, represent only a few outstanding examples of the myriad of other holy men and women who are fully united with the Lord. The canonized saints are not meant to be looked upon as an exclusive 'club' but as examples and models of holiness, representing all of the saints in heaven. The diversity of the canonized saints provides models for every Christian. Some saints led public lives and interacted with thousands of people while they lived. Other saints were obscure or little-known during their lives, but later their holiness was acknowledged by reports about their lives or by miracles worked through their prayers of intercession to God. The canonized saints include people from every state or situation in life: men and women, married and celibate, 'active' and 'contemplative' Christians, young and old, rich and poor, beggars and kings.

But why should Christians imitate the saints at all? Shouldn't we model ourselves after Jesus? Isn't He our only model? Of course Jesus Christ is the ultimate model for all Christians, but he is not our only model. His life is reflected in splendid and varied ways in the lives of those of the past and present who earnestly follow Him. This is another illustration of the incarnational principle. God works through his body, the Church. He knows that as a human being we necessarily model our lives on the lives of other persons, both living and dead. Indeed, one of the reasons why we imitate Jesus Christ is to reflect his life to those around us. As St. Paul boldly said, 'Be imitators of me, as I am of Christ' (1 Cor 11:1) and 'Brethren, join in imitating me, and mark those who so live as you have an example in us.' (Phil 3:17) The Second Vatican Council expressed this point as well:

'For when we look at the lives of those who have faithfully followed Christ, we are inspired with a new reason for seeking the city which is to come. (Heb 13:14, 11:10) At the same time we are shown a most safe path by which... we will be able to arrive at perfect union with Christ, that is, holiness. In the lives of those who shared in our humanity and yet were transformed into especially successful images of Christ (cf. 2 Corinthians 3:18,) God vividly manifests to men His presence and His face. He speaks to us in them, and gives us a sign of His kingdom to which we are powerfully drawn, surrounded as we are by so many witnesses (cf. Heb. 12:1) and having such an argument for the truth of the Gospel.'" [4]

I will mention briefly the life story of a few Catholic saints: St. Francis of Assisi, St. Patrick and St. Ignatius Loyola.

St. Francis of Assisi – Birthplace: Assisi, Italy

Feast Day: October 4

Francis was born in 1182 to a merchant couple who imported luxurious fabrics and sold them in Italy. His parents thought Francis would also become a successful fabric merchant. Instead, he decided to join the second crusade and had a fancy suit of armor made for him. But on his first night out, he had a vision: the Lord was sending him back. He then faced the jeers of his neighbors, who thought him a coward. Francis, undeterred, turned away from war to peace and vowed he would await a further sign from God.

Francis then had a vision in which God told him to repair His church. Francis took this literally and with his own hands began to rebuild the church where he had been praying. But God meant a bigger church: Francis's mission was to help rebuild the whole faith. Francis preached about humility, poverty, simplicity, and prayer to everyone, even the birds, which he thought of as God's special creations. While others took up arms in the later crusades, Francis went to the Muslim leader with a message of peace. He attempted to express God's brotherhood by truly living by the Gospel. But his life of poverty and wandering, while good for his soul, was hard on his body. Although he died in 1226, the Order he founded, the Franciscan Friars, carries on his humble teachings in every corner of the globe.

So often you hear, "There are no easy answers," but Francis never did anything the hardest way. He always looked for the simplest solution to every problem, believing that simplicity is one of the greatest virtues, one that helps lead to peace.

Francis's peacemaking abilities are the subject of legends, including one that has Francis making peace between a man-eating wolf and the village that was terrified of it. Perhaps that's just a legend, but there are simple things we can do to promote a peaceful life for our neighbors and ourselves, like finding time to pray everyday for peace, even if it's only a minute or two.

Prayer of St. Francis

"Lord, make an instrument of Your peace

Where there is hatred, let me sow love.

Where there is injury, pardon.

Where there is doubt, faith.

Where there is despair, hope.

Where there is darkness, light,

And where there is sadness, joy.

O Divine Master, grant that I may not so much seek to be consoled

as to console

to be understood, as to understand;

to be loved, as to love;

for it is in giving that we receive;

It is in pardoning that we are pardoned;

And it is in dying that we are born to eternal life.

(Copyright MMI IMP AB, "Ordinary People" produced under license by IMP Inc.)

St. Patrick – Birthplace: Scotland

Feast Day: March 17

Although he is the patron saint of Ireland, Patrick was not a native of that country; he was born in Scotland in 385. When he was just 14, he was captured and taken to Ireland, where he was enslaved. During this time of trial, he turned to God for comfort and strength; and he felt no sadness.

After Patrick had been in Ireland for six years, God came to him in a dream and told him to go home. Patrick escaped and was reunited with his family, but he still heard the Irish calling to him in dreams. Patrick entered the priesthood and eventually became a bishop; after many years of doing great work in Rome, Patrick was sent to Ireland to spread the message of the Gospel because he was able to speak Celtic, and was also able to communicate with the Irish. Patrick's mission was not an easy one. Druidism (an ancient Celtic religion,) was widely practiced in Ireland, and many Druids would rather have killed Patrick than convert; he and his followers were imprisoned and sentenced to death many times. But Patrick's faith in God was strong, and he knew he could keep going, "spreading God's name everywhere with confidence and without fear." Patrick preached all over Ireland, using a shamrock to explain the Trinity and converting thousands with his quiet, un-assuming manner and gentle way of speaking.

As a man of God, Patrick was known for his humility and disinterest of material wealth. He wouldn't accept gifts from admirers, and often retreated in quiet prayer. By the time he died in 461, Patrick had converted virtually all Ireland to Christianity, and he is a reminder that God speaks to us through His servants.

One way or another, we all face the same challenge that Patrick did: we may be asked to do things that don't make sense to us at the time, or be asked to forgive people that wronged us, or we find ourselves in situations that are not what we had planned. But each of us can find the courage to do God's will if we trust in Him and believe in His love for us.

Prayer of St. Patrick

"I bind to myself God's power to guide me, God's might to

uphold me, God's wisdom to teach me, God's eye to watch over

me, God's ears to hear me, God's word to give me speech,

God's hand to guide me, God's shield to shelter me, God's host to secure me...

Against the snares of demons, against the seduction of vices,

Against the lust of nature, against everyone who meditates injury to me,

Whether far or near, few or many." (Copyright MMI IMP AB, "Ordinary People" Under license by IMP Inc.)

St. Ignatius Loyola

Birthplace: Spain

Feast Day: July 31

Born Inigo de Loyola in 1491, Ignatius came from a noble family in northern Spain. A page at the age of 16, he quickly learned the pleasures of court life.

He eventually joined the army, and was severely wounded when he was 30. He recuperated but was disfigured with one shortened leg and a protruding bony knob below his knee. Because of his vanity, he insisted that the knob be sawed off (without the benefit of anesthesia,) and the shortened leg be stretched, which proved unsuccessful.

During his long recuperation, he began to read books written on the life of Christ and the saints. During this time he discovered that when his thoughts turned to Christ and the saints, he experienced a sense of peace and serenity, his conversion had begun.

His Mystical Encounters –While on a journey to Barcelona, Ignatius had a vision of God, which gave him a whole new outlook on creation, and led him to the belief that God could be found in all things. With this new insight, he joined the priesthood. On a trip to Rome, he had another mystical encounter, in which God told him he would one day be in the company of Christ.

The Start of New Order – Once in Rome, he and his companions started the Society of Jesus, an order that was under the direct order of the Pope. Members called Jesuits traveled wherever their help was needed, and Ignatius spent the rest of his life in service to the poor and in writing and teaching adults and children—always underscoring the omnipresence of God.

The spirituality of St. Ignatius espoused is still flourishing today within the Society of Jesus, which now has 25,000 members scattered throughout the world. In keeping with his love for teaching and service to God.

- The society of Jesus is affiliated with 28 U.S. colleges and 46 secondary schools
- Jesuits serve throughout the U.S. and 112 countries.

- Many of heir social ministries address the need of the poor and helpless.

But ministries are not only for the clergy. We too can live a faith-filled life and share our talents with others. As St. Ignatius believed, God can be found in all things—including each one of us. Why not take time to find a way to share your faith? (Copyright MMI IMP AB, "Ordinary People" under license by IMP Inc.)

Prayer of St. Ignatius

"Teach us to be generous, good Lord;

Teach us to serve You as You deserve;

To give and not to count the cost,

To fight and not heed the wounds,

To toil and not to seek for rest,

To labor and not to ask for reward

Save that of knowing we do Your will."

--St. Ignatius Loyola

Saint or Sinner

The Bible says that our righteousness is like a filthy rags and that all have sinned and come short in the glory of God. We are all sinners saved by the grace of the Almighty God through Jesus dying on the cross. John said: "If we say that we have no sins, we deceive ourselves, and the truth is not in us. If we confess our sins, He is faithful and just to forgive us our sins and to cleanse us from all our unrighteousness. If we say that we have not sinned, we make Him a liar and His Word is not in us." Also, in his letter to the Romans, Paul wrote:

"As it is written:

There is none righteous, no not one;

There is none who understands;

There is none who seeks after God.

They have all gone out of the way;

They have together become unprofitable;

There is none who does good, no not one.

Their throat is an open tomb;

With their tongues they have practiced deceit,

The poison of asps is under their lips,

Whose mouth is full of cursing and bitterness.

Their feet are swift to shed blood;

Destruction are in their ways;

And the way of peace they have not known.

There is no fear of God before their eyes."

(Romans 3:10-18)

"But now the righteousness of God apart from the law is revealed, being witnessed by the Law and the Prophets, even the righteousness of God which is through faith in Jesus Christ to all and on all who believe. For there is no difference; for all have sinned and fall short in the glory of God, being justified freely by His grace through the redemption that is in Christ Jesus." (Romans 3:21-25)

For new believers who do not know his or her new position in Christ after their salvation, will have a hard time believing that they are called saints. As a believer, we are sanctified in Christ. If we live a surrendered life to Jesus, the holiness of Jesus will become ours and will be exhibited in us. The most wonderful secret of living a holy life does not lie in imitating Jesus, but in letting the perfect qualities of Jesus exhibit themselves in our human flesh. In Colossians 1: 27 it says; "To them God willed to make known what are the riches of the glory of this mystery among the Gentiles: which is Christ in you, the hope of glory." Sanctification is "Christ in you.... It is His wonderful life that is imparted to us in sanctification – imparted by faith as a sovereign gift of God's grace."

"Sanctification means the impartation of the holy qualities of Jesus Christ to me. It is the gift of His patience, love, holiness, faith, purity, and godliness that is exhibited in and through every sanctified soul. Sanctification is not drawing from Jesus the power to be holy—it is drawing from Jesus the very holiness that was exhibited in Him, and that He now exhibits in me. The perfection of everything is in Jesus Christ, and the mystery of sanctification is that all the perfect qualities of Jesus are at my disposal. Consequently, I slowly but surely begin to live a life of inexpressible order, soundness, and holiness—'.... kept by the power of God...'" (1 Peter 1:5) 5

In the Old Testament the saints are mentioned in Psalms:

"And to the saints who are on the earth, they are excellent ones, in whom is all my delight." (Psalm 16:3)

"Oh, love the Lord, all you saints! For the Lord preserves the faithful." (Psalm 31:23)

"For the Lord loves justice, and does not forsake His saints; they are preserved forever, but the descendants of the wicked shall be cut off." (Psalm 37:38)

Paul in his letter to the Corinthians states: "Paul, a called apostle of Christ Jesus through the will of God, and Sosthenes the brother, to the church of God which is in Corinth, to those who have been sanctified in Christ Jesus, the called saints, with all those who call upon the name of our Lord in every place, who is theirs and ours." (Cor.1:1-2) The believers in Christ are called saints, not called to be saints. This is a positional matter, sanctification in position with a view of sanctification in disposition. To call upon the name of the Lord implies to believe in Him.

"For through Him we both have access by one Spirit to the Father. Now therefore, you are no longer strangers and foreigners, but fellow citizens with the saints and members of the household of God." (Ephesians 2:18-19)

Therefore, a saint is the term used as Jesus' followers and disciples. Based in St. Paul's teaching, we can rightfully say we are saints. Instead of saying: "I am just a sinner saved by the Almighty grace of God," now we can rightfully say, "I am a saint saved by the Almighty grace of God."

Chapter 19

HEAVEN

"O Death, where is thy sting?

"O grave, where is thy victory?

(1 Cor. 15:55 KJB.)

Most people who are interested in knowing about heaven are the elderly and the people with terminal illness. You know the reason why, because they are closer to getting there.

Besides, looking forward in getting to heaven, meanwhile, we need to address the common problem that most elderly person experiences. As an elderly person myself, I need to cope or learn to overcome this problem.

"Depression is common to general elderly population. In a study of well functioning adults over the age of sixty, 20 to 25 percent were determined to be at least mildly depressed. In a longitudinal study of elderly patients with chronic illness, 47 percent of these patients have diagnosable depression." [1]

When a person looses their spouse on top of their existing depression and chronic illnesses, their grief and pain can be overwhelming in spite of medications and counseling, like my beloved mother in law Raj Chopra. After her husband of 60 years passed away, she passed away a year and a half later. I used to tell her, "Mom, I prayed for your long life and happiness," and her respond, "Not long life please just good health!"

Without a deeper relationship with God, it will be very hard to shake off this problem of depression. When I was going through my loneliness and depression because of the divorce, I tried to find my satisfaction with God as I went through life living by myself. It was not easy making adjustments to coming home to an empty house, with no one expecting your return, and I was scared more than I wanted to admit, especially at night. Every day I surrendered my life to Him (Jesus.) I took my suffering of pain and loneliness as an act of obedience to His divine will. Pain as C.S. Lewis said, is God's megaphone. He whispers to us in our joys, speaks to us in our conscience, and shouts to us in our pain. The pain of loneliness is one way in which God wants to get our attention.

Divorce is a terrible thing. Divorced people like me hate it almost as much as God does, but it is happening all the time, smashing families and individual lives to bits, and creating chaos in church and society. The loneliness and pain caused by divorce is just as painful as losing a husband or wife through death.

Elizabeth Elliott, former missionary and author of many books, said: "Loneliness comes over us sometimes as a sudden tide. It is one of the terms of our humanness, and in a sense, therefore, incurable. Yet I have found peace in my loneliest times not only through acceptance of the situation, but making it an offering to God, who can transfigure it into something for the good of others."

When we think of being lonely, we usually mean that there are no people around, no one with us, no one to talk to. Or else we find that the people around us are not our wavelength; they don't understand us, and that can be worse than no company at all. So loneliness in my experience and what my mother in law experienced, is not relieved by just anyone's company. My mother in law was never left alone. Her family made sure that someone was with her. Yet she was very lonely because she was missing her husband. When you are lonely you need that someone special—someone who understands you, someone who can listen and be there when you need them. Out of all my friends, not one person could be with me all the time, and even if they could, none of them had the power to do anything about my situation. It was ultimately my problem.

Yet in the Bible, God is saying in Psalm 68:6: "God makes a home for the lonely." God could do something about our loneliness. If you look at the rest of the Psalm, it says that God can "do something" about a lot of things. Nothing is too difficult for Him.

The Psalmist goes on to elaborate from history exactly what that means: God is always on the side of His people in their battle for survival, from the massive exodus from Egypt to the individual plight of widows and orphans. God cares about justice. He is full of mercy. The giant scope of His power in world affairs does not cause Him to overlook our individual concerns. And He has come to earth to prove it, because of that, He can sympathize with our weakness.

He understands our feelings because when being human, He experienced loneliness too.

"We may be missing the fact that it is here, where we happen to be at this moment and not in another place or another time, that we may learn to love Him – here where it seems He is not at work, where His will seems obscure or frightening, where He is not doing what we expected Him to do, where He is most distant or absent. Here and nowhere else is the appointed place. If faith does not go to work here, it will not go to work at all." 2

The response of faith is different from the response of the rest of the world. I say that I found peace in my faith. The kind of peace that the world cannot give comes to me not by the removal of suffering, but in another way through acceptance. Amy Carmichael knew a good deal about suffering of many kinds, including loneliness. She knew the temptation to try to escape by forgetting, by drowning the trouble with activity, by shutting oneself off to the world, by surrendering to defeat and sullen resentment. She also knew that none of the above would lead to peace. She found what does lead to peace, here and now:

> He said, "I will forget the dying faces;
>
> The empty places,
>
> They shall be filled again.
>
> O voices moaning deep within me, cease."
>
> But vain the word; vain, vain:
>
> Not in forgetting lieth peace.

Heaven

He said, "I will crowd action upon action,
The strife of faction
Shall stir me and sustain;
O tears that drown the fire of manhood, cease."
But vain the word; vain, vain:
Not in endeavor lieth peace.

He said, "I will withdraw me and be quiet,
Why meddle in life's riot?
Shut be my door to pain.
Desire, thou dost befool me, thou shalt cease."
But vain the word vain, vain:
Not in aloofness lieth peace.

He said, "I will submit; I am defeated.
God hath depleted
My life of its rich gain.
O futile murmurings, why will ye not cease?"
But vain the word; vain, vain:
Not in submission lieth peace.

He said, "I will accept the breaking sorrow
Which God tomorrow
Will to His son explain."

Then did the turmoil deep within him cease.

Not vain the word,, not vain;

For in acceptance lieth peace.

"Loneliness will not disappear at once. We have to remind ourselves that we are made for God's purpose. Loneliness can be a wilderness but it can be a pathway to God. What we can do of our loneliness right now is to receive it. We have to receive it willingly as of God then offer it thankfully back to God. In doing this, you will find that you will be alone but not be lonely. You will find solace in solitude, and your sacrifice will bring you a step closer to spiritual maturity." 3

This particular scripture helped me in dealing with my pain and sufferings:

"We can be full of joy here and now even in our trials and troubles. These very things will give us patient endurance; this in turn will develop a mature character, and a character of this sort produces a steady hope, a hope that will never disappoint us." (Romans 5:3-5)

The passing of my mother in law is causing a lot of pain and grief to the family. My sister-in-law, Tony's sister, in her eulogy in her mother's funeral, she described my mother-in-law exactly as I have known her for forty years. She is one of the most important people in my life and I feel I need to include it here:

MY MOM

"Thank you for joining us today in paying our last respects to my mother. My brother Amrit (Tony) and my sister Elma, who are now the elders in our family and loved Mom immeasurably, could not be here in person but their thoughts are most definitely with us.

I am sure that my brothers share my sentiments when I say that we were especially privileged and blessed to have her as our mother. Over the last few days I've been told by many people that they feel like they, too, have lost their "Mom." This is a testament to her loving nature. Both my parents had the ability to make people feel that they were a part of their family. Dad always said that Mom was a fountain of love.

How can words even begin to describe the incredibly special person who was my Mom? She was the epitome of kindness; a gentle and caring soul whose heart was filled with concern and compassion for everyone. She never judged others and always had a sympathetic ear and a helping hand for anyone who needed it. She chose to see only the good in others. Although quiet and simple, she was a pillar of strength. She displayed immense strength in coping with physical and other challenges that life brought her and didn't complain. Her wisdom was imparted lovingly but only when asked. She had a deep understanding of spirituality. Dad would ask her questions on various religious, spiritual matters and her answers always amazed him. That's why he referred to her as his Guru.

My Mom and Dad shared a very special relationship. They got married when they were only in their teens and were together on this earth for sixty years. They say marriages are made in heaven. Theirs certainly was. If any two people were meant for each other, it was them. The tremendous love and respect that each felt for the other was clearly evident. They complemented each other beautifully. As far as I can remember, my Mom always had a glow and a smile on her face. She lost both the day that Dad passed away along with her will to live. In the year that she lived with me after Dad went, I could tell that she was totally lost without my Dad and saw no purpose in going on, when life meant it had to be lived without him. She repeatedly said that she wanted to go without suffering, quickly and peacefully and join Daddy in heaven. She got her wish, I'm absolutely sure, on both counts.

She spent her life doing "seva" (service) for others; for family, for friends and, of course, until the end, Narayan seva (service to the needy in the name of God.) She was a devoted wife, a dutiful daughter-in-law, a dedicated mother and non-interfering mother–in-law, a very proud Grandma and Bari Nani (great grandma,) a loving sister and Bhabhi, a caring Aunt, and a compassionate friend. She touched many lives.

It is said that "mother is our consolation in sorrow, our hope in weakness. She is the source of love, mercy, sympathy and forgiveness. He who loses his mother loses a pure soul who blesses and guards him constantly.

On Friday April 20 2007, We lost our mother, our friend, our angel. Mom, we hope you're breathing easier now. You are a very pure soul and we love you more than words could ever say. A part of us went with you. We will love you and treasure your memories always. You will live in our heart until the end of our days."

Tina Chopra Chetan

Heaven

There are many jokes about mother-in-law, but I never can accept or laugh at them. Although there is some truth in them as some acquaintance of mine shared their experiences as to how bad their relationship with their mother-in-law had been. I can never sympathize with them because my mother-in-law was superb and exceptional. She really was capable of loving everyone unconditionally including myself. You could not help but love her back. I know I was lacking in so many ways and I was not as dutiful a daughter-in-law as I was supposed to be, but I never heard her complain about me. All I heard was praises, saying good things about me that I know I really did not deserve.

I feel that I lost a real mother, not a mother-in-law. I grieved for her terribly as much as I grieved when my mother passed at the age of forty-five. I remember my mother-in-law most especially during this particular incident. A few months after we got married, we had our first big fight. My mother-in-law came over to see me. She never drove a car so she asked someone to drive her to our apartment. She tried to console me, holding my hand and sometimes touching my face. She never took sides but just listened intently. Just to make me feel better she asked me, "What do you want me to do with Tony?" I said, "I don't know but I am really mad and angry at him." Then Mom said, "Don't worry the next time I will see Tony I will pull his hair for you!" Before leaving she said, "Rani, you have to stop this and make up, okay?" "Rani" means "queen" in Hindu language. Queen is my affectionate name from Tony's mother and his grandmother. Can you believe that? In spite of my being a Filipino, different from their own culture, Tony's family accepted me whole-heartedly. Being alone with no family in Canada, and with no savings,

Tony's family shouldered all our wedding expenses, (except for my wedding dress.)

"God makes a home for the lonely" can also be translated as "God sets the lonely in families," I have come to know the reality of another family in "the Chopra family," other than my natural family. Even though I was already divorced with Tony, they still cared for me. My mother-in-law still continued to care and keep in touch with me. She listened to my complaints and problems, cried with me and encouraged me.

Thank God I was able to honor and show my love and respect for my mother-in-law during my son's wedding. As I was thanking our guests, and as I welcomed Mala to our family, I said: "I hope I will be a good mother-in-law to you Mala just like my mother-in-law Raj Chopra, she is the best mother-in-law in the whole world!" And I asked her to wave to identify herself in the crowd, which she gladly did beaming with a smile. Now that she is gone, I am thankful to God that I was able to let her know that I appreciated and loved her even though I did not tell her as often as I should have. I looked forward to seeing my in-laws, especially my mother-in-law, along with my own parents in heaven. What a day it would be to have a reunion with them in heaven after this life.

Now that I am in the winter years of my life, heaven comes to my mind every now and then. Heaven is much closer to me now. I can't wait to be with my Lord Jesus forever. You might ask me how I can be so sure that I am going to heaven. My answer is, not because I earned it. I know that I am going to heaven because Jesus said so. "Most assuredly, I say to you, unless one is "Born Again", he cannot see the kingdom of God." "Most assuredly, I say unto you, unless one is born of water and the Spirit, he cannot enter the kingdom of God." (John 3: 3,6) If you will ask me, "How about those of other religions, are they going to heaven?" My answer is that it is only God who can answer this question. I only believe what is in the Bible about my Christian faith. "Born Again" experience is available to everyone who accepts or receives Jesus as their personal savior, if you ask Jesus to forgive all your sins and finally if you live your life totally surrendered to Him only, you also have the assurance of heaven: "In My Father's house are many mansions; if it were not so, I would have told you. I go to prepare a place for you. And if I go to prepare a place for you, I will come again and receive you to Myself; that where I am, there you may be also." (John 14: 2-3) And, "Then we who are alive and remain shall be caught up together with them in the clouds to meet the Lord in the air. And thus we shall always be with the Lord." (1 Thess. 4:17)

I heard a joke about a taxi driver and a preacher that died and went to heaven. The taxi driver was met by St. Peter and was ushered to a nice mansion. The preacher said to himself, "Wow! My mansion should be much bigger and much nicer because I was preaching the word of God." Then St. Peter took the preacher to a small and not so nice mansion. The preacher complained to St. Peter and asked, "How come the taxi driver got a nice and big mansion he was not even serving God!" St. Peter replied, "You see my friend when you preached you put your congregation to sleep, when the taxi driver drove, his passenger prayed!"

Some people think Heaven will be dull and boring. But I say it will not be boring because our heavenly Father is not boring. God is the source of everything; therefore the desire of pleasure and joy comes from Him. Man is boring but not God. The Bible states: "Behold, I tell you a mystery: We shall not all sleep, but we shall all be changed – in a moment, in the twinkling of an eye, at the last trumpet. For the trumpet will sound, and the dead will be raised incorruptible, and we shall be changed. (1 Cor. 15:51-52) "For our citizenship is in heaven, from which we also eagerly wait for the Savior, the Lord Jesus Christ, who will transform our lowly body that it may be conformed to His glorious body, according to the working by which He is able even to subdue all things to Himself." (Philippians 3:20-21)

We will all be changed so we will not be boring anymore. Heaven is not boring because our Father's house is a happy home, because our friends and our families here on earth will be there. Just like being in a strange place and having the joy of seeing a familiar face. Not one of us who enters the Father's house will feel lonely or strange, for we who have put our trust in Jesus are part of His family, sharing Heaven's joys forever with all our brothers and sisters in Christ. "But you have come to Mount Zion and to the city of the living God, the heavenly Jerusalem, to an enumerable company of angels, to the general assembly and church of the firstborn who are registered in heaven, to God the Judge of all, to the spirits of just men made perfect." (Hebrews 12:22-23)

Heaven will be a happy home because we will be working there. There will be work to do for God's saints. We will be servants of God. "Therefore they are before the throne of God, and serve Him day and night in His temple. And He who sits on the throne will dwell among them." (Rev.7:15) Heaven will be a comfortable place because there will be no more hunger or thirst, because the Lamb of God (Jesus) will shepherd and lead us to the living fountains of waters. "They shall neither hunger or thirst anymore; the sun shall not strike them, nor any heat; for the

Lamb who is in the midst of the throne will shepherd them and lead them to living fountains of waters. And God will wipe away every tear from their eyes." (Rev. 7:16-17) In our final judgment, God's elect or saints, His faithful servants will enter and enjoy His kingdom and will be rulers of many. "His Lord said to him, well done good and faithful servant; you were faithful over a few things, I will make you ruler over many things. Enter into the joy of the Lord. (Matt. 25:21)

St. Peter told us about new world; new heaven and the new earth: "But the heavens and the earth which now exist are kept in store by the same word, reserved for fire until the day of judgment and perdition of ungodly men." (2 Peter 3:7) "But the day of the Lord will come as a thief in the night, in which the heavens will pass away with a great noise, and the elements will melt with fervent heat; both the earth and the works that are in it will be burned up." (2 Peter 3:10)

In the book of Revelation, it also states: "And I saw a new heaven and a new earth; for the first heaven and the first earth passed away, and the sea is no more. And I saw the holy city, New Jerusalem, coming down out of heaven from God, prepared as a bride for her husband." (Rev.21:1-2) "And anything common and he who makes an abomination and a lie shall by no means enter to it, but only those who are written in the Lamb's book of life." (Rev.21:27) This new world is promised by God, and He has not broken a promise. He kept His promise to send God (Jesus) to die for our sins. The promise world, the prospective world – the new world which is "heaven" (2 Peter 3:12-13) is designed for God's glory where righteousness dwelleth and cannot be destroyed. "Therefore, since all these things will be dissolved, what manner of persons ought you to be in holy conduct and godliness. Nevertheless we, according to His promise, look for new heavens and new earth in which righteousness dwells. Therefore beloved looking forward for these things, be diligent to be found by Him in peace without spot and blameless."

Some people do not believe that there is heaven or hell, but I do because Jesus said so. In His parable He gave: "The kingdom of heaven is like treasure hidden in a field. When a man found it, he hid it again, and then in his joy went and sold all he had and bought that field. Again, the kingdom of heaven is like a merchant looking for the pearls. When he found one of great value, he went away and sold everything he had and bought it." (Matt.13:44-46)

The way to heaven cannot be found through works. In Philippians 3, Apostle Paul tells us that if anyone could have confidence in earning righteousness, he himself would be the one. Paul achieved the highest level of righteousness through the Hebrew laws, but he knew that none of it meant a thing in bringing him purity before God. Paul said: "Whatever things were gain to me, those things I have counted as loss for the sake of Christ." (Philippians 3:7) He knew that he must give up any claim to righteousness of his own doing. He knew that his righteousness came from Jesus because of what He did, dying on the cross to save all of us. The way to heaven is found through rebirth. Jesus told Nicodemus, "Unless one is born again he cannot see the kingdom of God." (John 3:3) Nicodemus wanted to know how a person could re-enter the mother's womb to be born a second time. Jesus meant a new kind of birth. In the original language of this Gospel the term "born again" is also translated as "born from above." When we are physically born, we have earthly limitation; rebirth is the work of God from above through the Holy Spirit.

Heaven

Some day you and I will meet Christ the King; the King of Kings in heaven. His presence we can only bow and praise. Our cry will be that of Revelation: "You are worthy O Lord, to receive glory and honor and power." (Rev. 4:11) I hope my friend, that you are ready to see Jesus face to face. The time for you to prepare is now, by committing your life to Jesus Christ and begin to live as a child of the King.

The best description of what heaven is like is in Revelation Chapter 21. Pastor McGee described this chapter as the unveiling of eternity. Apostle John said, "And I saw a new heaven and a new earth: for the first heaven and the first earth passed away: and the sea is no more." (Rev.21:1) The scripture clearly teaches that this present order of creation is to pass away in order to make room for a new heaven and a new earth. The Lord Jesus Christ Himself said, "Heaven and earth shall pass away...." (Matt. 24:35) The old creation was made for the first Adam. Christ, the last Adam, has a new creation for His new creatures. "For, behold, I create new heavens and a new earth: and the former shall not be remembered, nor come into mind." (Isaiah 65:17) "For as the new heavens and the new earth, which I will make, shall remain before me, saith the Lord, so shall your seed and your name remain." (Isaiah 66:22) [4]

"And I John saw the holy city, New Jerusalem, coming down out of heaven from God made ready, as a bride adorned for her husband." (Rev. 21:2). The following is Pastor McGee's commentary on this particular verse. He said: "This is a part that should interest us. I believe that the New Jerusalem is where those of us who are children of God are going to live. When you talk about going to heaven, what do you think about it? To most it is just 'a beautiful isle of somewhere.' However, it is a definite place. It is a city called the New Jerusalem. It is a planet within itself. Very candidly, very little is said in Scripture about heaven – but here it is, and that is the reason this ought to be important to us.

'I saw the holy city, new Jerusalem, coming down out of heaven from God, made ready as a bride adorned for her husband.' This New Jerusalem should not be identified as the old Jerusalem, the earthly Jerusalem down here.

I cannot think of a lovelier description than this: 'made ready adorned for her husband.' It has been my privilege in my many years in the pastorate to marry several hundred couples. I have never seen an ugly bride – they are always lovely. At the wedding ceremony, after the solos have been sung, the preacher walks in followed by the bridegroom and the best man. Nobody pays any attention to the bridegroom except his mama. She smiles at him and thinks he's wonderful, but nobody looks at him. In a minute here comes the bride-to-be and I tell you everybody stands up and looks at her. I have never yet seen an ugly bride. On occasion when I would return from a wedding which my wife did not attend, she would always ask me, 'Was the bride beautiful?' And I would always answer, 'Yes, I've never seen an ugly one.' Don't think I am just a doting old man when I say that. I have seen some brides before they got married or after the wedding, and I have wondered if she were the same girl who had come down the aisle. God gives to them at that time a radiance and beauty. That is a thrilling moment for the bridegroom to look down the aisle and see the one whom he is going to make his own – she will belong to him. It seems that for that moment God transforms every girl into a lovely bride.

I think the reason He does it is that the New Jerusalem where we are going to live is like the bride adorned for her husband. What a picture we have here! The New Jerusalem is the habitation, the eternal home that is prepared for the church. The Lord Jesus said: 'I go to prepare a place for you, and if I go to prepare a place for you, I will come again, and receive you unto myself; that where I am, there ye may be also.' (John 14:2-3) You could not have a lovelier or more appropriate picture given. We have seen in Revelation 17:7-8 that ushering in the millennial period, actually before Christ returned to the earth, was the marriage of the Lamb, and the bride was the Church. At the judgment seat of Christ, there will be the straightening out and the judging of believers. Everything that is wrong will have to be corrected. All sin will be dealt with there. Rewards will be given out. And He is going to do something else – He is going to clean the Church with the Word. The Word of God is a mighty cleansing agent. 'That he might present it to himself a glorious Church, not having spot, or wrinkle, or any such thing; but that it should be holy and without blemish.' (Eph.5:27) 5

Billy Graham in one of his sermons, made the following statement, "If I believe in the reality of heaven, then I must also believe in the reality of hell. I know some people do not believe in hell but I do. In the New Testament, the word hell is used to translate two words, (1) Hades, generally meaning the same as Sheol, the place of the dead (2) gehenna, the place of retribution for evil deeds. (Concordance) Jesus said, "I am He who lives, and was dead, and behold, I am alive forevermore. Amen. And I have the keys of Hades and death." (Rev. 1:18) Jesus also said, "But I say to you that whoever is angry with his brother without a cause shall be in danger of judgment.

And whoever says to his brother, 'Raca!' shall be in danger of council. But whoever says, 'You fool!' shall be in danger of hell fire." (Mathew 5:22) ("Raca" is defined by the New Testament Recovery Version as an expression of contempt.) You see, Jesus believed in hell, so we should also believe it. Some people ask, "How can a loving God send people to hell?" Billy Graham answered this question very clearly:

"God is a God of love, but it is important to remember that He is also a holy, righteous and just God who cannot overlook sin. Sin is far more terrible than any of us can imagine—and we are all guilty of sin in God's sight. Provision for its forgiveness cost the very Son of God His life.

It is not God's desire that any person should suffer an eternity in hell. The Bible says, 'He is patient with you, not wanting anyone to perish, but everyone to come to repentance.' However, God will not force anyone to go to heaven. If we willfully refuse to turn from sin to God, with faith in Jesus' sacrifice for sin, God has no alternative. His justice demands that those who disregard and reject His loving offer of pardon will pay the penalty for their own sins forever in hell.

Don't take the terrible risk of losing your soul by delaying your decision. Choose Christ and eternal life now! The Bible says, 'Now is the time of God's favor, now is the day of salvation." [6]

I will include in this topic another joke, this was sent to us by my sister in law, Tina. This confirms the statement I heard frequently "Everyone wants to go to heaven but no one wants to die or every one is afraid to die."

Heaven

From: Ram Lakhan
Date: 11/24/04 09:58:22
To: Ram Lakhan
Subject: emailing to a loved one!

A man checked into a hotel. There was a computer in in his room, so he decided to send an e-mail to his wife.

However, he accidentally typed the wrong e-mail address,

Meanwhile.....somewhere in Houston, a widow had just

returned home from her husband's funeral. The widow decided to check her e-mail, expecting messages from relatives and friends. After reading the first message, she fainted. The widow's son rushed into the room, found his mother on the floor, and saw the computer screen which read:

To: My Loving Wife

Subject: I've reached

Date11/12/04

I know you are surprised to hear from me. They have Computers here now, and you are allowed to send e-mails to your loved ones. I've reached and have been checked in. I see that everything has been prepared for your arrival tomorrow. Looking forward to seeing you then! Hope your journey is as uneventful as mine was.

I strongly feel the Holy Spirit leading me to tell you about my dream in 2003. I dreamt that I was in the church or a temple with other people. It was like a graduation ceremony. I can remember my garment vividly. We were all wearing white. The reason I remember most about my white dress is because this robe was very simple; cut like a hospital patient's gown with an opening in the back. This white robe was made of satin, silky material, the best kind I ever saw. Surprisingly, this robe, like a hospital patient's gown fit me perfectly, very nicely fitted, just like a wedding gown, and I felt like I was getting married. I had such a joyful feeling while waiting patiently for the ceremony to start. It reminded me of my wedding day, full of happiness and excitement. All of a sudden I heard at the back someone call my name. I looked back and it was Tony. Then I woke up.

The dream was so unusual that I wrote it down immediately in my journal. I seldom have dreams, and when I do, I usually forget it when I wake up. When I told Tony about my dream, his comment was, "I told you I would make it to heaven." I do not know if this dream had something to do with heaven, I know that I have read somewhere in the Bible, about white robes, but when I looked it up in the Concordance, Revelation 9 mentioned white robes; "After these things I looked, and behold, a great multitude which no one could number, of all nations, tribes, peoples, and tongues, standing before the throne and before the Lamb, clothed with white robes, with palm branches in their hands, and crying out with a loud voice, saying, 'Salvation belongs to the God who sits in the throne, and to the Lamb.' And all the angels stood around the throne and the elders and the four living creatures, and fell on their faces before the throne and worshiped God, saying:

'Amen! Blessing and glory and wisdom, Thanksgiving and honor and power and might, Be to our God forever and ever. Amen.' Then one of the elders answered, saying to me, 'Who are these arrayed in white robes, and where did they come from?' And I said to him, 'Sir, you know.' So he said to me, 'These are the ones who come out of the great tribulation, and washed their robes and made them white in the blood of the Lamb.' (Rev. 7: 9-14) Also, in Revelation19:7-9 it tells about the Lamb's marriage and His marriage dinner. In verse 9, it says: "Then he said to me, Write Blessed are those who are called to the marriage supper of the Lamb! " And he said to me, "These are the true sayings of God." The marriage dinner of the Lamb here is the wedding feast in Matt.22:2. It will be a reward to the overcoming believers.

The lesson I can get from this dream is for me to stay focused on Jesus, to stay holy and worthy to be able to stand before my Heavenly Father and my Lord and Savior when I will meet Him face to face in heaven.

"Only one life, twill soon be past;

Only what's done for Christ will last.

Life is a glorious opportunity if it is used to condition us for eternity. If we fail in this, though we succeed in everything else, our life will have been a failure. There is no escape for the man who squanders his opportunity to prepare to meet God.

You will never live this day again; once it is gone, it is gone forever. How will you spend it – for yourself or for Christ? Remember: Only what is done for Christ will last." [7]

Heaven is full of unimaginable glory and splendor. I can't help but remember the chorus of the song:

"…When Jesus comes back receiving His Bride/ There will be no more pain / No more sorrow / No waiting for elusive tomorrows / There will be no more pain / No more sorrow / No more strivin or strain/ No more pain."

The verses of the song were taken from Revelation 21:4, "And God will wipe away every tear from their eyes; there shall be no more death, nor sorrow, nor crying; and there shall be no more pain, for the former things have passed away." And in verse 25, "Its gates shall not be shut at all day there shall be no night there."

Another song was also taken from this wonderful Bible verse:

"What a day that will be, when my Jesus I shall see,

And I look upon His face, the One who saved me by His grace…

There'll be no sorrow there, no more burdens to bear,

No more sickness, no pain, no more parting over there.

And forever I will be with the One who died for me;

What a day, glorious day, that will be." (See Rev.21:4) 8

"But until then, my heart will go on singing, until then with joy I'll carry on

Until the day my eyes behold the city, until the day God calls me home." 9

A most recent popular Gospel song "I Can Only Imagine," is my favorite, and I think it is an anointed song because most of the time when I listen, it brings tears in my eyes:

"I can only imagine what it will be like

When I walk by your side

I can only imagine what my eyes will see

When your face is before me

I can only imagine

Chorus:

Surrounded by Your glory

What will my heart feel?

Will I dance for You Jesus, or in awe of You be still?

Will I stand in Your presence or to my knees

Will I fall? Will I sing Hallelujah?

Will I be able to speak at all?

I can only imagine, I can only imagine.

I can only imagine when that day comes

And I find myself standing in the Son

I can only imagine when all I will do is

Forever, forever worship You

I can only imagine, I can only imagine.

I can only imagine when all I will do is forever, forever worship you." 10

In 2 Timothy 4:6-8, St. Paul wrote to Timothy:

"For I am already being poured out as a drink offering, and the time of my departure is at hand. I have fought the good fight, I have finished the race, I have kept the faith. Finally, there is laid up for me the crown of righteousness, which the Lord, the righteous Judge, will give to me on that Day, and not to me only but also to all who have loved His appearing."

St. Paul was saying that he was ready for his departure, his death, and he was confident of his eternal security in heaven because he fought the good fight, finished the race and kept the faith as a Christian. He also had the assurance that he would get the "crown of righteousness" as his reward.

Like St. Paul, we can also end our life here on earth, full of confidence and unafraid to die if we acknowledge our sinfulness and receive Jesus as God's payment for our sins.

As a believer in Jesus, if we follow Him and keep the faith without wavering, (based on the truth we have known,) if we live a sanctified life, trusting Him through it all, our eternal security once and for all is secure. Lastly, we can get our reward, the "crown of righteousness" waiting for us when we go to heaven.

I look forward to being with the risen King, Lord Jesus, and He will be sharing His heaven's glory with all of us, His children.

Chapter 20

MY PILGRIMAGE TO NAJU, KOREA

In the middle of March 2007, I received a call from Carmelita, my friend and my previous co-worker. She asked me if I was interested in going with her for a pilgrimage to Naju, Korea, where mother Mary cried tears, and tears of blood, many times. Carmelita added, "I wish you could go so we could be room-mates." I was about to tell her that I was not interested since I was scheduled to go to Canada, Turkey, and the Philippines. Instead I said, "I will pray about it!" Then Carmelita said before hanging up the phone, "I will also pray about it, but you have to give me an answer by Monday."

After I hung up the phone I thought to myself that this pilgrimage might renew my relationship with Virgin Mary the mother of God. Since I became "Born Again," because of the Baptist denomination influence, the focus of my prayer was mainly Jesus and the Blessed trinity. I completely stopped praying the Rosary and I seldom prayed the Hail Mary. Before I slept that night, I prayed the following prayer:

"Lord Jesus I only want to do your will, please tell me if you want me to go to this pilgrimage." Then I prayed the

"Our Father," "Hail Mary," and ended it with "Glory be to the Father, to the Son and to the Holy Spirit." That night I dreamt that I was in a plane with a group of people that I didn't know and when I looked around the plane I saw Carmelita, then I woke up. I took that dream as God's approval. Monday morning before my daily walk I told Tony; "Guess what! I am going to Korea for a pilgrimage!"

We stayed overnight in Seoul, Korea and the next morning we left for Naju, Korea. That same day in the evening we attended a prayer meeting held in the Lady of Naju chapel. I felt the warm and kind welcome of the Korean people. I was tired because of the jet lag but we had to attend this prayer meeting. The chapel was filled to the capacity; about two hundred people. We prayed the joyful, sorrowful, glorious and luminous mysteries of the rosaries, then the thanksgiving, worship songs and the prayer for Blessed Mother's intercession. Among our group from Los Angeles, only four of us were first timers. Most of them had been to this pilgrimage more than three times. Our pilgrimage coordinator had been to this pilgrimage many times. She told us that after she had been to Naju the tenth time, she stopped counting. I have the feeling that it is her ministry now to take people to Naju for pilgrimage. Several of the pilgrims in our group had the conversion experience while in Naju. We learned later, that one of the pilgrims in our group would relate her conversion experience in the next overnight prayer service that we would be attending in a few days.

The second day of our itinerary was a visit to the Blessed Mother's mountain in Naju. The Blessed Mother's mountain is known to be a special place of graces. This mountain is a sacred place chosen by her and blessed with miraculous changes in the Eucharistic species twice, descent of the Eucharist twice, and descent of Our Lord's

My Pilgrimage To Naju, Korea

Precious Blood and Our Lady's tears of blood seven times between 1995 and 2003. This mountain is also the site of a miraculous spring, which has been instrumental in numerous physical healings. Frequently, the air on the mountain becomes filled with a fragrance of roses. The area above the spring has been landscaped in the design of the reverse side of the Miraculous Medal of the Blessed Mother. Apparently, the Blessed Mother instructed Julia Kim in a vision to come to this mountain. Above this area, there is a replica of Mt. Calvary with a large crucifix and statues of Our Lady, St. John, Mary Magdalene, and a Roman soldier. Encircling this whole area is the way of the cross with fifteen stations. This mountain is located five miles west of Our Lady's Chapel where her statue, which wept and exuded oil, is being preserved and honored.

On January 18, 1990 Jesus promised Julia, "In the not-too-distant future, through my mother, I will give you a miraculous spring close to your place, which will be overflowing with love and grace and through which souls and bodies can be healed." On August 26, 1992, while praying, Julia saw a vision of the Blessed Mother climbing up a mountain, carrying several large bundles of soiled clothes and linens, one on her head, two in her hands, and more pushed forward with her feet. She stopped near a large creek with crystal clear water and began washing the clothes and linens. Down the stream, not far from where the Blessed Mother was, many people were drinking the water and washing themselves with it. Some were playing joyfully in the creek. The next day Julia went to the place that she had seen in the vision and began digging with her bare hands the ground where she had seen the creek. Every time she dug the ground water came out and a stream of water began, and this was repeated until there were seven streams of water. When she dug the eighth time, the seven streams merged into one. In her message to Julia on the same mountain on May 27, 1993, the Blessed Mother said, "I will make this place a shrine of mine and wash numerous souls who are walking towards hell." [1]

My first impression of the Blessed Mother's mountain was the awesomeness of the place. The serenity and the vibration of the place charged me spiritually. As soon as we arrived our pilgrimage coordinator took us to the area where we could drink the water coming from the miraculous spring. Then I started praying in front of the statue of Jesus in Gethsemane, then to the grotto of the Blessed Mother. Just before our lunch I bathed in the area provided for the pilgrims. Pilgrims that needed healing bathed here. The water here came from the miraculous spring. I heard that many were healed after bathing. I didn't have any ailment, but I bathed anyway in behalf of my sister–in-law and my friend who were ill. After our lunch, our group prayed the Rosary, followed by the Chaplet of Divine Mercy prayer. After our group prayer I asked Carmelita if she would like to join me in doing "The Way of the Cross," and she agreed. The atmosphere and the experience of climbing the mountain while doing the way of the cross made me feel so close to Jesus and made me feel very bad that He had to go through all the sufferings for my sins. I felt like crying but I held it back. When we reached the fourteenth station, I saw a perfect round light about the size of the Eucharist host just below the picture of Jesus being buried. The light moved from one spot to another, but stayed within the boundary just below the picture of Jesus. As soon as we finished our prayer for this station, I started to check where the light came from. I thought it was the reflection of the sun or my watch. Then I asked Carmelita if she saw what I saw. She said, "Yes," and said, "I am also wondering where that light come from." After this happened I tried to meditate more deeply the significance of this miraculous event in my life.

FIRST SATURDAY VIGIL

May 5, 2007 was the first Saturday vigil in honor of Blessed Mother's Day. When we arrived at the Blessed Mother's mountain, the place where we gathered for service was filled to capacity. I heard that there were more than 2000 people there. At three in the afternoon, the way of the cross began. I noticed that many people who followed the way of the cross were walking bare foot against the tiny, sharp rocks of the footpath. I don't know how they did it. I had a hard time climbing without sliding down the mountain with my good shoes, how much more without shoes. Again, I was touched with the whole experience and felt deeply the sacrifice and the sufferings of Jesus. I felt that the glory of God's presence was with us at this moment. This time I was not ashamed to cry. I cried freely because I was not the only one crying. Many were crying. The person leading the way of the cross was crying also. When the way of the cross was over, most of the crowd stayed at the scene of Calvary at the statue of the crucified Jesus. I was glad to see Carmelita on my way down because I got separated from her because of the crowd.

As we were talking and walking down, a Korean lady told us to look up to see the sun. When I looked up, I saw a bright light of white rays first, then I saw the sun radiating with different rainbow colors, blue, green, purple, yellow, red and gold. Then I saw the sun starting to move up and down like a pulsating movement. Carmelita saw it too and we were both exited. When I reached at the foot of the mountain, I met Mary, our co-pilgrim, and in my excitement I also told her to look at the sun. In her amazement she said, "I thank God to allow me to see this!" Then she made this comment to me, "You are blessed to see this manifestation at the age of 64, you will still see more. I am already 84." When I told my pilgrim guide about the sun, she told me, "It happened a few times here before; it is similar to the "Dancing sun of Fatima." Then I remembered reading about it in some religious book many years before, but did not pay much attention to it. Maybe it is because I had a hard time believing myself that this phenomenon could occur.

We had a one and a half hour break for supper, and then the procession of Blessed Mother statue followed. We began the recitation of the Rosary along the route of the Way of the Cross. Followed by the procession we were all provided with lighted candles. The 2000 plus lit candles was a sight to see. It was so beautiful and amazing. Then the presentation of dances in praises and honor of our Blessed Mother and Jesus followed right after the procession.

At 1:00 A.M. Sunday, May 6, 2007 the Mass celebration started, celebrated by Father Ume from California. After the Mass the Holy Eucharist celebration followed. This ceremony was followed by Julia Kim's speech along with her interpreter. She was giving us the highlights of the messages that she received from the Blessed Mother and Lord Jesus over the years since she started receiving the visions.

The following are the major points of Julia's speech:

    1. Love the Lord and one another

2. Don't criticize others no matter what; recognize your fault before thinking of other's fault.
3. Pray for the conversion of sinners and follow Jesus and the Blessed Mother Mary
4. Offer your sufferings and sacrifices for the salvation of people.
5. Forgive one another
6. Do not be fearful
7. Offer your heart, mind and soul to experience resurrection
8. Enter the narrow gate of salvation
9. Be humble like a child
10. Repentance and sanctification; we should repent and be holy.
11. Take all the hatred, selfishness, jealousy, unforgiveness, sufferings and hardships and bring it to the Sacred heart of Jesus and the Immaculate Heart of Mary.

Julia Kim's talk was followed by two personal testimonies. One man stated that he had a genuine conversion experience after attending the overnight prayer meeting and reading the books about the messages that Julia received from Jesus and the Blessed Mother. The second testimony was about the lady pilgrim in our group. She was very shy to be on stage so the program coordinator of our group gave her testimony. She explained Fe's story of how they met and then she read Fe's Testimony.

Fe is a Filipino lady. Like most Catholics, (including myself, before I became born again,) she considered herself Catholic by name only. She hardly attended Mass, even on Sundays. If she did attend a Mass, she looked for a Church that was known to have the shortest sermon or liturgy. After her retirement, she heard about the apparition of Blessed Mary in Naju, Korea. As a retired person she had all the time in the world and free from any obligations. Her husband encouraged her to join the group for a pilgrimage to Naju. Reluctantly, she agreed to come for the reason of just checking it out. During the all night prayer, when Julia prayed for her, she was slain by the Holy Spirit. "Slain by the Holy Spirit" is the term commonly used by the Charismatic and Pentecostal Christians when all of a sudden you become unconscious and fall to the ground. I have seen this phenomenon many times on T.V. during religious crusades, but not in Catholic services or gatherings. I understand how Fe felt when one of the pilgrims told her, "Wow you were slain by the Holy Spirit!" She became upset hearing this comment because she did not know what it meant and she never heard about this phenomenon. She was even awe-struck as to what happened to her.

When Fe went home after her pilgrimage, her husband noticed the great change in her. He wondered what had happened to Fe. He later told Judy, the pilgrimage coordinator, that Fe was now a loving, sweet and kind wife. He added, "I wish I had met you Judy one week after our wedding!" Fe made changes in her home as well. She told her family, "From now on I want this house to be God's house." She started a prayer service in her house every week and prayed the

My Pilgrimage To Naju, Korea

Rosary every day. Her life revolved around Jesus and Mary.

Some months after her conversion experience, she was involved in a near fatal car accident. She was in a coma for two weeks. Her family prayed for The Sacred Heart of Jesus and for the intercession of the Immaculate Heart of Mary. She was out of the coma after two weeks, but her recovery was difficult. She was discharged home with very bad headaches and she was unable to sleep lying down, but her faith never wavered. She considers her recovery the greatest miracle of her life, and she is still praising the Lord and the Blessed Mother until now for this miracle. She strongly believed that God gave her a second life. Most of her friends made this comment about her, "This lady didn't go to church previously, now she won't leave the Church!" Fe is very active in her Church. She assists the priest everyday during the Mass and volunteers to help distribute food for the homeless in her parish every Wednesday. Her main reason to come to this pilgrimage this time with us was to give her testimony and to thank the Lord Jesus and the Blessed Mother for her healing miracle and for the miracle of her new life.

The last part of the overnight vigil service was for the priest to bless the people and for Julia to pray for the people one by one. I noticed several people who were slain by the Holy Spirit, but no one seemed surprised because it had been happening quite often in this particular service. It took three hours for the priest and Julia to bless and pray for the people. I looked at my watch; it was already 8:00 o'clock in the morning. I was a bit tired but not at all sleepy because of the emotional and the spiritual excitement. We then went back to the hotel. During our breakfast I told everyone in our group, "If my whole trip was only to attend the overnight vigil service, it was all worth the trip for me." Then I said, "The light that I saw on the fourteenth station during my way of the Cross on the mountain and the 'Dancing sun similar to Fatima,' was my bonus from the Blessed Mother." I had been praying for a sign before leaving Los Angeles and I received it.

The day before leaving Naju we had our farewell dinner with Julia. I was surprised with this special treatment from her, but I heard that she always tries to meet the pilgrims in private, especially our pilgrim coordinator's group (Judy.) She was bringing many pilgrims to Naju, so Judy became a very special person to Julia. I find Julia a very nice person with great humility. I could see that Julia is one of God's anointed, used by our Lord Jesus and the Blessed Mother.

May 9, 2007, my last day in Naju, Korea, We attended our last Mass in Naju celebrated by Father Ume. He thanked us for our kindness and for our zeal in our faith and in our prayers. Because of the many miracles we heard: Blessed Mother weeping tears and tears of blood, descent of the Eucharist twice, changes in the Eucharistic species twice, descent of our Lord's precious blood, and many others, my mind boggled at times. I was thankful that Father Ume made the following comment in his homily; he made me feel a lot better. Father Ume stated that in the book of Hebrew in the Bible, God revealed Himself in so many ways and even now in our present days Jesus is still working in many ways to make Himself known to us. As soon as the Mass was over, I wrote down what Father Ume said in his homily.

The following day, at home, I read every chapter of the book of Hebrew. In Hebrew 1:1-2 states: "God who at various times and in different ways spoke in times past to the fathers by the prophets, has in these last days spoken to us by His Son, whom He has appointed heir of all things, through whom He made the worlds." It was not very clear to me, so in order to gain more understanding I looked it up in the Recovery Version Bible and it states: "God revealed Himself in the Old Testament not once for all and in only one way but in many way but in many portions and in many ways; in one portion to the Patriarchs, in another way to Moses, another to David, to Prophets in several different ways." This verse in the Bible, along the many testimonies I heard and read about the miracles in Naju, helped me to gain my faith back in the Blessed Mother and her many miracles. I mentioned it earlier that my prayer directed to Mary was lessened or weakened when I became born again because of the Protestant Christian influence in my faith. I remember a Christian brother who quoted the scriptures in Mathew 12:46-50, it states,

"While He was still talking to the multitudes, behold, His mother and brothers stood outside, seeking to speak with Him. Then one said to Him, 'Look, Your mother and your brothers are standing outside, seeking to speak with You.' But He answered and said to the one who told Him, 'Who is My Mother and who are My brothers?' And He stretched out His hand toward His disciples and said, 'Here are My mother and My brothers! For whoever does the will of My Father in heaven is My brother and sister and mother.'" I think He pointed this verse to me because as a Catholic he thinks I worship Mary. After I returned from my pilgrimage, I studied this scripture. I learned that in this scenario Jesus was explaining to the disciples about the Jews rejection of Christ. After breaking with the Jews, Christ turned to the Gentiles. Thenceforth, His relationship with His followers was not in the flesh but in the spirit. This passage of the scripture does not mean that Jesus did not honor Mary as His mother, but Jesus is telling us that in the kingdom of God, His Word and Himself are more important than flesh and blood relationships.

Similarly, another Christian sister also pointed to me the scripture in Luke 11:27-28 that states, "And it happened, as He spoke these things, that a certain woman from the crowd raised her voice and said, 'Blessed is the womb that bore You and the breasts that nurse You!' But He said, 'More than that, blessed are those who hear the Word of God and keep it!' Jesus was saying here that people who listen and obey His Word are more blessed and more important than mother and child relationships.

There are many testimonies of genuine conversion and healing written in the book Messages of Love, and I would like to include a few testimonies of the people who witnessed the miracles and experienced healing in their lives.

Personal testimony to the happenings on the night of the 19th of October, 2005 while celebrating the 19th Anniversary of the shedding of tears of blood by our Blessed Mother Mary on the Blessed Mother's mountain in Naju.

Msgr. Paul Chee, Sibu, Sarawak, Malaysia

My Pilgrimage To Naju, Korea

(October 23, 2005)

It was the celebration of the 20th Anniversary of the shedding of tears by our Blessed Mother's mountain that I witnessed and saw with my own eyes the miracle of the "dancing sun" of the Fatima for the second time and which I had read so much about in books. I remembered it was about 3:15 p.m. that day when the overcast sky suddenly opened up. Two members of our pilgrimage group, Paul Lau and Joseph Song took video pictures of this "dancing sun." I wasn't prepared for the unexpected. What turned up after both films were being developed at home in Sibu were the divine mercy rays – white and red in colors 'raining down' from the bright sun.

This has led me to the totally unexpected pilgrimage trip to Naju again led by Peter Ting and Felicia Lim, this time for the celebration of the 19th Anniversary of the shedding of tears of blood by our Blessed Mother Mary which fell on October 19, 2005.

It was after the Eucharist celebration that Archbishop Nicholaus, Fr. Bosmans, Fr Pham, Fr. Tito, Julia and myself with all the people present went up the mountain just before 11:00 p.m. After the presentation of dances in praises and honor of our Lady and Jesus, at about 12:10 a.m., we began the recitation of the Holy Rosary along the route of the Stations of the Cross.

It was during the third decade of the Rosary when we arrived at the scene of the Cavalry. I stared at "Jesus hanging on the cross." Jesus looked alive on the cross if my eyes did not deceive me! I was a step behind Julia with Archbishop Nicholaus on her right side and Fr. Bosmans was beside me. With in split seconds, Julia, who was in front of me, was thrown backward as if by force and fell flat on the ground.

I was momentarily stunned as I turned and looked down at her on the ground. Her aides rushed to her assistance and within less than a few minutes, Julia was on her feet again. We then continued the recitation of the Holy Rosary until we reach Julia's room inside the tent. It was then that I came to know from Julia that Jesus has spewed His blood from His side at the scene of the Cavalry! Julia's dress was covered with fresh blood of Jesus. So, too also was the Archbishop Nicholaus suit.

As I and other photographers were busily taking photo shots of Julia and the Archbishop, there was a commotion behind my back.

One photographer noticed the back of my windbreaker was also covered with the precious blood of Jesus. I was then asked to take off my windbreaker and I laid it on the flat surface to be photographed. There and then, I really saw some large drops of fresh blood, few streaks of fresh blood and many tiny droplets of fresh blood all over the back of my woolen windbreaker!

I felt awe-struck by this event and was wondering what this could mean.

This testimony, which I now attest, is the true happenings as I saw it happen on the Blessed Mother's mountain in Naju, South Korea on the night of the celebration of the 19th anniversary of the weeping of the years of blood by our Blessed Mother which fell on 19th of October, 2005.

N.B.: Later on, during the same night, two pilgrims, Helen and James from my group of Singaporeans and Malaysians personally approached me to tell me that they saw Jesus alive on the cross oozing streams of copious blood from His wounds that night at the scene of the Cavalry.

After this happening, and for the remainder of the trip, I did not share with anyone my own same personal experiences as theirs. I really believed that my eyes have not deceived me as I just wore my newly made pair of glasses before this trip! 2

Angela Lim, Busan, Korea (June 1992)

"My name is Angela Lim living in Busan, South Korea. I divorced my husband 18 years ago and have been raising two children. No one will understand how many times I have cried or how much pain I have endured. Tears of blood have been flowing inside me.

I was resentful and decided to take revenge by earning as much money as possible and raising the children in the best way possible. I worked like an ox, even though I had some sickness. My heart was always sizzling with resentment and anger, unable to forgive. I was angry with the world and sometimes, even with God.

On December 8, 1987, I had an opportunity to visit Naju. There was a prayer meeting for the consecration of the new Chapel, to which the Blessed Mother's statue was moved from Julia's apartment. At that meeting, Julia relayed the Blessed Mother's messages to us:

'The just anger of God the Father is overflowing. Do not criticize or judge others, but convert yourself... Families are sick. Sanctify your family by loving one another. Never blame others, but always blame yourself only. Those who accept my messages will experience a renewal of their souls through my messages of love...'

I was totally shaken up by these messages and Julia's testimonies. I was crying loudly. Until that time, I always thought that I was right. I never admitted any fault on my part, as I had always been blaming others and been full of anger, I felt so shameful before the Lord and the Blessed Mother. My heart was shaken up in an indescribable way and I was crying uncontrollably. I cried and cried as I was deciding to accept my husband.

People around me in the Chapel asked me to control the noise. So, I crawled out and began cleaning the bathroom floor. I cleaned it thoroughly remembering Julia's words: 'Let us become a mop to clean souls.' I wanted to become a mop for cleaning my husband, who was sick both spiritually and physically. I continued cleaning other corners around the Chapel. I felt so grateful to Julia, who suffered pains for the conversion of others, including me.

I went to the place where my husband was staying. He was in bed alone and very sick. He also had many debts. Momentarily I felt angry, but soon this was replaced with an overwhelming sense of pity. We came home together and the Blessed Mother gradually restored his health. I got my spouse back after 18 long years, thanks to the Blessed Mother and her love. "My dear children! Love even your enemies." If you live according to the love of God, you will be saved.' These words of the Blessed Mother given to us through Julia were the medicine that gave our family a new life.

How can we say we love the Lord without loving our spouses, regardless of the situation? When I see his shortcomings, I realize they are truly my shortcomings. My husband now looks like St. Joseph to me, as the Blessed Mother is filling my ignorant heart with her love.

The grace I received was so precious that I have been encouraging others to accept the Blessed Mother's love too. Sometimes we rent a bus, as there were quite a few people who wanted to visit Naju. Many around me, my relatives, friends and neighbors, have been baptized. Sometimes even Buddhist monks and Protestant clergyman joined the group and converted with tears in front of the Blessed Mother's statue in Naju. My husband is always anxious that I do not miss the trip to Naju. Often he cannot come along because of the business. When I go to Naju without him, he waits for me at home praying with a candlelight lit.

Now, whenever we had difficulties or pains, I rush to the Blessed Mother in Naju. So far, she has taken care of all our problems, whether they are spiritual or physical. Whenever we rush to her, trusting her, she helps us- not just me but my whole family. We have experienced this so many times. Our Lord also cures, through the Blessed Mother, physical sicknesses, which were declared incurable by doctors.

Before visiting Naju, I had tried many other ways: charismatic prayer retreats, fasting, overnight prayers, and so on. But I could not find peace of mind from them. The Blessed Mother cured my hardened heart and liberated me with love in Naju.

I am writing this testimony in immense gratitude to the Lord for curing my spiritual and physical sicknesses. I hope that others who are in difficulties will also find the boundless love of the Blessed Mother in Naju. Our Blessed Mother frequently said that we could reach glory only through suffering.

I cannot write here about all the numerous sufferings I went through before conversion. Now I realize that even those many sufferings were given to me, because the Lord loves me. I give the Lord and the Blessed Mother my endless gratitude. I pray that each and every family in the whole world experience this healing and become a small church."

Eli Siason, Manila, Philippines (1992)

"I am Eli Siason, living in Paranaque, MetroManila. I am 53 years of age, married, and have seven children.

I have been a professional musician playing the guitar and the piano for the past 35 years and am presently employed as musical director and pianist/singer at Concourse Bar of the Nikko Hotel Manila Garden.

Life was good to me, and although there were ups and downs in my life, no major tragedy had happened to me not until September 6, 1991, when I lost the use of my right arm and right leg while I was driving my car. I had to deliberately swerve my car with my left hand to an electric post to stop the vehicle, since my right foot could not step on the brakes.

A bystander helped me and brought me to the Makati Medical Center. Four doctors of Makati Medical Center initially suspected a heart problem. However, after further medical examinations and heart scanning, they found nothing wrong with my heart. Two doctors, Dr. Jamora and his associate recommended a brain scan. Four brain scans were done on me, and it was then that they discovered a brain tumor. Doctors recommended an immediate operation, a mass or tumor as big as an egg was removed from the left side of my brain. This tumor was found to be malignant. After a recuperation of three months, I was able to acquire the use of my right arm and to walk with a limp, as my right leg had not fully recovered.

Tragedy struck me again when sometime during Holy Week, particularly Good Friday, I lost my left eyesight. My left eye had gone completely blind and only my right eye was functioning. I underwent laser treatment four times in my left eye, but nothing happened. There was no improvement to my left eye no matter how slight. During this time, although I had recovered the use of my limbs, I was still limping due to the weakness on my right leg. According to my doctors, the damage to my left eye and right leg was done by the malignant tumor, which had been removed.

I confided this problem to Attorney Nordy P. Diploma. I told him that I was afraid of a recurring malignant tumor, considering that we could not be sure that everything was removed. Atty. Diploma advised me to attend a healing Mass at Greenbelt Chapel on May 12, 1992, as at that time there was a visiting visionary from Korea, whom I later found out to be Julia Kim. During Julia's prayers and meditation, I smelled the sweet fragrance of roses filling the entire Chapel. Such sweet smell, I am sure was experienced by the entire congregation in the Chapel.

The following day, there was another healing Mass celebrated in a church in Katipunan St. Quezon City. After the Mass, Julia prayed and meditated. While she was relaying the messages of the Virgin Mary to the congregation, she felt some pain in her head. She announced that somebody in the congregation, who was in a brain illness was being cured. She repeated this announcement twice since she must have felt much pain in her head. After Mass, I felt considerably better and proceeded to the residence of Atty. Diploma. It was there that his aunt and sister noticed a sweet fragrance of roses from me, which my children also smelled when I reached home about two hours later.

The following day Atty. Diploma and I went to Mrs. Mercy Tuazon's residence, where Julia was staying. I was introduced to Julia when we arrived. Julia then felt pain in her left eye and in her head. She was also limping. She then went to her room to rest. When Julia came out, she prayed for other people and then came to me and touched my left eye and left temple. She prayed for me in her own Korean language. While she was praying for me I felt coldness in my body. After Julia prayed for me, Atty. Diploma motioned for us to leave. I indicated to Atty. Diploma to wait awhile. I then noticed that my vision was becoming clearer. I covered my right eye to test whether my eyesight on the left eye had been restored. Praise God! My left eye could see now! I told my friends the astonishing news, I thank for this cure bestowed on me.

Atty. Diploma and I went home after the session at Mrs. Mercy Tuazon's residence.

Later that week I contacted the eye doctors who had treated me and told them the good news and the healing of my eye. They could not believe me. They told me that it must have been a miracle. Yes, there is no doubt in my mind that a miracle happened to me. Deep in my heart, however, I know it was more than just a miracle of healing my cancer, it was a miracle having been given back by Almighty God my playing skills as a pianist and my voice as a singer to be of better service again to my fellow men.

I have tried to tell this personal account of my healing with only one purpose in mind, which is to tell what happened to me as accurately as possible, without adding or subtracting from what actually happened. I give this testimony with no other intention than to glorify the infinite goodness and mercy of God Almighty. 3 ("Messages of Love" Appendix A-17)

Mrs. Mercedes Diploma, Manila, Philippines (November 14, 1994)

"While I was visiting a friend's house earlier this month, I became ill, experiencing much difficulty breathing and feeling extremely dizzy. I felt that I was dying and went to a hospital. Doctors diagnosed my condition as stenocardia, (the narrowing of the vessels in the heart.) My blood pressure was 240/130. To make things worse, they also found out that my lungs were filled with fluid. They sent me to intensive care unit.

For almost four days, I was in coma and did not know what was happening to me. Because I was not getting any oxygen, doctors decided to insert a tube through a hole in my neck. At that moment, my son, Nordy Diploma, asked the doctors to wait for a few minutes and gave me a piece of cloth that had absorbed the fragrant oil from Our Lady's statue in Naju. Julia Kim had given that cloth to Nordy. When the cloth was placed on me, a miracle happened. My blood pressure came down to 140/80. I felt that my condition was improving.

Later, this cloth was lost while I was still in the hospital room. So, Nordy gave me his handkerchief that Julia had prayed on during her visit to the Philippines. I touched various parts of my body with that handkerchief. My health continued improving and soon I was out of the hospital. Now, I am healthier than before. Thank you so much."

Marcia M. Czarnicki, Mechanisburg, Pennsylvania (January 14, 1995)

"Dear Julia,

I want to thank you for coming to Toronto, Canada so that I could hear Our Blessed Mother's messages given to you. I received many graces that evening and continue to do so through reading the book, The Miracle in Naju, Korea – Heaven Speaks to the World, and watching the videos concerning the miracles in Naju.

The greatest miracle I have received is the grace to see what the will of God is for my life and to desire it alone. Before hearing the Our Blessed Mother's messages to you at Naju, I wasn't sure what she and her Son Jesus were asking of me, especially in my relationship with my husband. I was on the road of doing my own will and doing what made me happy instead of doing what made Jesus and Mary happy. The messages from Naju seem particularly made for me and all sinners who have lost their way and are feeling very discouraged by their weakness and sinfulness.

When I heard Mary's word in the video, 'Tears of Love,' 'How can you say you love me and my Son when you don't love those in your family.' I heard Our Blessed Mother calling me to unity, by loving, trusting, respecting, and being faithful to my husband. It was as if a light went on penetrating my darkened mind and softening my hardened heart. I heard Our Blessed Mother calling me to be obedient to my spiritual director, to renounce myself and my selfish desire, to suffer gracefully, without complaining, uniting your sufferings with Jesus for the salvation of souls, to pray for priests, bishops and the Holy Father, and most specially to a profound love and a deeper belief in the Real Presence of Jesus in the Eucharist.

In trying to respond Our Lady's messages to you at Naju, my marriage has been saved after twenty-two years of enormous struggles and pain. My husband has had a profound conversion. He is now the husband that Jesus calls all husbands to be. We pray together daily as a family and share our Joys and sufferings.

On October 25, 1994, when you walked into the Convocation Hall at the University of Toronto, a beautiful perfume emanating from you filled the room. You smiled at us with such love that I felt the presence of Jesus and Mary in the room. The vision you shared with us that you had during the Eucharistic miracle on September 24, 1994 about the large ships which were sailing in the ocean, showed me I was stepping out of the safe boat with the

Eucharistic Jesus, Mary and the Heavenly Father, into the other boat where my desires for worldly happiness would be satisfied.

Later that evening I cried and I heard many others crying while you prayed out loud in our behalf for the healing and for the loving hands of Jesus and Mary to touch our hearts. I felt a great hope and renewed courage to follow only Jesus and Mary as you left the room.

To my amazement, you gave me the awesome gift of inviting me to meet you after you spoke. Before going to Toronto, I told my spiritual director my great fear of being in your presence because I had heard you had been given the grace to read souls. Because of my sinfulness, I was sure you would ask me to leave the auditorium before speaking to us that evening. Father promised me that not only would you not throw me out, but I would get to meet you personally and that you would hug and kiss me! You did just that! You stood up as I came downstairs and walked towards me, took both my hands, smiled at me and hugged and kissed me! I truly felt Jesus and Mary telling me through you that they still loved me even though I was a terrible sinner and that they were helping me to stand up and begin again with their love and strength to support me.

Whenever I have sinned again since then, I have received the grace to make a sincere Confession and begin anew. I sincerely believe it is because of your sufferings and prayers for the conversion of poor sinners that I have received these graces. I feel Our Blessed Mother's powerful intercession and her merciful love for her children. I feel her leading me ever nearer to the Eucharist Heart of her Son.

I have always believed in the Real Presence of Jesus in the Eucharist, but after seeing the video, on Naju and reading about the seven miracles that you have had, my love and devotion for Jesus in the Eucharist has increased hundredfold.

Thank you Julia, for being Our Blessed Mother's most humble and obedient servant. In doing so, you are showing me and others the narrow way Jesus and Mary want us to follow to bring peace to our hearts and homes and to enter Heaven someday." 4

Fr. Francis Su, Sarawak, Malaysia (August, 1995)

I, Francis Su Haw Hoo, a Catholic priest from the Diocese of Sibu, Malaysia, wish to offer a testimony to the recent miracles which occurred in Naju, Korea during the tenth anniversary of the Blessed Mother's first tears (1985.) I went to Naju with a group of Singaporeans and Malaysians. We arrived at Naju on June 29,1995 and spent exactly four nights there, and we participated in the overnight vigils for three consecutive nights in the Chapel (The Blessed Mother's house.) The Chapel was occupied with lots of pilgrims coming from different countries. The whole place was filled with a fragrance of roses from the statue of Mother Mary.

On the first night (Thursday, June 29, 1995) our group brought a lot of flowers for Mamma Mary. Julia Kim asked me to crown Mother Mary. I felt so privileged to be given the honor to crown Mother Mary. Thank you Mamma Mary!

On Friday, June 30, we went to the mountain to collect water from the miraculous spring. The water had the fragrance of roses, indicating the presence of Mother Mary, her friendship and love for us, her children. After we all had collected the miracle water, some came to me for Confession. After that we prayed the Rosary. While praying the Rosary, many looked up towards the sun, which moved up and down. It started spinning and formed the shape of a big Host. Later, we heard that a group of people saw the sun coming down slowly in the form of a Host and resting on the roof of the Blessed Mother's House.

In the evening at 7:30, we participated in the 10th anniversary concelebrated Mass in the Parish Church, which was packed to full capacity with pilgrims coming from all over the world. The Mass was said and presided by the Parish Priest, Rev. Fr. Julio Kim, in Korean language. The response was very good. Four priests helped distribute Holy Communion. Julia, who was sitting in the back of the Church due to the huge crowd, received Holy Communion last. She went back to her seat, and after a few minutes, the Host in her mouth started to bleed. She was then surrounded by large crowds of people who witnessed this occurrence. Immediately after the Mass, the concelebrants also went and witnessed this. I saw the Host in Julia's mouth look like flesh mingled with blood. This is a confirmation to me that a consecrated Host is truly the Body of Jesus Christ in the form of bread so that it can easily be consumed.

After this we all went back to the Chapel for another overnight vigil. This night was completely jammed with people both inside and outside the Chapel. Many people gave testimonies. I was also given the opportunity to give testimony about my experiences during my first visit to Naju in May 1995, when I witnessed the pain that Julia had to suffer for people who had aborted their unborn babies. While I was still giving my testimony, Julia who was sitting behind me, was in pain again. Her stomach became big just like a pregnant woman. This was witnessed by over a thousand people. I asked the people to pray and implore God's mercy and forgiveness on those people who are responsible for killing so many unborn babies. Many cried and begged mercy and pardon from God. After a while, Julia's stomach returned to normal size. Today the greatest evil is abortion – the killing of the innocents. At about 2:30 a.m. (Saturday morning,) Julia asked me to anoint her forehead and hands with the holy oil which I brought along with me. I did the same with Julio, her husband. She held our hands in deep prayers and cried in front of the statue of the Blessed Mother. I felt very much like a child holding the hand of Mother Mary. I felt drowsy but very peaceful. I could then feel the very strong presence of Mamma Mary.

At 3:45 a.m. Julia still holding my hand, suddenly jumped up and reached her hands towards the crucifix above the statue of Our Lady. In that split of the moment as I jumped up with her, I felt she was asking me to catch something falling down. As she opened up her hands, I saw to my amazement, communion Hosts being placed in front of Our Lady's statue on the altar. I counted the Hosts, and there were seven. The Chapel was ecstatic, as many present had witnessed this miracle, and their curiosity turned into worship and prayer, worthy of our Lord Jesus in the Eucharist.

On Saturday (1st of July1995,) being the first Saturday of the month, we again had the overnight vigil. The night was crowded and filled with songs, prayers and testimonies from priests and lay people on how Our Lady had brought them closer to the Lord through healings and the Eucharistic miracles. On Sunday (July 2) morning at about 5:30 a.m., I led the people to adore the Blessed Sacrament as taught by Michael the Archangel to the three children of Fatima, Lucia, Francisco and Jacinta, after which I took one piece out of seven miraculous Hosts to bless the people present. Then, the people lined up in a long queue to see the miraculous Hosts and pay homage and adore the Eucharistic King. Julia and myself then prayed over the people one by one or family by family. It took us more than two hours to finish praying over them. I felt very sleepy and exhausted. I looked at my watch; it was 8:oo o'clock in the morning.

By Sunday night (July 2,) most of the pilgrims had left Naju. That night, there were only about a hundred people in the Chapel: 45 of us from Singapore and Malaysia, 6 from Hong Kong, 2 Australians, and the rest were Koreans.

In obedience to the instruction by Archbishop Yoon in Naju area, we decided to consume the seven Hosts. I was given the privilege to receive the first Host from Fr. Pete M. Marcial, Julio (Julia's husband,) Rufino (administrator of the Chapel.) Kap-Joo Choi (Chairman of Naju City Council,) Andrew (a helper) and lastly to Julia. Before Julia received the Host, she felt very uneasy. But after she received the last Host, she bowed her head in deep union with the Lord. I laid hands on her head and prayed over her. After a few minutes, she lifted up her head and opened her mouth. Her mouth was filled with blood again. Those around us cried and worshipped the Lord. I put my finger on her tongue, and it was covered with blood, and I showed it to the people. I wiped my finger with a linen cloth and the stain of blood remained there. This linen with the stain of blood is being kept in the Chapel as evidence and for further scientific laboratory tests.

I asked myself, 'Why all these occurrences in such a short period of time?' I began to understand that this is a gift from Mother Mary as a reassurance and reemphasis on the Eucharist. Many have lost the sense of the Real Presence of Our Lord in the Eucharist. As a priest, I have been given the power to make Jesus present in the lives of people through the Eucharist. The Eucharistic occurrences on these few days have increased my faith and strengthened my ministerial Priesthood. The celebration of the Mass and the Consecration of the Eucharist will be a different experience to me henceforth. I testify and reaffirm the presence of Jesus in the Eucharist and will give witness to these occurrences.

Monday, July 3 at 4:15 a.m., Yo Han (one of the volunteers from the Blessed Mother's house) came to our hotel to fetch us to the Chapel to witness the big statue of Our Lady in the garden outside the Chapel. It also shed tears. Within a short stay in Naju, I witnessed at least eight miracles. Our trip to Naju is very meaningful and significant to me, especially the Eucharistic Miracles.

I believe wholeheartedly that Mamma Mary had led me to Naju to experience all these wonderful miracles in such a short time for a grave reason. She has undoubtedly put in my heart a strong desire and sense of urgency in responding to her pleas and repeated requests to pray for the world peace and for conversion of sinners. 'Pray, pray a great deal and make sacrifices, for many souls go to hell because they have no one to make sacrifices and to pray for them.' (Our Lady of Fatima on 19th August 1917)

'Come to me and spread my messages of love courageously so that people may be freed from the Red Dragon and that the Kingdom of the Lord may come. In union with the Pope and all the bishops, let the victory of the Resurrection reach the whole world. In this age, the devil is becoming more active to control humans by means of human powers. My numerous poor children are following the Red Dragon and walking toward the deep darkness, hell, in their extreme pride. They are working in many different cunning ways to confuse people about the messages that I give.

Oh, my poor children. My priests hold the hands of so many of my children who are recklessly walking into darkness.

There are some priests who have broken away from me and do not follow the will of Jesus. But, through my priests and on this soil made fertile by the blood of so many martyrs, many souls are growing under the light from my Son and me. On the other hand the Red Dragon is becoming more violent. So, tell people to be awake and pray.

Oh, my dear priests! I want even the most corrupt souls to receive the light from me. Therefore, be loyal to Jesus so that they may convert. Also, do not let my tears and blood flow in vain. I want my beloved priests to become sacrificial victims for the conversion of sinners.

Oh, my beloved priests! My precious ones who perform the amazing miracle of the sacrament! Do not turn your eyes away from my messages, but have complete trust in my Immaculate Heart and entrust everything to my guidance. Rely totally on my Immaculate Heart through unending sacrifices and penances in order to crush the devil who are trying to afflict you by all kinds of cunning methods.

My Immaculate Heart will surely triumph. You will certainly see the victory, if you accept my words." 5

My Pilgrimage To Naju, Korea

Reverend Tae Hyung Kang, Kwangmin Presbyterian Church, Kwangju, Korea (1995)

"I am a Protestant clergyman at Kwangmin Presbyterian Church in Kwangju. First of all, I would like to express my deepest gratitude to the Lord for allowing me an opportunity today to write a testimony on the numerous graces that I have received from the Blessed Mother and also on my beliefs.

Earlier I had worked in the Kyungki Province, but the Lord led me to the city of Kwangju in 1993. One of the most important events that have happened to me since I moved to Kwangju has been that I have been frequently visiting the Blessed Mother's House in Naju. In the course of these visits, I have clearly experienced the love and graces from the living Lord and have acquired an understanding that Jesus, in whom I had believed since a long time ago, sent the Blessed mother to all of us, sinners. In other words, I have discovered the important lesson that the Marian devotion, as taught by the Catholic Church, is pleasing to Jesus. For this reason, I, as a Protestant minister, am ready to face any disadvantages that may fall upon me because of the call by my loving Jesus and my devotion to the Blessed Mother. The fact that I, who am unworthy, have acquired the Marian devotion, has not been associated by anyone in this world. I only hope that the Lord will protect me to the end. Sometimes, I have also restrained my desire to visit the Blessed Mother's House to avoid inconveniencing the workers of Our Lady by frequent visits by a Protestant clergyman, even though these visits have not been caused by mere curiosity.

The Bible says that faith is a gift of the Holy Spirit (1 Cor. 12:9.) Therefore, my Marian faith is also a gift of the

Holy Spirit, which may have some bearing of my vocation, which I don't know yet. On September 24, 1994, the Blessed Mother gave us a message of love, especially for the Protestants:

'The small, separated churches have not accepted me yet, but will gradually accept me as the mother of the Church... Spread my words of love not just to Catholics but to all my children.'

How wonderful it would be if the churches which have been divided since the 16th Century discontinue all the enmity and fighting and become one based on brotherly love through the grace from the Blessed Mother! St. John of the Cross said: 'Most merciful God! Please give me the Spirit of thy Son to all the souls. Without thee we cannot do anything.'

The Bible further says that not even a bird will fall from the sky, unless God allows it (Mathew 10:29.) It can also be said that the Reformation would not have occurred without God's permission. The important lesson from this is that this unfortunate event in Church history was caused by human sins and represented a chastisement from God.

Anyhow, the Blessed Mother's messages give a new mission and hope to both Catholics and Protestants. All of us should walk toward the Blessed Mother, hold her warm hands, listen to her loving voice, be embraced in her bosom and become one as brothers and sisters and, thereby, accomplish the important historical event of becoming one in the Love of Jesus.

The Blessed Mother has appeared and given messages at many places around the world during the past several centuries. Particularly, in Naju, Korea, she has been giving us very special signs and messages. In Naju, she has been revealing to us numerous signs, such as tears and tears of blood, fragrant oil, fragrance, Eucharistic miracles, and messages for the past ten years since 1985. I understand that there is no place in the world with such powerful and objective manifestations for such a long time at one same location. Until now, numerous people have personally seen, heard, touched, smelled, and received the miraculous Communion, drunk the water from the mountain, and experienced graces! In addition, countless people who had lost faith and left the Church have repented and returned to the Lord!

In the Bible, we find two persons who are contrasting examples. One is Judas Iscariot, who had accompanied Jesus for three years and yet betrayed Him and fell into eternal damnation. The other is the thief on the right hand of Jesus on the Cross, who believed the Lord and was saved at the moment of his death. What made the difference was 'faith.' No matter how long one may have been a believer, how lofty a position one may be in, and how much recognition one may get from others, he will be deserted if he does not have the kind of faith that Jesus can accept. (Mathew7:21-27) The leaders of Israel at the time of Jesus believed in God, but refused to believe in Jesus. Even the great St. Paul had not only been an unbeliever in Jesus, but judged Him as the head of heretics and persecuted His disciples before his conversion. We need to remember the following words of God which apply to our world as well as to the past:

'But I know that you do not have the love of God in you.' (John5:42)

This means that those who believed in God but lacked the love for God failed to recognize Jesus as the Son of

God and the Messiah. The Kingdom of God is not in speech but in power (1 Cor. 4:20.) According to John 7:31 and 9:30, a person who had been blind from birth and was cured, was wondering why the Jewish leaders and Pharisees did not believe Jesus. The same kinds of things are happening in today's world. Again, it is a matter of 'faith.' At the time of Jesus' public life, humans were tested on their belief in God's work through their acceptance of Jesus. Now in this end time, we are being tested in our belief in the work of Jesus through our acceptance of the Blessed Mother. What is important is the ability to discern. This ability is the power from the Lord, which He gives to those who truly love Him.

As stated in John 10, we should become God's people who recognize His Voice through Jesus. By the same token, we should become the Lord's sheep who recognize His Voice through the Blessed Mother.

As stated in John 17:20, God and Jesus are One and the Blessed Mother is with Jesus. The early Fathers of the Church had this faith and the Saints possessed it. We should become people who inherit his tradition of faith. True faith means that one should have a sincere desire for childlike innocence and truth and courage to deny oneself, and willingly carry the cross for the Lord.

If anyone refuses to believe, continues to doubt, and throws vicious accusations despite so many signs and anxious calls by the Blessed Mother in Naju, he would not only be persecuting the workers of the Blessed Mother, but foolishly poking the eyes of Jesus. The Blessed mother is the Mother of all people. She is the loving Mother to Catholics, Protestants, and unbelievers. I sincerely hope that her messages be spread to many people. As the Blessed Mother says, the corruption of humans worsens day after day, and the world is standing at the edge of a cliff, inviting its own destruction. Even the Church has been affected by the secular spirit and is sick. All of us must hurriedly arm ourselves with the Immaculate Heart of Mary, wake up from sleep, and change our lives based on the Blessed Mother's messages, which in turn, are based on the Gospels. I pray in the Name of Jesus that we become one in the Lord and the Blessed Mother. Amen. 6

I purposely included this particular testimony last mainly to help explain my point of why my faith and devotion to Mother Mary was strengthened after my pilgrimage. Many pilgrims that go to Naju, I believe, go there out of curiosity to see if the miracles are real or not. Like me, I was skeptical at first. Then I came to realize that when it comes to spiritual things, instead of doubting, we should keep our minds open and pray more to the Holy Spirit. Our "Faith" is a gift of the Holy Spirit. The Bible, in 1 Corinthians 12: 4-13 states: "But the manifestations of the Spirit is given to each one for the profit of all: for to one is given word of wisdom through the Spirit, to another the word of knowledge through the same spirit, to another faith by the same Spirit, to another gifts of healings by the same Spirit, to another the working of prophecy, to another discerning of Spirits, to another different kinds of tongues, to another the interpretation of tongues. But one and the same Spirit works all these things, distributing to each one individually as He wills. For as the body is one and has many members, but all the members of that one body, being many, are one body, so also is Christ. For by one Spirit we were all baptized into one body – whether Jews or Greeks, whether slaves or free—and have all been made to drink into one Spirit."

Also, our Heavenly Father, the Father God, has the paternal and maternal attributes. Mother Mary represents the maternal attribute of God's love. The Blessed Mother is important in our faith because we all need to experience this kind of love in our life. To experience the love of God more fully and completely we need Our Blessed Mother. However, we should not lose focus and get confused with Our Lord Jesus and the Blessed Mother's role in our faith, and place the Blessed Mother above Jesus. We only ask for her intercession, and give respect to her position as the earthly mother of Jesus.

"The main message of the appearance of Mary at Lourdes, France, in 1858, to fourteen-year–old Bernadette Soubirous, was Mary herself. God presented the Immaculate Conception as a model of holiness who reflects the grace and holiness of the Church. Thousands of people who have visited Lourdes have been healed and turned to Christ.

Perhaps the most striking appearances of Mary in our time occurred at Fatima, Portugal, in 1917. Mary appeared to three children, aged seven to ten, and presented a disturbing message about the perilous situation of the world and the dire consequences in store if humans did not repent and return to God. Mary revealed that the destiny of both individuals and nations hinged on whether people prayed and interceded for salvation. In particular, Mary asked for the consecration of Russia to her immaculate heart. She warned, 'If my requests are heard, Russia will be converted and there will be peace. If not, she will spread her errors throughout the entire world, provoking wars and persecution of the Church...' At that time, Russia was a poor country torn by civil war, and this prediction seemed almost laughable, but history has proven it true. Mary's appearance at Fatima reminds Christians that the things we do now and our prayers and faith have consequences, for our own salvation and for that of the world. As Pope John Paul 11 stated in his homily at Fatima on May 13, 1982:

'If the church has accepted the message of Fatima, it is above all because that message contains a truth and a call whose basic content is the truth and call of gospel itself, 'repent and believe in the gospel.' (Mark 1:15): these are the first words that the Messiah addressed to humanity, The message of Fatima is, in its basic nucleus, a call to conversion and repentance, as in the Gospel.'

At Fatima, Mary promised a sign of the validity and truth of her appearances there. It is estimated that about 100,000 people witnessed this sign—the sun dancing at midday. Many secular observers witnessed this sign, and have not been able to explain it. It has often been ignored, but never effectively denied." [7]

One of the essential marks of a consecrated life, or a person with genuine conversion, is the zeal for spreading the authentic Christian Faith. There are so many people in this world who are in desperate need for spiritual nourishment and yet have no one to reach and help them. At the same time, this world is continuously being inundated with useless information and evil influences. This problem can be overcome only if more of us offer up fervent prayers everyday and become missionaries for spreading the authentic teachings of the Church and the true messages of Mary. In Fatima, Portugal, Mary said, "Many poor sinners go to hell because they have no one to pray or make sacrifices for them" In Naju, Korea, Our Lady said, "Spread my messages of love vigorously to all the children so that the lost love of God may be restored in every corner of the world." [8]

Since my pilgrimage to Naju, in obedience to follow Mother Mary's messages, everyday, I pray for conversion of sinners, sanctification of families, priests and ministers, and our leaders of the whole world, for peace in the world and for unification of our churches through the infinite merit of the Sacred Heart of Jesus and the intercession of the Immaculate Heart of Mary.

Chapter 21

MY HOPE

My hope is that more people will accept Jesus to be their savior so that more people will go to heaven.

My greatest hope is for all denominations to try and learn each other's beliefs. In doing so, they will be able to respect each other's belief, this will prevent them from being judgmental. Our Pope Benedict on his visit to Turkey in November 2005 appealed to everyone to respect the differences of each other's faith.

My hope is mainly for Catholics and Evangelical Christians to be more united as Christians and to bond together to defend the essential Christian faith that we received from the church against the relativism and unbelief that is rampart in our world today.

I also hope that every Christian, Catholic, Protestant and those who are searching for God's truth will read the Bible cover to cover. Reading the Bible is the only way to have a changed life. In reading the Bible we come to know who God really is. We will know His ways, His love, His laws and principles, and the purpose of why He created us.

Daniel Webster made this statement: "If there be in my style or thoughts to be commended, the credit is due to my kind parents for instilling into my mind an early love for the scriptures." What about you today Christian parent? Are you making a Daniel Webster in your home, or a little rebel? Webster also made this statement: "I have read it (the Bible) through many times. I now make it a practice of going through it once a year. It is the book of all others for lawyers as well as divines. I pity a man who cannot find in it a rich supply of thought and rules for conduct." [1]

"Born in the East and clothed in Oriental form and imagery, the Bible walks the ways of the entire world with familiar feet, and enters land after land to find its own hundreds of languages to the heart of man. It comes into the palace to tell the Monarch that he is a servant of the Most High, and into the cottage to assure the peasant that he is the Son of God. Children listen to its stories with wonder and delight, and wise men ponder them as parables of life. It has a word of peace for the time of peril, a word of comfort for the time of calamity, a word of light for the hour of darkness. Its oracles are repeated in the assembly of the people, and its counsels whispered in the ear of the lonely. The wicked and the proud tremble at its warnings, but to the wounded and the penitent it has a mother's voice. The wilderness and the solitary place have been made glad by it, and the fire on the hearth has lit the reading of its well-worn pages. It has woven itself into our dearest dreams; so that love, friendship, sympathy and devotion, memory and hope put on the beautiful garments of its treasured speech, breathing of frankincense and myrrh." - Henry Van Dyke [2]

My Hope

An unknown author wrote an awesome statement about the Bible, it says:

"This book contains the mind of God, the state of man, the way of salvation, the doom of sinners and the happiness of believers. Its doctrines are holy, its precepts are binding, its histories are true, and its decisions are immutable. Read it to be wise, believe it to be safe, and practice it to be holy. It contains light to direct you, food to support, and comfort to cheer you. It is the traveler's map, the pilgrim's staff, the pilot's compass, the soldier's sword and the Christian's character. Here paradise is restored, heaven opened and the gates of hell disclosed. Christ is its grand object, our good is its design, and the glory of God its end. It should fill the memory, rule the heart, and guide the feet. Read it slowly, frequently, and prayerfully. It is given you in life and will be opened in the judgment and will be remembered forever. It involves the highest responsibility, will reward the greatest labour, and will condemn all who trifle with its contents."

__ Author Unknown

I heard this mentioned many times in Christian T.V. programs, that the meaning of **BIBLE** is: Basic Instructions Before Living Earth. Dr. Charles Stanley also said that the Bible is the blueprint of our life. It is God's instruction book of life. In the Bible there is an answer to every question, and it tells us how to live. If we believe that there is God who made us, then we should also believe that as our Creator, He would give us the instruction book on how to live this life. The Bible is our life's manual book.

Lee Stroebel, former legal editor of Chicago Tribune, and an award –winning journalist with Masters of Studies in Law Degree from Yale Law School, got converted from Atheism after reading the Bible. He was reading the Bible to find faults and flaws in the Bible, to examine and to find credible evidence that Jesus of Nazareth really is the Son of God. He wrote a book, <u>The case For Christ,</u> which is a "must- read" for every skeptic and baby Christian that still has doubts about the reality of God and His Word.

My hope is one of the reasons that I wrote this book. My hope, aside from winning souls for Christ, is for both Christians and Catholics to understand each other, learn from each other, and to work together to win the whole world for Christ. I have attended many Evangelical Christian services and I can say that there are things that Catholics can learn from them to improve their spiritual walk. In Christian or Evangelical Churches, their Bible studies before their service, and the preaching during the service was great. (When I was searching for the truth, I couldn't seem to get enough of God's Words.) The Christian Church preachers are excellent in expounding God's Words. They have the knack in making the scriptures alive, therefore making it easy for the layperson to understand. The emphasis of their Church is teaching God's Words. Therefore, each individual member of their church is more knowledgeable about the Bible than the Catholics. In Catholic Church of course, we have priests that are good in giving sermons, but I guess the time allotted for the sermon is not long enough. Besides, they have to be conscious not to exceed the time limit or the congregation will complain about the overtime.

Another thing is that at the end of their service the pastor asks anyone who would like to accept Jesus as their personal Savior or re-commit their life to Him, to come forward (in public.) This is to follow what Jesus said in Luke Chapter 12, "Also, I say to you, whoever confesses Me before men, him the Son of Man also will confess before the angels of God." (Luke 12:8) In Catholic Church we are encouraged to have ongoing repentance and renewal of our faith, and we can do it privately.

In Christian Church they are very serious in sharing their faith with others. Besides sending many missionaries all over the world, they encourage every single believer to share their faith. This is surprising to me because we Catholics tend to be very private and quiet about our faith. I remember my Catholic friend when she was asked by a Christian pastor if she was "born again," and her response was, " I am sorry but my faith is private to me!" I did not know that we had to share our faith verbally aside from living out or putting it into practice every single day. One pastor told me that if we are a Christian believer we all have a story to be shared and told.

I only mentioned a few of the things that attract some Catholics, but I must say that they don't need to transfer to another Christian Church unless they strongly feel that they are not fed enough of God's Words or unless they feel the Holy Spirit leading that God can use them better in that particular Christian Church. On the other hand, it is also up to you to make your Catholic Church meet your needs. To begin with, we need to study the basics of our Catholic faith. You can read books and study the Bible in groups and by yourself regularly, or seek other venues to improve your knowledge of God. There are different tools you can use to improve your Bible knowledge. There are Bibles that have interpretation notes, or you can attend Bible classes in an Evangelical Christian Church like Harvest Church, if it is not offered in your Church. Knowing God completely will make you a better Catholic and a better Christian.

Knowing Him will enable you to love Him and because you love Him, you will become obedient to His teachings and commandments. God's commandments are not burdensome to you anymore, but easy to follow. You will gladly serve Him and you become His disciple. Religion is not but a hindrance to your faith. Religion will not satisfy your soul, only Jesus our Savior will. Therefore it is the knowledge of our Lord Jesus that counts. I strongly believe this is what is lacking in all Christian denomination. We all know about Jesus but there is no love relationship, because if you truly loved Him, you would be a changed person. This love relationship with Him enables you to feel His glory and His presence. His desires will become your desires. You will have new purpose: To love God and your neighbor, and you will have His strength to keep getting up every morning with excitement. As what the prophet Ezekiel prophesied: "Then I will give you a new heart, and I will put a new spirit within you; I will take the heart of stone out of your flesh, and give you a heart of flesh. " I will put My Spirit within you and cause you to walk in My statutes, and you will keep My judgments and do them, you shall be My people, and I will be your God," (Ezekiel 36:26-28.)

Since I mentioned what I like about the evangelical Christian Church, I should also mention what I like most about our Catholic Church. First and foremost, I like their well- structured organization. Another thing is that the Catholic Church never demeans other Churches or denominations. The Catholic Church believed in the intercessions of Saints, (not worshipping them like we worship our Triune God.) Regarding the Sacraments, I know that our Christian brothers and sisters don't agree with Infant baptism, not to forget we also have the sacrament of confirmation to confirm the Infant baptism and for the infilling of the Holy Spirit. This is done during the child's middle school years and in the age of accountability. This is the time when they ask for the infilling of the Holy Spirit. During confirmation they also have adult sponsors that have the responsibility to help the parents when this particular child fails to follow their faith.

The Catholic Church does not give rise to the preacher's ego; their priests live a life of modesty and humility, unlike some Christian Church preachers that live a luxurious life style. The Icons, which the evangelical Christians say we worship, actually brings the attention of some Catholics to their spirituality, but they don't worship them per se. Catholics don't worship the icons; we venerate them, we give them "supreme respect." Last but not the least, the Catholic Church history and lineage came from the original Christ Church. The sacrifice of the holy Mass, (called service in Evangelical Church,) is solemn, you can really feel the glory of God and God's presence. The worship part of the Mass is also great.

I feel that all Christians can learn to love each other and work together. As what one priest said: "In essentials unity, in non-essentials liberty and charity." I feel that to be unified with each other is to focus on what Jesus prayed in John's Gospel, Chapter 17 in verse 17: "Sanctify them by Your truth. Your word is truth." In verse 18 it says: "As You sent Me into the world, I also have sent them into the world." In verse19: "And for their sakes I sanctify Myself, that they also may be sanctified by the truth." In verse 20: "I do not pray for these alone, but also for those who will believe in Me through their word;" verse 21: "that they all may be one, as You, Father, are in Me, and I in You; that they also may be one in us, that the world may believe that You sent Me." (John 17:17-21.) To explain verse 17; "To be sanctified (Eph.5:26, 1 Thes.5:23) is to be separated from the world and its usurpation unto God and His purpose, not only in position, (Matt.23:17) but also in disposition (Rom.6:19, 22) God's loving word works in the believers to separate them from anything worldly. This is to be sanctified in God's word, which is the truth, the reality. The explanation of verse 21; This is the second aspect of the believers' oneness, the oneness in the Triune God through sanctification, separation from the world by the word of God. In this aspect of oneness the believers, separated from the world unto God, enjoy the Triune God as the factor of their oneness." [3]

The essentials here are that we believe in the same Jesus, the Holy Trinity; God the Father, the Son and the Holy Spirit. We also have the believers' "oneness" that John was talking about in Chapter 17. But most of all we can be united in the Eucharist. Whether we partake Jesus symbolically, as what our Christian brothers believe, or actually partake Jesus' body as what we Catholics believe, as long as we are partaking in communion and believe in what Jesus said: "Most assuredly, I say to you, unless you eat the flesh of the Son of Man and drink My blood, you have no life in you. Whosoever eats My flesh and drinks My blood has eternal life, and I will raise him up in the last day," (John 6:53-54) we are united. The unifying force of the Eucharist is that we all believe that we have eternal life if we eat His flesh and drink His Blood, and hopefully we all will abide in Him as He promised: "He who eats My flesh and drinks My blood abides in Me and I in him." (John 5:56) I have to remind everyone though, not to take the Eucharist for granted by just taking it without sincere repentance of sins prior to receiving it. Also, there are some people who say they are a believer but never take communion. I cannot express enough what they have been missing. Not only that they are missing forgiveness, but also their healing, physical, mental, and spiritual healing.

As one pastor said, when we all go to heaven, there will be no denomination there, only souls facing his final judgment. One of our Catholic Hymns, "One Bread One Body" written by John Foley, S.J. explains more about the Eucharist:

"One Bread, One Body, One Lord of all

One cup of blessing which we bless,

And we though many throughout the earth,

We are one body in this one Lord.

Gentile or Jew, servant or free,

Woman or man, no more.

Many the gifts, many the works,

One in the Lord of all.

Grain for the fields, scattered and grown,

Gathered to one for all."

The things that both Catholics and Christians can work together on, I believe are the following:
1. Stop criticizing each other, (I don't mean the leaders of the churches, but the members; parishioners of the Catholic Church and the members of the congregation of the Christian church.)

2. We should not focus in interpretations, rules and regulations, religion and which doctrine to follow.

3. We should work together in stopping the media (movies) that dishonor our Lord Jesus and His Name.

4. We should sincerely pray together to get rid of the spiritual problem in our world which is "sin," and we should pray together to bring prayer back in all of our American Schools.

5. We should work even harder to spread the Gospel – in making Jesus known. Only Jesus can change a human heart. With Jesus, our souls can know peace and we will have peace with God, peace in our hearts and peace with each other. It is the only way to change the people and our world.

6. Criticizing and putting each other down will frustrate and discouraged the non-believers or the nominal Christians. We should concentrate in praying and encouraging all the nominal Christians to become "born again" Christians. "As we walk in the light, (Jesus,) we have fellowship with one another.

My journey as a Catholic Christian is been exiting and awesome. I knew Jesus since I was 30 years old, and how I wish I had known Him sooner. My life is full of hope, confidence and courage because I trust in Jesus. I know that I know that His grace and his Holy Spirit is there to help me every single day, moment by moment. I am saved by His grace, and I can also live by His grace every step of the way. Because of His grace, I am able to love even those who don't deserve to be loved, and I am able to forgive even those who don't deserve forgiveness. Through Jesus, my sins of the past, present, and future are forgiven, and by His Holy Spirit my life has been changed and renewed. My sin, confusion and disillusionment are replaced with righteousness, peace, joy, contentment and hope. I know His will for my life is the best because He is my loving Father. Jesus said: "I am the way, the truth, and the life. No one comes to the father except through Me." (John 14:6)

Therefore my friends, if you are without hope and purpose (even if you are rich), if you are not sure that you are going to heaven, if you think you are not forgiven, if you think you are spiritually blind or spiritually bankrupt, if you hunger and thirst for God although you may not even realize it – come to Jesus. God will change and transform you. Jesus will give you a new beginning. He gave me new attitude to face my present and future problems. From now on, if you give your life to Jesus, you are not alone in facing your problems. Jesus will face it with you.

Looking back to who I was, and who I am now, it is hard for me to believe that I am the same person. Letting Jesus have control of my life was really hard, it could only have happened through the grace of God and the power of His Holy Spirit.

CONCLUSION

I hope that I have cleared some misunderstanding and misconception among Catholic Christians and Evangelical Christians about my being a "Born Again" Catholic. As a "Born Again" Catholic, some Christian told me that I was not really "Born Again" because I believe in Mary and the Pope. My Catholic friends and relatives said that I was more Protestant Christian than a Catholic because of my ways. I love to listen to Protestant Christian Preachers and attended their conferences sometimes; I often listen to them in T.V. and radio and support them. Most of all I am comfortable to have fellowship with other denominations.

One example of why my relatives think that I am more in the Protestant denomination than a Catholic, is because: When I went home to the Philippines to do my ministry work, my cousin asked me the name of my foundation. When I told her, "New Life Family Outreach," she then asked me,

"Are you a Protestant now? Did you change your religion?" I chose this name, "New Life Family Outreach" because there is a universalty ring to it and because my main goal and purpose for this ministry is for every individual to have a new life with Jesus. Once again, I want to emphasize that denomination is not important. What is important is our relationship with Jesus our Savior, and to live a holy life serving and following Him.

Our Heavenly Father inspired me to write this book and the Holy Spirit sponsored it, there is no doubt about it. As His servant I have to obey. As what Pastor Charles Stanley said, "Be obedient to God and leave all the consequences to Him." This is a good Christian slogan or motto to live by and to follow. This book is a journey of my faith in Jesus. I can say that this faith has been proved and withstood the test. I shared my life experiences with honesty and sincerity and I hope that it will impact others and lead them to salvation, then, to a deeper faith in our Lord and Savior Jesus.

Had I known Jesus and followed Him wholeheartedly at a younger age, it would have made a whole life of difference. I have learned after many years of walking with Him, that salvation is not enough. God wants us to go deeper in our relationship with Him, and that is to live a holy life. We are set apart by God for God alone, (this is sanctification,) living with intimate fellowship with Him, following His ways, and being obedient to His commands. It is the only way to live in peace, contentment, victory, and with sense of purpose.

Had I known what I know now, I would have not married without praying and seeking God for His will for the life partner that He intend me to have. Only God knows what is best for me because He knows me well, as He is my Creator. Besides, He will give me the best because it is His nature to give only the best out of His love for me. Billy Graham said in one of his classic crusades that he gave up his first love because deep in his spirit God told him that she was not the will of God as his life partner. He continued to serve God and waited until God found him his perfect partner, Ruth Graham. Billy Graham often said that he could not have carried out the ministry God entrusted to him without his wife, Ruth, by his side. Looking at the lives

Conclusion

they lived together, and looking at their children and grandchildren! They are all serving Jesus. Billy Graham's legacy of faith changed millions of lives throughout the whole world. Together with Pope John Paul 11, Pope Benedict and Mother Theresa, the Graham's are my Christian heroes. The Grahams have great influence to all of us and many look up to them because they refused to compromise in matters of honesty, integrity and morality. They are effective witnesses to Christ.

I was transformed and changed because I have come to know the Triune God; God the Father, God the Son, and the Holy Spirit. I know Jesus because of His Word, the Holy Bible. If you are seeking for the real truth then follow Jesus. Jesus did not say, "I am one of the ways," but Jesus said: "I am the way, the truth and the life. No one comes to the Father except through me." (John 14:6)

I wish that our Churches today, all over the world, would be like the Church of Philadelphia. (Rev. 3:7) Pastor McGee mentioned this Church in his book as the "revived Church." This is the Church that has turned back to the Word of God. Pastor McGee writes: "Today Protestantism and Roman Catholic Church, there are multitudes of people who are turning to the Word of God. Mail which I received from all over the world indicates that there are people wanting to hear the Word of God and who are hungry for it. This period is pictured in the Church of Philadelphia" [1]

Pastor McGee continued to expound in these two verses in Revelation 3:7-8:

"And to the angel of the Church in Philadelphia write: These things saith he that is Holy, he that is true, he that hath the key of David, he that openeth, and no man shutteh; and shutteth and no man openeth. (Rev.3:7)

In each of these messages, the Lord always draws something from that vision of Himself as the glorified Christ, our Great High Priest. Here He reminds them that He is holy. He was holy at His birth, He was holy at His death, and He is holy today in His present earthly office. He was so called at His birth when the angel said to Mary, "...therefore also that holy thing which shall be born of thee shall be called the Son of God," (Luke 1:35) and in His death He was holy. We are told in Acts 2:27: "Because thou wilt not leave my soul in hell, neither wilt thou suffer thine Holy One to see corruption." He was holy in His death and resurrection. What a marvelous thing this is! He is also holy today in His priestly office. "For such an high priest became us, who is holy harmless, undefiled, separate from sinners, and made higher than the heavens." (Heb.7:26)

He that hath the keys of Hades and death, which we saw in Chapter 1, verse 18. This speaks of His regal claims as the Ruler of this universe. "He shall be great, and shall be called the Son of the Highest: and the Lord God shall give unto him the throne of his father David: And he shall reign over the house of Jacob for ever; and of his kingdom there shall be no end." (Luke 1:32-33) He will sit on the throne of David in the Millennium, but today He is sovereign, sitting at His Father's right hand, waiting for His enemies to be made His footstool.

"He that openeth, and no man shutteth: and shutteth and no man openeth." He is the one today who is able to open and to close, and because of that He is a comfort to us. (see Matt. 28:18-20)

"I know thy works: behold, I have set before thee an open door, and no man can shut it: for thou hast a little strength, and hast kept my word, and hast not denied my name." (Rev. 3:8) 2

The church of Philadelphia was the Church which was true to the Word of God. In our day the church that it represents could not be called the Protestant church or the Roman Catholic Church or any other church. Actually, it represents all churches over the world – regardless of their labels ---which still remain true to the word of God.

The Lord commends the Philadelphian church on seven counts:

1. " I know thy works." The Lord Jesus is looking for fruit; He is looking for works in the lives of believers. "For by grace are ye saved through faith; and not of yourselves: Not of works, lest any man should boast. For we are his workmanship, created in Christ Jesus unto good works, which God hath before ordained that we should walk in them." (Eph. 2: 8-10)

   My friend, there is something wrong with your faith if it doesn't produce works. Good, old, practical, camel-kneed James was a great man of prayer who said, "…shew me thy faith without thy works, and I will shew thee my faith by my works." (James 2:8) Works are not works of law but works of faith. Calvin said, Faith alone saves, but faith that saves is not alone. Saving faith produces works.

2. "Behold, I have set before thee an open door, and no man can shut it." This could be a door to the joy of the Lord or to knowledge of the scriptures. I personally believe that it is a door to the

knowledge of the scriptures, which means that if He opens the door, He intends for you to move in because He will open a door of opportunity for witnessing and for proclaiming the Word of God. I believe that both go together.

3. "For thou hast a little strength (dunamin.) Dunamin is the Greek word from which we get our English word dynamite. He says, 'You have little power.' This was a humble group of believers which did not have impressive numbers, buildings or programs. I get a little weary today hearing every Christian group making reports. Even here at <u>Thru the Bible,</u> we like to tell you how many radio stations our broadcast is heard on. My, how we like to talk about those things! My friend, that type of thing is not worth anything. We like to talk about the hundreds of letters we receive from those who have accepted Christ—that's nothing. The important thing is whether or not we are getting out the Word of God. He will do the counting. God has His own computer which is registering all this, and He tells us that we had better not. The apostle Paul said, 'I don't even judge myself' (see 1 Cor. 4:3) Why not? In effect he is saying, 'I may report too many converts. I may speak 'evangelistically' and give you a wrong figure. I may look at this a little differently than God does. I need to wait until I get into His presence for the accurate rendering of it.'"

4. "And hast kept my word." In a day when there was a denial of the inspiration of the Scriptures, this church believed the Bible to be authoritative, inspired Word of God. A twentieth-century theologian, of course of the liberal ranks, stated

that no intelligent person could believe the verbal inspiration of the Bible. Well, that sure put me in the bad light! I am, therefore, not an intelligent person because I do believe in the inspiration of the Bible—That is, if his definition is right, but I do not think that he is right even about that.

5. "And hast not denied my name." In a day that when the deity of Christ is blatantly denied by seminary and pulpit, here is a group of believers who have remained true to Him by proclaiming the God-man and His substitution death for sinners.

This church of Philadelphia has been labeled many things. Some have called it a missionary church, some have called it the serving church, some have called it a live church—all of these are accurate. I personally like to call it the revived church or the Bible believing church. The thing that the Lord Jesus emphasizes is this: "Thou ...hast kept my Word and hast not denied my name." In this day of unbelief and skepticism, the Lord Jesus is commending this church because it has kept His Word. This is the church that got out the Word of God, and, as far as we know, this church lasted longer than any other of the seven churches mentioned here. Until the thirteenth century, it had a continued existence. The Seljuk Turks destroyed it when they came in and brutally murdered all the believers who were left in this church. It was also a missionary church. It is the belief now that the fact that Christianity penetrated into India as early as it did was because this church had sent out missionaries.

6. "Behold, I will make them to come and worship before thy feet, and to know that I have loved thee." The Lord Jesus says here that He will make the enemies of the Philadelphian church to know that He loves this church.

7. "Because thou hast kept the word of my patience, I also will keep thee from the hour of temptation, which shall come upon all the world, to try them that dwell upon the earth (Rev. 3:10.) This last commendation is that this church kept the Word of Christ in patience. This is evidently the patient waiting for the coming of Christ for His own. (See 2 Thess.3:5)

I believe that God is still patient with a world that has rejected His Word. It is not like it was back in the days of Noah. They didn't have the written Word of God, yet God judged them, (they did have a man bringing the message to them.) But today we do have the Word of God. There is a Gideon Bible in practically every hotel and motel room throughout the world. In the different countries of Europe, Asia, and Africa, I find that the Word of God has penetrated all of these areas. The Philadelphian church is the church that believed in the Word of God. "I will also keep thee from the hour of temptation, which shall come upon all the world, to try them that dwell upon the earth."

Christ's final word of encouragement to His church is that it will not pass through the Great tribulation. The church is to be removed from the world, (see 1 Thess.4:13-18,) which is its comfort and hope. (See Titus 2:13) Such is the patient waiting of the church "...who through faith and patience inherit the promises" (Heb.6:12.) The church is not anticipating the Great Tribulation with all of its judgment (see John 5:24, Rev. 13:1-8,11-17,) but rather it is looking for Him to come. "The hour of temptation" is definitely a reference to the Great Tribulation—it's worldwide. After the preliminaries are put down in chapters 4-5, and in chapters 6-19 you have presented the Great Tribulation Period. This is the period that He says is coming upon the entire world to test those that are upon the earth. "I also will keep thee from the hour of temptation." He says that He will keep them not only from that awful holocaust that is coming on this earth, that period of judgment, but also from the hour of temptation. Therefore, this is to my judgment a complete deliverance. When He says, "keep thee out of the hour of trial." By any stretch of the imagination, you could not say that this church is going through the Great Tribulation Period. I believe that the period of the Philadelphian church continues right on through to the rapture of the church. This is the church which will go out at the time of the Rapture. [3]

Now that we know about the commended church of Philadelphia, we should also look at the church that our Lord has no word of commendation about. This is the church of Laodicea. The letter of Christ to the church in Laodicea is the last of these seven letters. Sir William Ramsay calls Laodicea "the city of compromise." Laodicea was a place of great wealth and of Greek culture. It was a place of great commerce where they made clothing. It was a place of science and literature. It boasted an excellent medical school, which again, was very primitive and heathen. Here is where they developed what was known in the Roman world as Phrygian powder, a salve for the ears and the eyes. Laodicea was also a center of industry with extensive banking operations. Cicero held court there. It is said that he brought notes here to be cashed in this city. Jupiter, or Zeus, was the object of worship in Laodicea.

"I know thy works, that thou art neither cold nor hot: I would thou wert cold or hot. So then thou art lukewarm, and neither cold nor hot, I will spew thee out of my mouth." (Rev. 3:15-16)

A cold church actually means a church that has denied every cardinal doctrine of the faith. It is given over to formality and is carrying on in active opposition to the Word of God and the Gospel of Christ. You find today in liberalism that they are in active opposition to the Gospel of Christ. Hot, speaks of those with real spiritual fervor and passions like the Christians in Ephesus, although even then, they were getting away from their best love. The spirit of God had brought them to a high pitch in their personal relationship to Christ, but the Laodicean church was neither hot nor cold, just lukewarm. I would say that this is the picture of many, many churches today in the great denominations that have departed from the faith.

"Because thou sayest, I am rich, and increased with goods, and have need of nothing; and knowest not that thou art wretched, and miserable, and poor, and blind, and naked."(Rev.3:17)

The Laodicean thought that they had need of nothing because they had everything. But Christ tells them that though they think they are rich, they are really wretched, miserable, poor, blind and naked. Christ offered to them an invitation to fill the hole that they were experiencing in their soul. He invited them to leave their preoccupation with materialism and to turn to Him. He asked them to come to Him for everything they needed.

Conclusion

"I counsel thee to buy of me gold tried in fire, that thou mayest be rich; and white raiment, that thou mayest be clothed, and that the shame of thy nakedness do not appear; and anoint thy eyes with eye-salve that thou mayest see." (Rev.3:18)

The first thing Jesus offers in the marketplace of His provisions is "gold refined by fire." Gold in those days was the ultimate wealth by which you could secure whatever you wanted and needed. Christ says that He offers the ultimate resource for all we need and want. In fact, He says that if we have the pure gold He offers, we will become truly rich.

"And white raiment, that thou mayest be clothed, and the shame of thy nakedness do not appear." This speaks of the righteousness of Christ. This white garments were purified by His finished work on the cross. What Christ was offering here is the prosperity of Himself and the pleasure of His purity.

"And anoint thine eyes with eye-salve, that thou mayest see." This speaks of the Holy Spirit who opens the eyes of believers today. This is no doubt a reference to the fact that when we fully rely on Jesus Christ, He enables us to see with discernment and accuracy so that we can judge correctly in all that we do and pursue.

"The church of Laodicea, as we shall see, is an organization which will continue on in the world, although the Lord gives a marvelous invitation to it, and many even in that Laodicean church will turn to Christ and be taken out at the time of the rapture. But there is a church that goes through the Great Tribulation Period, sand that is the apostate church, the church of Laodicea." [4]

I hope that we can all learn from the letter of Jesus to the Church of Laodicea.

The inscription on the cathedral in Lubeck, Germany, is still true:

Thus speaketh Christ to us:

Ye call Me Master and obey Me not.

Ye call Me Light and see Me not.

Ye call Me Way and walk Me not.

Ye call Me Life and choose Me not.

Ye call Me Wise and follow Me not.

Ye call Me Fair and love Me not.

Ye call Me Rich and ask Me not.

Ye call Me Eternal and seek Me not.

Ye call Me Noble and serve Me not.

Ye call Me Gracious and trust Me not.

Ye call Me Might and honor Me not.

Ye call Me Just and fear Me not.

If I condemn you, blame Me not.

In 1992, I found these two sentiments that I adopted from my patient who was eighty-three years old in the nursing home where I worked. It was written at the back of her Bible. I was given permission by one of her family member to copy these two excerpts.

Conclusion

The Ways of the Lord

"I asked God for strength that I might achieve…..
I was made weak that I might learn humbly to obey.
I asked for help that I might do greater things…..
I was given infirmity that I might do better things.
I asked for riches, that I might be happy…..
I was given poverty that I might be wise.
I asked for all things that I might enjoy life….
I was given poverty that I might enjoy all things.
I got nothing that I asked for but everything I had hope for.
Despite myself my prayers were answered.
I am among all men most richly blessed."

--Unknown –

"Anything that drives my vision of Christ Jesus
And restraint my testimony of Him
And take away my desire to read my Bible
And of worshiping my Blessed Savior
And prevents me from praying
And causes me to neglect my prayer life
And ministry to the sick and the needy
And does not inspire me to be charitable, compassionate,

And kind to all humanity in love ……

Is not of God and I as a Christian must turn away from it.

I will end this book with Peter Kreeft's words:

"The world's purest gold is only dung without Christ. But with Christ, the basest metal is transformed into the purest gold.... With Him, poverty is riches, weakness is power, suffering is joy, to be despised is glory. Without Him, riches are poverty, power is impotence, happiness is misery, glory is despised." [5]

Conclusion

God's Invitation:

" For God so love the world that He gave His only begotten son, that whoever believe in Him should not perish but have everlasting life." [John 3:16]

This verse in the Holy Bible is God's invitation to everyone. Today is your day of salvation. Make it personal to you by praying these words.

Dear God, I am sorry for all my sins. Lord Jesus Christ, Son of God, have mercy on me, a sinner. I repent of my sins and I ask You to wash them away through Your holy blood shed on the cross. Thank You for dying in the cross for me. Fill me with Your Holy Spirit. Fill me with Your love and Your presence as I forgive everyone I need to forgive. I now confess You as my Lord and Savior. In Jesus name, I pray. Amen

Now that you are "Born Again," I encourage you to read the Bible everyday and to attend Church regularly.

If you've been touched by this book and want to help make it available for others, and want to participate in our missionary adventure or support please contact us:

New Life Family Outreach

4138 Rosemead Blvd.

Pico Rivera, Ca. 90660

Notes

Chapter 1

1. Billy Graham; <u>Hope For Each Day</u>. Copyright 2002

Chapter 2

1. J. Vernon McGee; "<u>Thru The Bible</u>." pp. xi-xiii

2. Ibid.

3. Billy Graham; <u>Hope For Each Day</u>. Copyright 2002

Chapter 3

1. Oswald Chambers; <u>My Utmost For His Highest</u>. March 20

2. Billy Graham; <u>Hope For Each Day</u>.

. J.I. Packer; "<u>Really Knowing God.</u>" Decision Magazine Nov.2006

Chapter 4

1. Francis Cardinal Arinze; <u>Religion for Peace.</u> p.89

2. Ibid

3. Warren Wiersbe; <u>Quiet Time-Quite a Time</u>. p.39

4. Ibid

5. Oswald Chambers; My Utmost For His Highest.

6. Linda Schubert; Miracle Hour; a method of Prayer that will Change Your Life Copyright 1991 p.4

Chapter 5

1. Jill Briscoe; Prayer That Works. Tyndale House Publishers Inc. Copyright 2002, p.172

2. Ibid p.172

3. Billy Graham; Prayer. The Billy Graham Sermon Series Copyright 1955, Rev.2006

Chapter 6

1. Richard J. Foster; Celebration of Disciple. Copy right 1978, pp139-140

2. Linda Schubert; Miracle Hour; a Method of Prayer Copyright 1991

3. Richard Foster; Celebration of Disciple.

4. Ibid

5. James Pittman; "Decision" Magazine BGEA

Chapter 7

1. Charles Stanley; "It Is Good To Give Thanks To God." Life Principles Notes /LPO 61119.

2. Linda Schubert; <u>Miracle Hour; a method of Prayer</u>. 1991

Chapter 8

1. <u>"New Testament Recovery Version"</u> Living Stream Ministries 1985 Rev.1991

2. J. Oswald Chambers; <u>My Utmost For His Highest</u>. 1990

3. Pope Paul II; <u>Private Prayers of Pope Paul II Atria Books N.Y.</u>

4. Ibid

Chapter 9

1. J. Vernon McGee; <u>"Thru the Bible."</u> Vol. 3 p. 1021

Chapter 10

1. Joseph M. Stowell; <u>Coming Home.</u> 1998 p.187

2. Ibid pp.154-155

3. Charles Stanley; <u>"Life Principles Notes"</u> LPO 060910

Chapter 11

1. Joyce Myer; <u>Seven Things That Steals Our Joy.</u> 2004

Conclusion

2. Lewis B Smedes; <u>Forgive and Forget</u>. 1984 p. 182-184
3. Ibid pp.192-193
4. Joyce Myer; <u>Seven Things That Steals Our Joy</u>.2004

Chapter 12

1. Billy Graham; "True Repentance, Real Change" Decision Magazine January 2007 p.2
2. Ibid
3. Linda Schubert; <u>Miracle Hour</u>. 1991
4. <u>Catechism of The Catholic Church</u> # 1285
5. Billy Graham Evangelistic Association
6. Oswald Chambers; <u>My Utmost For His Highest</u>. March 9
7. Alan Schreck; <u>Catholic and Christian</u>. Copyright 1984-2004 p. 147
8. Charles Stanley; <u>Handbook For Christian Living</u>. Copyright 1966 p. 204

Chapter 13

1. Oswald Chambers; <u>My Utmost For His Highest</u>. July 2
2. Ibid. July 24

Chapter 14

1. Richard J. Foster; Celebration And Discipline Harper and Row Copyright 1978
2. Ibid p. 114
3. Ibid p. 114
4. Ibid p.115
5. Ibid p.116

Chapter 15

1. Charles Stanley; <u>Handbook For Christian Living.</u> Copyright 1996 p.352
2. Ibid p.353
3. Ibid p.354
4. The New King James Bible
5. Oswald Chambers, <u>My Utmost for His Highest</u>.

Chapter 16

1. Alan Schreck; <u>Catholic and Christian</u> Copyright 1984-2004
2. Ibid p.26
3. Ibid p.30
4. Ibib pp. 30-31
5. Ibid p. 32
6. Ibid p. 116-117

   A. Sacraments

    1. Alan Schreck; <u>Catholic And Christian</u>.

    2. Ibid p.26

Conclusion

    3.Ibid p. 151

    B. Hierarchy of Truth

1. Alan Schreck; <u>Catholic And Christian</u> Copyright 1984-2004

    2. Ibid p.9-10

    C. Mass Celebration

    1.Alan Schreck; <u>Catholic And Christian</u> Copyright 1984-2004 p.141

    2.Ibid pp. 142-143

    3. Pope Paul II <u>The Private Prayer Of Pope Paul II</u> Atria Books 2005.

    D. Common Questions Other Denomination Asks About Catholic Faith

1. Paul Whitcomb; <u>Catholic Church Has The Answer.</u> Copyright 1986
2. Ibid

    E. Catholic Prayers

1. Spiritual Theology; Aumann p.97

    F. Ecumenism

1. Thomas P. Rausch; <u>Catholics And Evangelicals.</u> Paulist Press Copyright 2000.
2. Alan Schreck; <u>Catholic And Christians.</u> p. 65
3. Ibid p. 66
4. Ibid p.67
5. Ibid p.45
6. Thomas P. Rausch; <u>Catholics And Evangelicals.</u> Paulist Press 2000 p.47
7. David E. Bjork; <u>Catholics And Evangelicals.</u>Paulist Press 2000
8. Cecil M. Robeck, Jr.; "<u>Evangelicals And Catholics Together.</u>" Catholics And Evangelicals Paulist Press Copyright 2000, pp.30-33

Chapter 17

1. Pope John II; <u>Private Prayers of Pope Paul II</u>. Atria Books N.Y. p. 40
2. Ibid p. 41
3. Ibid p.42

Chapter 18

1. Alan Schreck; <u>Catholic And Christian</u>. p.162
2. Ibid p.163
3. Wikepedia.org. "<u>Canonization.</u>" July 4,2003
4. Alan Schreck; <u>Catholic And Christian.</u> p. 169

Conclusion

5. Oswald Chambers; <u>My Utmost For His Highest</u>. July 23

Chapter 19

1. Bryan Kemp et al, <u>"Gerontology"</u> A College Hill Publication 1990 p. 253
2. Elizabeth Elliot; <u>Loneliness.</u> 1988 p.22
3. Ibid
4. Vernon McGee, <u>"Thru The Bible"</u> p. 1063
5. Ibid pp.1063- 1064
6. Billy Graham; <u>"Answers To Difficult Questions"</u> Decision Magazine March 1999
7. Billy Graham; <u>Hope For Each Day. P.46</u>
8. James V. Hill; <u>What A Day That Will Be.</u> Copyright 1955
9. Stuart Hamblen; <u>Until Then.</u> Copyright 1958
10. Simpleville Music; <u>"I Can Only Imagine."</u> Copyright 1999

Chapter 20

1. Mary's Touch Magazine 2007

2. " <u>Messages of Love</u> " Appendex A-17

3. Ibid Appendex A-23

4. <u>Message to Julia Kim</u> Naju July 5 1989
5. <u>" Messages of Love"</u> Appendex A 24-27
6. <u>Ib id Appendex A 24-27</u>
7. Alan Schreck; <u>Catholic And Christian</u> <u>Copyright1984,2004</u> p. 201
8. <u>Message to Julia Kim</u> Naju, Korea July 5, 1989 Mary's Touch Magazine

Chapter 21

1. The New Testament Recovery Version pp.446-447
2. J. Vernon McGee; <u>"Thru The Bible"</u> Volume 1 p .X
3. Ibid

Conclusion

1. J. Vernon McGee <u>"Thru The Bible"</u> p. 916
2. Ibid p.916
3. Ibid p.918-919
4. Ibid p.919
5. Joseph Stowell; <u>Coming Home</u>. P. 61

Breinigsville, PA USA
14 August 2010
243609BV00001B/1/P